AQUINAS ETHICUS:

OR,

THE MORAL TEACHING OF ST. THOMAS.

A TRANSLATION OF THE PRINCIPAL PORTIONS OF THE SECOND
PART OF THE "SUMMA THEOLOGICA,"

WITH NOTES.

BY

JOSEPH RICKABY, S.J.

Vol. II.

LONDON:
BURNS AND OATES,
LIMITED,
GRANVILLE MANSIONS, W.
1892.

230.6
Su6a
1892
v.2

88/5268

CONTENTS OF VOL. II.

SECOND DIVISION, OR SECUNDA SECUNDÆ.

QUESTION XLVII.
OF PRUDENCE.

		page
Art. 12.	Is prudence in subjects or only in superiors?	1
Art. 13.	Can there be any prudence in those who live in sin?	2

QUESTION XLVIII.
OF THE PARTS OF PRUDENCE.

Art. 1.	Are there three assignable parts of prudence?	4

QUESTION LV.
OF THE PRUDENCE OF THE FLESH.

Art. 1.	Is the prudence of the flesh a sin?	5
Art. 6.	Is it lawful to entertain solicitude for temporal things?	5
Art. 7.	Ought one to be solicitous about the future?	6

QUESTION LVII.
OF RIGHT.

Art. 1.	Is right the object of justice?	7
Art. 2.	Is right properly divided into natural and positive right?	8
Art. 4.	Is paternal right to be placed in a special category?	9

QUESTION LVIII.
OF JUSTICE.

Art. 1.	Is justice aptly defined to be a standing and abiding will to give every one his due?	11
Art. 2.	Is justice always to another?	11

			page
Art. 4.	Is the will the subject of justice?	.	12
Art. 5.	Is justice a general virtue?	.	13
Art. 6.	Is justice, inasmuch as it is a general virtue, essentially identical with all virtue?	.	14
Art. 7.	Besides general, is there any particular justice?	.	15
Art. 8.	Has particular justice any special subject-matter?	.	16
Art. 9.	Does justice deal with the passions?	.	16
Art. 11.	Is it the act of justice to render to every man his own?	.	17

QUESTION LIX.
OF INJUSTICE.

Art. 3.	Can one suffer injustice willingly?	.	18

QUESTION LX.
OF JUDGMENT.

Art. 3.	Is judgment unlawful when it proceeds upon suspicion?	18
Art. 4.	Is a favourable construction to be put upon dubious proceedings?	20
Art. 6.	Does usurpation make judgment void?	21

QUESTION LXI.
OF THE PARTS OF JUSTICE.

Art. 1.	Is it proper to assign two species of justice, commutative and distributive?	22
Art. 2.	Is the mean taken in the same way in distributive as in commutative justice?	23
Art. 3.	Is the matter of each of these two species of justice the same?	23

QUESTION LXII.
OF RESTITUTION.

Art. 1.	Is restitution an act of commutative justice?	26
Art. 3.	Is it enough to restore the simple amount that has been taken away?	27
Art. 4.	Is any one bound to restore what he has not taken away?	27
Art. 5.	Is restitution always to be made to the person from whom the thing was taken?	29

			page
Art.	6.	Is he always bound to restitution, who has taken the thing?	30
Art.	7.	Are they bound to restitution, who have not taken the thing?	32

QUESTION LXIII.
OF THE RESPECTING OF PERSONS.

Art.	1.	Is the respecting of persons a sin?	34
Art.	2.	Is there room for the respecting of persons in the distribution of spiritualities?	35
Art.	3.	Has the sin of respecting of persons any place in the showing of honour and reverence?	38

QUESTION LXIV.
OF HOMICIDE.

Art.	1.	Is the killing of living creatures in all cases an unlawful act?	39
Art.	2.	Is it lawful to slay sinners?	40
Art.	3.	Is it lawful for a private person to slay a sinner?	42
Art.	5.	Is it lawful for any man to kill himself?	42
Art.	6.	Is there any case in which it is lawful to kill an innocent man?	46
Art.	7.	Is it lawful to slay a man in self-defence?	47
Art.	8.	Is the guilt of homicide incurred by killing a man accidentally?	48

QUESTION LXV.
OF MUTILATION OF MEMBERS.

Art.	1.	Can mutilation in any case be lawful?	49
Art.	2.	Is it lawful for fathers to flog their sons?	50
Art.	3.	Is it lawful to put a man in prison?	51

QUESTION LXVI.
OF THEFT AND ROBBERY.

Art.	1.	Is the possession of exterior things natural to man?	53
Art.	2.	Is it lawful for any one to possess anything as his own?	53
Art.	3.	Does the essence of theft consist in the secret taking of the property of another?	55
Art.	6.	Is theft a mortal sin?	56

CONTENTS.

			page
Art. 7.	Is it lawful to steal on the plea of necessity?	.	57
Art. 8.	Can robbery be committed without sin?	.	59
Art. 9.	Is theft a more grievous sin than robbery?	.	60

QUESTION LXVII.
OF INJUSTICE IN A JUDGE.

Art. 1.	Can it be just to sit in judgment on one who is not a subject of the court?	60
Art. 2.	Is it lawful for a judge to give sentence against what is to him the known truth, on the ground of the evidence that is brought forward to the contrary?	61
Art. 3.	Can a judge condemn where there is no accuser?	62
Art. 4.	Can a judge lawfully remit the penalty?	62

QUESTION LXVIII.
OF WHAT RELATES TO AN UNJUST ACCUSATION.

Art. 1.	Is accusation a duty?	64

QUESTION LXIX.
OF SINS AGAINST JUSTICE ON THE PART OF THE ACCUSED.

Art. 1.	Is an accused party guiltless of mortal sin, in denying the truth that would lead to his condemnation?	67
Art. 2.	Is it lawful for an accused party to set up a fraudulent defence?	68
Art. 3.	Is it lawful to escape sentence by an appeal?	69
Art. 4.	Is it lawful for a condemned criminal to take what steps he can in the way of self-defence?	69

QUESTION LXX.
OF INJUSTICE IN THE PERSON OF THE WITNESS.

Art. 1.	Is it a duty to give evidence?	71
Art. 4.	Is false witness always a mortal sin?	74

QUESTION LXXI.
OF INJUSTICE ON THE PART OF COUNSEL AT LAW.

Art. 1.	Is counsel bound to take up the case of poor clients?	75
Art. 3.	Does a lawyer sin by defending an unjust cause?	76
Art. 4.	Is it lawful for a lawyer to take money for his pleading?	77

QUESTION LXXII.
OF INJURIOUS LANGUAGE OUT OF COURT, AND FIRST OF CONTUMELY.

Art. 1.	Does contumely consist in words?	78
Art. 2.	Is contumely a mortal sin?	79
Art. 3.	Ought a man to bear the contumelies put upon him?	80

QUESTION LXXIII.
OF DETRACTION.

Art. 1.	Is it a suitable definition of detraction, that it is a blackening of another's character by words?	82
Art. 2.	Is detraction a mortal sin?	83
Art. 3.	Does detraction stand pre-eminent above all the rest of the sins that are committed against one's neighbour?	84
Art. 4.	Does the listener sin grievously who endures a detractor?	85

QUESTION LXXIV.
OF MISCHIEF-MAKING.

| Art. 1. | Is mischief-making a distinct sin from detraction? | 87 |
| Art. 3. | Is detraction a more grievous sin than mischief-making? | 88 |

QUESTION LXXVI.
OF CURSING.

| Art. 1. | Is it lawful to curse any one? | 89 |
| Art. 3. | Is cursing a mortal sin? | 90 |

QUESTION LXXVII.
OF FRAUDULENT DEALING IN BUYING AND SELLING.

Art. 1.	May one lawfully sell a thing for more than it is worth?	91
Art. 2.	Is a sale rendered unlawful by a defect in the thing sold?	93
Art. 3.	Is the seller bound to mention any flaw there is in the thing sold?	94
Art. 4.	Is it lawful in trade to sell an article at more than cost price?	96

QUESTION LXXVIII.
OF THE SIN OF USURY THAT IS COMMITTED IN LOANS.

| Art. 1. | Is it a sin to take usury for the lending of money? | 98 |

Art. 2.	Is it lawful to ask a consideration of another kind, in return for loan of a money?	.	101
Art. 4.	Is it lawful to borrow money at usury?	.	103

QUESTION LXXIX.
OF THE INTEGRAL PARTS OF JUSTICE, WHICH ARE TO DO GOOD AND TURN AWAY FROM EVIL.

Art. 1.	Are turning away from evil, and doing good, parts of justice?	.	104
Art. 2.	Is transgression a special sin?	.	106
Art. 4.	Is the sin of omission graver than the sin of transgression?	.	107

QUESTION LXXX.
OF THE POTENTIAL PARTS OF JUSTICE.

Art. 1.	Is the list of virtues annexed to justice duly made out?	.	108

QUESTION LXXXI.
OF RELIGION.

Art. 3.	Is religion one virtue?	.	110
Art. 4.	Is religion a special virtue distinct from others?	.	111
Art. 5.	Is religion a theological virtue?	.	112
Art. 7.	Does religion involve any external act?	.	112
Art. 8.	Is religion the same as holiness?	.	113

QUESTION LXXXII.
OF DEVOTION.

Art. 1.	Is devotion a special act?	.	115
Art. 2.	Is devotion an act of religion?	.	115
Art. 3.	Is contemplation, or meditation, a cause of devotion?	.	116
Art. 4.	Is joy an effect of devotion?	.	118

QUESTION LXXXIII.
OF PRAYER.

Art. 2.	Is it proper to pray?	.	120
Art. 5.	Should we in prayer ask anything definite of God?	.	121
Art. 6.	Ought a man in prayer to ask of God temporal blessings?	.	121
Art. 8.	Ought we to pray for our enemies?	.	122

		page
Art. 12.	Should prayer be vocal?	124
Art. 13.	Is it a necessary condition of prayer that it should be attentive?	125
Art. 14.	Ought prayer to be lengthy?	126
Art. 16.	Do the prayers of sinners obtain anything of God?	129

QUESTION LXXXIV.
OF THE EXTERIOR ACTS OF DIVINE WORSHIP.

| Art. 2. | Does worship suppose any bodily act? | 131 |

QUESTION LXXXV.
OF SACRIFICE.

Art. 1.	Is it of the law of nature to offer sacrifice to God?	133
Art. 2.	Ought sacrifice to be offered to God alone?	134
Art. 3.	Is the offering of sacrifice a special act of virtue?	135
Art. 4.	Are all persons bound to offer sacrifices?	136

QUESTION LXXXVI.
OF OFFERINGS.

| Art. 2. | Are offerings due only to priests? | 138 |

QUESTION LXXXVIII.
OF A VOW WHEREBY SOMETHING IS PROMISED TO GOD.

Art. 1.	Does a vow consist in a mere purpose of the will?	139
Art. 2.	Must a vow always be of the better good?	139
Art. 4.	Is it expedient to make any vow?	141
Art. 6.	Is it more praiseworthy and meritorious to do a thing by vow than without a vow?	142
Art. 8.	Are those debarred from vowing who are subject to another's control?	143
Art. 10.	Does a vow admit of dispensation?	144
Art. 12.	Is the authority of a prelate requisite for the commutation or dispensation of a vow?	146

QUESTION LXXXIX.
OF OATHS.

| Art. 1. | Is swearing a calling on God to witness? | 148 |
| Art. 2. | Is it lawful to swear? | 149 |

xiv   CONTENTS.

		page
Art. 3.	Are these three duly enumerated accompaniments of an oath—justice, judgment, and truth?	149
Art. 5.	Is swearing something desirable and frequently to be practised, as a thing useful and good?	150
Art. 8.	Is the obligation of an oath greater than that of a vow?	153
Art. 9.	Has any one any power to dispense from oaths?	153

QUESTION XCI.
OF THE TAKING OF THE DIVINE NAME TO INVOKE IT IN PRAYER OR PRAISE.

Art. 1.	Is God to be praised by word of mouth?	156
Art. 2.	Ought singing to be employed in the divine praises?	157

QUESTION XCII.
OF VICES OPPOSED TO RELIGION, AND FIRST OF SUPERSTITION.

Art. 1.	Is superstition a vice opposed to religion?	158

QUESTION XCIII.
OF THE SPECIES OF SUPERSTITION, AND FIRST OF SUPERSTITION BY UNDUE WORSHIP OF THE TRUE GOD.

Art. 1.	Can there be anything pernicious in the worship of the true God?	160
Art. 2.	Can there be anything superfluous in the worship of the true God?	160

QUESTION XCIV.
OF IDOLATRY.

Art. 1.	Is idolatry rightly set down as a species of superstition?	162
Art. 2.	Is idolatry a sin?	164
Art. 3.	(p. iii. q. 25.) Is the image of Christ to be adored with the adoration of *latria*?	195

QUESTION XCV.
OF THE SUPERSTITION OF DIVINATION.

Art. 1.	Is divination a sin?	168
Art. 2.	Is divination by invocation of evil spirits lawful?	170
Art. 8.	Is divination by lot unlawful?	170

QUESTION XCVI.
OF SUPERSTITIOUS OBSERVANCES.

Art. 2. Are those observances unlawful, that are directed to produce changes in animal bodies, health, and the like effects? 174
Art. 3. Is it unlawful to observe omens of good or bad luck? . 175

QUESTION XCVII.
OF TEMPTING GOD.

Art. 1. Does tempting God consist in certain proceedings, in which an effect is looked for that is possible to divine power alone?. . . . 176

QUESTION XCVIII.
OF PERJURY.

Art. 2. Is all perjury a sin? 178
Art. 3. Is all perjury a mortal sin? . . . 179

QUESTION XCIX.
OF SACRILEGE.

Art. 1. Is sacrilege the violation of a sacred thing? . . 180
Art. 2. Is sacrilege a special sin? . . . 180
Art. 3. Are the species of sacrilege distinguished according to the distinction of sacred things? . . 181

QUESTION C.
OF SIMONY.

Art. 1. Is simony a will of deliberate choice to buy or sell something spiritual, or annexed to what is spiritual? 183
Art. 2. Is it always unlawful to give money for the sacraments? 184
Art. 4. Is it lawful to take money for what is annexed to spiritualities? 186

QUESTION CI.
OF NATURAL AFFECTION.

Art. 1. Are there certain definite persons who come within the range of natural affection? . . . 187
Art. 2. Does natural affection find sustenance for parents? . 188

Art. 3. Is natural affection a special virtue, distinct from others? 189
Art. 4. Is religion an occasion for laying aside the offices of natural affection to parents? . . . 189

QUESTION CIV.
OF OBEDIENCE.

Art. 2. Is obedience a special virtue? . . . 192
Art. 3. Is obedience the greatest of virtues? . . 194
Art. 5. Are subjects bound to obey their superiors in all things? 197
Art. 6. Are Christians bound to obey civil authority? . 199

QUESTION CVI.
OF GRATITUDE.

Art. 2. Is the innocent more bound to render thanks to God than the penitent? 200
Art. 4. Ought a benefit received to be requited on the spot? . 201
Art. 6. Ought the return of kindness to exceed the kindness received? 201

QUESTION CVII.
OF INGRATITUDE.

Art. 2. Is ingratitude a special sin? . . . 202
Art. 4. Are kindnesses to be withdrawn from the ungrateful? . 203

QUESTION CVIII.
OF VENGEANCE.

Art. 1. Is vengeance lawful? 204
Art. 2. Is vengeance a special virtue? . . . 207
Art. 3. Ought vengeance to be taken by means of the punishments customary amongst men? . . 208
Art. 4. Is vengeance to be exercised on those who have sinned involuntarily? 209

QUESTION CIX.
OF TRUTHFULNESS.

Art. 2. Is truthfulness a special virtue? . . . 213
Art. 3. Is truthfulness a part of justice? . . . 213

QUESTION CX.

OF VICES OPPOSED TO TRUTHFULNESS, AND FIRST OF LYING.

Art. 1.	Is lying always opposed to truthfulness?	214
Art. 3.	Is every lie a sin?	217
Art. 4.	Is every lie a mortal sin?	218

QUESTION CXI.

OF SIMULATION AND HYPOCRISY.

Art. 1.	Is all simulation sinful?	220
Art. 2.	Is hypocrisy the same as simulation?	221
Art. 4.	Is hypocrisy always a mortal sin?	222

QUESTION CXII.

OF BOASTING.

Art. 1.	Is boasting opposed to the virtue of truthfulness?	223

QUESTION CXIII.

OF SELF-DEPRECIATION.

Art. 1.	Is the self-depreciation by which a man feigns to possess lower endowments than he really has, a sin?	224

QUESTION CXIV.

OF THE FRIENDLINESS THAT IS CALLED AFFABILITY.

Art. 1.	Is friendliness a special virtue?	226

QUESTION CXV.

OF FLATTERY.

Art. 2.	Is flattery a mortal sin?	229

QUESTION CXVI.

OF THE SPIRIT OF CONTRADICTION.

Art. 2.	Is the spirit of contradiction a more grievous sin than flattery?	230

QUESTION CXVII.

OF LIBERALITY.

Art. 5.	Is liberality a part of justice?	232

QUESTION CXVIII.
OF COVETOUSNESS.

Art. 1.	Is covetousness a sin?	233
Art. 4.	Is covetousness always a mortal sin?	234
Art. 5.	Is covetousness the greatest of sins?	235
Art. 7.	Is covetousness a capital sin?	236

QUESTION CXIX.
OF PRODIGALITY.

Art. 1.	Is prodigality the opposite of covetousness?	237
Art. 2.	Is prodigality a sin?	238
Art. 3.	Is prodigality a more grievous sin than covetousness?	239

QUESTION CXX.
OF EQUITY.

Art. 1.	Is equity a virtue?	240
Art. 2.	Is equity a part of justice?	241

QUESTION CXXIII.
OF FORTITUDE.

Art. 1.	Is fortitude a virtue?	242
Art. 2.	Is fortitude a special virtue?	244
Art. 3.	Is fortitude about fears and ventures?	244
Art. 4.	Is fortitude about dangers of death only?	245
Art. 5.	Is fortitude properly conversant with the dangers of death that occur in war?	245
Art. 6.	Is endurance the principal act of fortitude?	247
Art. 8.	Does the man of fortitude find pleasure in the exercise of it?	248

QUESTION CXXIV.
OF MARTYRDOM.

Art. 3.	Is martyrdom the act above all others of greatest perfection?	250
Art. 4.	Is death essential to martyrdom?	252

QUESTION CXXV.
OF FEAR.

		page
Art. 1.	Is fear a sin?	253
Art. 4.	Does fear excuse from sin?	253

QUESTION CXXVI.
OF INSENSIBILITY TO FEAR.

Art. 1.	Is insensibility to fear a sin?	254
Art. 2.	Is insensibility to fear opposed to fortitude?	256

QUESTION CXXVII.
OF FIERY DARING.

Art. 1.	Is fiery daring a sin?	257

QUESTION CXXVIII.
OF THE PARTS OF FORTITUDE.

Art. 1.	Are the parts of fortitude suitably enumerated?	258

QUESTION CXXIX.
OF MAGNANIMITY.

Art. 1.	Does magnanimity obtain in the matter of honours?	261
Art. 3.	Is magnanimity a virtue?	262
Art. 8.	Do the goods of fortune contribute to magnanimity?	266

QUESTION CXXX.
OF PRESUMPTION.

Art. 1.	Is presumption a sin?	267
Art. 2.	Is presumption opposed to magnanimity by way of excess?	268

QUESTION CXXXI.
OF AMBITION.

Art. 1.	Is ambition a sin?	269

QUESTION CXXXII.
OF VAINGLORY.

Art. 1.	Is the seeking after glory a sin?	272
Art. 2.	Is vainglory opposed to magnanimity?	274
Art. 3.	Is vainglory a mortal sin?	275

		PAGE
Art. 4.	Is vainglory a capital vice?	275
Art. 5.	Are the daughters of vainglory properly stated to be disobedience, boasting, hypocrisy, contention, obstinacy, discord, and presumption of novelties?	276

QUESTION CXXXIII.
OF PUSILLANIMITY.

| Art. 1. | Is pusillanimity a sin? | 277 |

QUESTION CXXXIV.
OF MUNIFICENCE.

| Art. 3. | Are large expenses the matter of munificence? | 278 |
| Art. 4. | Is munificence a part of fortitude? | 279 |

QUESTION CXXXV.
OF PETTY ECONOMY.

| Art. 1. | Is petty economy a vice? | 281 |

QUESTION CXXXVI.
OF PATIENCE.

| Art. 1. | Is patience a virtue? | 282 |
| Art. 2. | Is patience the chief of virtues? | 283 |

QUESTION CXXXVII.
OF PERSEVERANCE.

| Art. 1. | Is perseverance a virtue? | 285 |
| Art. 2. | Is perseverance a part of fortitude? | 286 |

QUESTION CXLI.
OF TEMPERANCE.

Art. 2.	Is temperance a special virtue?	287
Art. 4.	Is temperance confined to the matter of the desires and delights of touch?	288
Art. 7.	Is temperance a cardinal virtue?	290

QUESTION CXLII.
OF VICES OPPOSED TO TEMPERANCE.

| Art. 1. | Is insensibility a vice? | 291 |
| Art. 2. | Is intemperance a childish sin? | 292 |

		page
Art. 3.	Is cowardice a greater vice than intemperance?	294
Art. 4.	Is the sin of intemperance especially shameful?	296

QUESTION CXLIII.
OF THE PARTS OF TEMPERANCE IN GENERAL.

Art. 1.	Does Tully suitably assign as the parts of temperance, continence, clemency, and decorum?	297

QUESTION CXLV.
OF PROPRIETY.

Art. 3.	Does propriety differ from utility and pleasurableness?	299

QUESTION CXLVI.
OF ABSTINENCE.

Art. 1.	Is abstinence a virtue?	300
Art. 2.	Is abstinence a special virtue?	301

QUESTION CXLVII.
OF FASTING.

Art. 1.	Is fasting an act of virtue?	302
Art. 3.	Is fasting of precept?	304
Art. 4.	Are all bound to observe the fasts of the Church?	305

QUESTION CXLVIII.
OF GLUTTONY.

Art. 1.	Is gluttony the greatest of sins?	307
Art. 4.	Are the species of gluttony distinguished according to these five conditions,—too soon, too expensively, too much, too eagerly, too daintily?	308
Art. 6.	Are the daughters of gluttony duly assigned as five,—inept mirth, buffoonery, uncleanness, much talking, and dulness of mind for intellectual things?	309

QUESTION CXLIX.
OF SOBRIETY.

Art. 3.	Is the use of wine altogether unlawful?	310
Art. 4.	Is sobriety more requisite in greater personages?	311

QUESTION CL.
OF DRUNKENNESS.

Art. 1.	Is drunkenness a sin?	312
Art. 2.	Is drunkenness a mortal sin?	313
Art. 3.	Is drunkenness the most grievous of sins?	314
Art. 4.	Does drunkenness excuse from sin?	315

QUESTION CLI.
OF CHASTITY.

Art. 2.	Is chastity a general virtue?	316
Art. 4.	Does modesty belong specially to chastity?	317

QUESTION CLII.
OF VIRGINITY.

Art. 2.	Is virginity unlawful?	318
Art. 3.	Is virginity a virtue?	320
Art. 4.	Is virginity more excellent than marriage?	322
Art. 5.	Is virginity the greatest of virtues?	323

QUESTION CLIII.
OF THE VICE OF LUXURY.

Art. 2.	Can there be no sexual act without sin?	324
Art. 3.	Can the luxury that is about sexual acts be a sin?	325
Art. 4.	Is luxury a capital vice?	326
Art. 5.	Are the daughters of luxury duly stated to be,—blindness of mind, inconsiderateness, headlong haste, inconstancy, self-love, hatred of God, affection for the present world, horror or despair of the world to come?	326

QUESTION CLIV.
OF THE PARTS OF LUXURY.

Art. 2.	Is simple fornication a mortal sin?	328
Art. 4.	Do touches and kisses amount to a mortal sin?	330
Art. 5.	Is nocturnal pollution a sin?	331

CONTENTS.

Art. 8.	Is adultery a determinate species of luxury distinct from the rest?	*page* 333
Art. 12.	Is unnatural vice the greatest sin of all the species of luxury?	334

QUESTION CLV.
OF THE POTENTIAL PARTS OF TEMPERANCE, AND FIRST OF CONTINENCE.

Art. 1.	Is continence a virtue?	335
Art. 3.	Is the concupiscible faculty the subject of continence?	336
Art. 4.	Is continence better than temperance?	337

QUESTION CLVI.
OF INCONTINENCE.

Art. 1.	Does incontinence belong to the soul or to the body?	338
Art. 3.	Does the incontinent man sin more than the intemperate?	339
Art. 4.	Is the man who is incontinent of anger, worse than him who is incontinent of concupiscence?	342

QUESTION CLVII.
OF CLEMENCY AND MEEKNESS.

Art. 1.	Are clemency and meekness quite the same thing?	343
Art. 4.	Are clemency and meekness virtues of the first rank?	345

QUESTION CLVIII.
OF IRASCIBILITY.

Art. 1.	Is it lawful to get angry?	346
Art. 4.	Is anger a very grievous sin?	349
Art. 6.	Should anger have a place among the capital vices?	349
Art. 7.	Are the daughters of anger duly assigned to be six,—brawling, swelling of spirit, contumely, clamour, indignation, and blasphemy?	350
Art. 8.	Is there any vice, the opposite of irascibility, arising from lack of anger?	351

QUESTION CLIX.
OF CRUELTY.

Art. 2. Does cruelty differ from savagery, or brutality?	353

QUESTION CLXI.
OF HUMILITY.

Art. 1. Is humility a virtue?	354
Art. 2. Is humility concerned with the appetitive faculty?	355
Art. 3. Ought a man in humility to take all men for his superiors?	356
Art. 4. Is humility a part of temperance?	357
Art. 5. Is humility chiefest of virtues?	358
Art. 6. Are the twelve degrees of humility duly marked in the scheme of Blessed Benedict?	360

QUESTION CLXII.
OF PRIDE.

Art. 2. Is pride a special sin?	362
Art. 3. Is the irascible faculty the subject in which pride resides?	363
Art. 5. Is pride a mortal sin?	365
Art. 6. Is pride the most grievous of sins?	366
Art. 8. Should pride be set down for a capital vice?	369

QUESTION CLXVI.
OF STUDIOUSNESS.

Art. 1. Is knowledge properly the matter of studiousness?	370
Art. 2. Is studiousness a part of temperance?	371

QUESTION CLXVII.
OF CURIOSITY.

Art. 1. Can there be curiosity in the matter of intellectual knowledge?	372
Art. 2. Has the vice of curiosity place in the matter of sensible knowledge?	374

QUESTION CLXVIII.
OF MODESTY, OR DECORUM, IN THE OUTWARD MOVEMENTS OF THE BODY.

Art. 1. Is there any virtue in the outward movements of the body? 375
Art. 2. Can there be any virtue in games and sports? . 376
Art. 4. Is there any sin in being too little disposed to sport and play? 380

QUESTION CLXIX.
OF MODESTY IN DRESS.

Art. 1. Can there be virtue and vice in matters of toilet? . 381
Art. 2. Is indulgence of the love of dress a mortal sin in women? 383

QUESTION CLXXXII.
OF THE COMPARISON OF THE ACTIVE LIFE WITH THE CONTEMPLATIVE.

Art. 1. Is the active life better than the contemplative? . 386
Art. 2. Is the active life of greater merit than the contemplative? 387
Art. 3. Is the contemplative life hindered by the active life? . 389

QUESTION CLXXXIII.
OF OFFICES AND VARIOUS STATES OF MEN IN GENERAL.

Art. 1. Does state (*status*) essentially denote the condition of liberty or slavery? 391
Art. 2. Ought there to be in the Church a variety of offices or states? 392
Art. 4. Does the difference of states answer to the difference between beginners, proficients, and perfect? . 394

QUESTION CLXXXIV.
OF WHAT RELATES TO THE STATE OF PERFECTION IN GENERAL.

Art. 1. Is the perfection of Christian life to be looked for in charity especially? 395
Art. 2. Can any one be perfect in this life? . . 396

		page
Art. 3.	Does perfection consist in the precepts or in the counsels?	398
Art. 4.	Is every one who is perfect, in a state of perfection?	400
Art. 5.	Are religious and prelates in a state of perfection?	401
Art. 8.	Are parish priests and archdeacons in positions of greater perfection than religious?	402

QUESTION CLXXXVI.

OF THE THINGS IN WHICH THE RELIGIOUS STATE PROPERLY CONSISTS.

		page
Art. 1.	Does religion mean a state of perfection?	406
Art. 2.	Is every religious bound to all the counsels?	407
Art. 3.	Is poverty a requisite of religious perfection?	410
Art. 4.	Is perpetual continence requisite for the perfection of religious life?	411
Art. 5.	Does obedience appertain to the perfection of religious life?	411
Art. 6.	Is it requisite for religious perfection that poverty, chastity, and obedience, should be made matters of vow?	413
Art. 7.	Is it proper to say that in these three vows religious perfection lies?	414
Art. 8.	Is the vow of obedience chief of the three vows of religion?	416
Art. 10.	Does the religious sin more grievously than the secular for the same kind of sin?	418

QUESTION CLXXXVII.

OF THE THINGS PROPER FOR RELIGIOUS TO DO.

		page
Art. 1.	Is it lawful for religious to preach and teach?	420
Art. 3.	Are religious bound to work with their hands?	422
Art. 4.	Is it lawful for religious to live on alms?	424
Art. 5.	Is it lawful for religious to beg?	426

QUESTION CLXXXVIII.

OF THE VARIETY OF RELIGIOUS ORDERS.

		page
Art. 1.	Is there only one religious order?	428
Art. 2.	Can a religious order be instituted for the works of the active life?	429

		page
Art. 3.	Can there be a religious order destined for military service?	430
Art. 4.	Can a religious order be instituted to preach or hear confessions?	432
Art. 5.	Is it right for a religious order to be instituted for purposes of study?	432
Art. 6.	Does the holding of property in common diminish the perfection of a religious order?	433
Art. 8.	Is a religious order living in community more perfect than an order of solitaries?	436

QUESTION CLXXXIX.
OF THE ENTRY INTO RELIGION.

Art. 1.	Ought they to enter religion, who have not been exercised in the observance of the commandments?	438
Art. 8.	Is it lawful to pass from one religious order to another?	440
Art. 10.	Is it a praiseworthy thing to enter religion without seeking the advice of many persons, and without long previous deliberation?	441

AQUINAS ETHICUS,

OR

THE MORAL TEACHING OF ST. THOMAS,

Translated from the Summa.

SECOND DIVISION, OR SECUNDA SECUNDÆ.

QUESTION XLVII.

OF PRUDENCE.[1]

ARTICLE XII.—*Is prudence in subjects or only in superiors?*

R. Prudence lies in the reason. Now reason's proper office is to rule and govern; and therefore it is proper to every one to have reason and prudence, in so far as he has any part in ruling and governing. But to rule and govern is not the office of the subject, inasmuch as he is a subject, but rather to be ruled and governed; and therefore prudence is not the virtue of the subject as such. But because every man, inasmuch as he is reasonable, has some share in governing according to the free choice of

[1] See *Ethics and Natural Law*, pp. 87—90. (Trl.)

his reason, to that extent it is proper to him to have prudence. Hence it is manifest that prudence is in the superior after the manner of a mastercraft, but in the subject after the manner of a handicraft.

§ 3. By prudence a man not only commands others, but also commands himself in the sense in which reason is said to command the lower powers.

ARTICLE XIII.—*Can there be any prudence in those who live in sin?*

R. Prudence may be understood in three senses. There is a false prudence, or a prudence metaphorically so called. For whereas he is prudent who arranges well what has to be done in order to a good end, he who with an evil end in view makes suitable arrangements for that end has a false prudence, inasmuch as what he takes for an end is not really good, but only has the likeness of good. In this sense, that man may be metaphorically styled *a prudent burglar*, who finds out suitable ways for committing burglary. Of this sort is the prudence of which the Apostle says: "The prudence of the flesh is death,"[1] that, namely, which places its last end in the delight of the flesh. There is a second prudence, true indeed, because it finds out ways adapted to an end that is truly good, but withal an imperfect prudence, because the good which this prudence takes for its end in view is not the common end and aim of all human life, but of some special department of business; as when one discovers fit and suitable methods of trade or navigation, he is

[1] Romans viii. 6.

called a prudent trader or seaman. But the third prudence is at once true and perfect, rightly counselling, judging and commanding in view of the end and aim of all human life; and this alone is absolutely called prudence; and it cannot be in those who live in sin: whereas the first-mentioned prudence is in sinners only, and the imperfect sort of prudence is common to good and bad.

ARTICLE XIV.

§ 3. *Acquired* prudence is caused by the exercise of acts; hence experience and time are needed to create it; and therefore it cannot be in young people either in habit or in act. But *gratuitous* prudence is caused by divine infusion: hence in baptized children that have not come to the use of reason, this prudence is found in habit, but not in act, as also is the case in idiots. But in such as have attained to the use of reason, this prudence is found in act also, for the things that are of necessity to salvation, but by exercise it merits increase until it is perfect, like the other infused virtues.[1]

[1] See I-II. q. 92, art. i. § 1. (Trl.)

QUESTION XLVIII.

OF THE PARTS OF PRUDENCE.

ARTICLE I.—*Are there three assignable parts of prudence?*

R. A *part* is threefold—*integral*, as *wall, roof,* and *foundation* are parts of a house; *subjective*, as *ox* and *lion* are parts of *animal;* and *potential*, as *nutritive* and *sensitive* are parts of the soul. In three ways, therefore, may we assign parts to any virtue. In one way according to the likeness of *integral* parts, calling those things parts of any virtue that must needs concur to the perfect act of the said virtue. Again, by the *subjective* parts of a virtue we understand its different species. In this way the parts of prudence, strictly considered, are the prudence with which a man governs himself, and the prudence with which he governs a people. Lastly, by the *potential* parts of a virtue are understood the adjoining virtues that are directed to secondary acts or matters, and have not the full force of the primary virtue.

QUESTION LV.

OF THE PRUDENCE OF THE FLESH.

ARTICLE I.—*Is the prudence of the flesh a sin?*
R. Prudence is conversant with those things that make for the end and aim of our whole life. And therefore that conduct is properly called *prudence of the flesh*, whereby one takes the goods of the flesh for the ultimate end of his life. Manifestly this is a sin: for hereby man is set in disorder with respect to his last end, which does not consist in the goods of the body.

§ 2. The flesh is for the soul, as the matter for the form, and the instrument for the principal agent. And therefore the flesh is lawfully loved, so that it be directed to the good of the soul as to its end. But if the last end is set up in the mere good of the flesh, the love will be inordinate and unlawful.

ARTICLE VI.—*Is it lawful to entertain solicitude for temporal things?*
R. Solicitude implies an earnestness of effort applied to the gaining of a purpose. Clearly a greater earnestness of effort is applied where there is fear of a failure: and where there is secure confidence of success, less solicitude comes in. Thus

then solicitude for temporal things may be unlawful in three ways. In one way, on the part of the object of our solicitude, if we seek temporal things as our final goal. In another way, by an excessive amount of pains bestowed upon obtaining temporal goods, whereby a man is withdrawn from spiritual things, to which he ought by preference to devote himself. In a third way, by an excess of fear, when a man fears that by his doing what he ought to do the necessaries of life may come to fail him.

§ 1. Temporal goods are subject to man that he may use them for his necessity, not that he may set up his rest in them, or be idly solicitous about them.

ARTICLE VII.—*Ought one to be solicitous about the future?*

R. No work can be virtuous unless it be clothed in due circumstances, one of which is due time, according to the text: "There is a time and opportunity for every business;"[1] which saying obtains, not only for outward works, but also for inward solicitude. For every time has it own befitting solicitude, as summer brings the solicitude of reaping, and autumn the solicitude of gathering in the fruit. Any one that in summer-time was already solicitous about gathering in the fruit, would be idly anticipating the solicitude of time to come. Hence our Lord forbids such solicitude as idle, saying: "Be not solicitous for to-morrow; for the morrow will be solicitous for itself;"[2] that is, will.

[1] Eccles. viii. 6.   [2] St. Matt. vii. 34.

have its own proper solicitude, which will be sufficient to afflict the soul. And this is the meaning of the addition: "Sufficient for the day is the evil thereof;" that is, the affliction of solicitude which it brings.

§ 1. The ant has a solicitude suitable to the season; and this is what is proposed to us for imitation.[1]

QUESTION LVII.

OF RIGHT.[2]

ARTICLE I.—*Is right the object of justice?*
R. The proper office of justice in its place among virtues is to direct a man in his dealings *with another*. For justice involves a certain equality, as the name itself shows; for the things that are equalized are said to be *adjusted;* and equality is a relation of one thing *with another*. Other virtues perfect a man only in what is his own private concern. They regard the agent, and the agent exclusively, in the rectitude of conduct which they determine and aim at as their object; but justice fixes its rectitude of conduct in reference to some one else—even passing over the agent. That is called *just* in our doings, which is in some sort of equality corresponding to

---

[1] Prov. vi. 6—8.
[2] In Latin, as in French, the same word stands for both *law* and *right*. An English translator must give the meaning which seems to him predominant each time the word occurs. (Trl.)

something else, as in the instance of wages corresponding to work done. So then that is just, which is the term of a just action, even irrespectively of the disposition of the agent. But in other virtues right action always supposes a certain disposition of the agent.[1] And therefore what is called *just*, that is, *right*, is determined to be the proper object of justice above other virtues.

§ 3. Because justice involves equality, and we cannot make an equivalent return to God, hence we cannot render to God what is *just* in the proper sense of the word. Justice, however, tends to this end, that man so far as he can, should make a return to God, subjecting his whole soul to Him.

ARTICLE II.—*Is right properly divided into natural right and positive right?*

R. *Right*, or a *just settlement*, is some work made adequate to another work according to some measure of equality. Now a man may get an adequate return in two ways: in one way, by the very nature of the thing, as when one gives so much to receive exactly as much; and this is called *natural right*. In another way, one thing is adequate to, or commensurate with another thing by convention, or some common resolve, that is, when a party reckons himself satisfied if he receives so much. And this may be either by private agreement or by public convention, as when a whole people agree that one thing be held adequate to and commensurate with another: or when the prince, who bears the person

[1] Cf I-II. q. 64. art. 2. (Trl.)

of the people, ordains this. And this is called *positive right*.[1]

§ 2. The will of men by common agreement can make a thing just in matters that of themselves are not irreconcilable with natural justice; and in these matters *positive law* has place. Hence the Philosopher says: "Legal justice is in a case where, to start with, it makes no difference whether the thing be so or otherwise; but when the enactment is made, it does make a difference." But whatever is of itself irreconcilable with natural law, cannot be made just by human will. Hence it is said: "Woe to them that make wicked laws."[2]

ARTICLE IV.—*Is paternal right to be placed in a special category?*

R. *Right*, or a *just claim*, implies the proportion of one thing to another. That is *absolutely other*, which is altogether distinct, as in the case of two men, one of whom is not under the other, though they are both under one civil ruler; and between such parties a transaction is possible that can be called *absolutely just*. In another way a being is called *other*, not absolutely, but as being a part of another being; and in this way the child is in a manner part of the father. And therefore the father is not matched with his child as with some-

---

[1] This does not coincide with the modern division of *natural* and *acquired* rights; nor does it show in what sense we affirm that a man has a *natural right* to live, to marry, to acquire property, &c. Cf. *Ethics and Natural Law*, pp. 244—246. (Trl.)

[2] Isaias x. 1.

thing absolutely other than himself; and therefore there is not here a case of absolute justice, or absolute right, but of a certain sort of right, namely, *paternal* right. Whereas, though the wife is part of the husband, standing to him as his own body,[1] still she is more distinct from the husband than the child from the father, inasmuch as she is taken into partnership in matrimonial life; and therefore there is more of the nature of justice between husband and wife than between father and child.

§ 1. It is a point of justice to render to every one what is by rights his own, on the supposition, however, of a diversity between the two parties; for if any one gives to himself what is due to himself, that is not properly called *just dealing*.

§ 2. The son, as a son, is his father's chattel; and in like manner the slave, as a slave, is his master's chattel. But both the one and the other, considered as a man, is something subsisting by himself distinct from other beings. And therefore, inasmuch as both the one and the other is a man, justice in some way extends to them. Therefore also there are sundry laws given for the dealings of a father with his son, or of a master with his slave. But to the extent that either son or slave is the chattel of another, the perfect idea of a *just claim* or *right* so far fails to be verified in them.

[1] Ephes. v. 28.

QUESTION LVIII.

OF JUSTICE.[1]

ARTICLE I.—*Is justice aptly defined to be a standing and abiding will to give every one his due?*

R. In the definition of justice, the first thing set down is *will*, to show that the act of justice ought to be voluntary; then *standing and abiding* is added, to mark the firmness of the act. And therefore the above is a complete definition of justice, except that the act of willing is put for the habit. And if any one wished to reduce it to the proper form of a definition, he might say that *justice is a habit, whereby with a standing and abiding will one gives every one his due.*

ARTICLE II.—*Is justice always to another?*

R. The name of *justice* implies an equality, and therefore justice is essentially *to another*: for nothing is equal to itself, but *to another*. And because it belongs to justice to rectify human acts, the equality that justice requires must be between different agents. Now actions are the actions of substances and wholes, not properly of parts and forms, or powers; for it is not properly said that the hand

[1] *Ethics and Natural Law*, pp. 102—108. (Trl.)

strikes, but the man with the hand; nor is it properly said that heat warms, but the fire through the heat. The other expressions are used, but they are analogical. Justice therefore, properly so called, requires a diversity between those who are parties to it; and holds consequently only of one man in relation to another. But analogically, we may take for different agents different principles of action in one and the same man, as *reason*, and the *irascible faculty*, and the *concupiscible;* and therefore, metaphorically, justice is said to obtain in one and the same man, inasmuch as reason rules the irascible and concupiscible faculties, and they obey reason, and generally inasmuch as to every part of man there is assigned its proper office. Hence the Philosopher styles this, *justice metaphorically so-called.*[1]

§ 4. The behaviour of a man in regard of himself is sufficiently rectified by the rectification of the passions, which is the work of the other moral virtues; but the behaviour of one man towards another man needs a special rectification, not in relation to the agent only, but likewise in relation to the other person with whom he deals. And therefore there is a special virtue concerned with that behaviour, namely, justice.

ARTICLE IV.—*Is the will the subject of justice?*

R. That power is the subject of justice, to the rectification of whose acts justice is directed. Now justice is not directed to the guidance of any

[1] This is aimed at the account of justice given by Plato, *Rep.* 443. 444. (Trl.)

cognitive act; for we are not called *just* for the fact of our knowing anything correctly. And therefore the subject of justice is not the intellect or reason, which is a cognitive power. But because we are called *just* in this that we do a thing rightly, and the proximate principle of action is the appetitive faculty, some portion of the appetitive faculty must be the subject of justice. Now the appetitive faculty is twofold: the will, which is in the reason; and the sensitive appetite that follows the apprehension of sense, which sensitive appetite is divided into *irascible* and *concupiscible*. But the rendering to every one of his own cannot proceed from the sensitive appetite; because the apprehension of sense does not extend to the consideration of the proportion of one thing to another: that is proper to reason. Hence neither the irascible nor the concupiscible faculty can be the subject of justice, but the will alone.

ARTICLE V.—*Is justice a general virtue?*

R. Justice directs a man in his relations with another. That may be either with another in his individual aspect, or with another in general, inasmuch as he who serves a community serves all the human beings who are comprised in that community. Justice in its proper essence may deal with either of these objects. All who are comprised in a community stand to the community as parts to the whole. Now all that the part is, belongs to the whole; hence everything good in the part is referable to the good of the whole. In this way then the goodness of every virtue, whether it directs a man in regard of himself, or directs him in regard of other individuals, is referable to the general good to which justice leads. And thus the acts of all the virtues may belong to justice, as that directs a man to the general good; and in this respect justice is called a *general* virtue. And because it is the office of law to direct a people to the general good, hence the above-described general justice is styled *legal justice*, because by it man keeps accord with the law that directs acts of all the virtues to the general good.

ARTICLE VI.—*Is justice, inasmuch as it is a general virtue, essentially identical with all virtue?*

R. The word *general* may be taken in two ways. One way is the way of *logical predication*, as *animal* is a general term with respect to *man* and *horse*. What is general in this way, must be identical in essence with the things about which it is general; because the *genus* belongs to the essence of the *species*, and is included in the definition of the same. A thing is otherwise called general in the way of efficiency. Thus a universal cause is general in reference to all its effects, as the sun in reference to all bodies that are illuminated or changed by its virtue. What is general in this way, need not be identical in essence with the objects in respect whereof it is general: because the essence of the effect and of the cause is not the same. In this latter way legal justice is said to be a general virtue, inasmuch as it directs the acts of the other virtues to its own end, or sets in motion by its command all the other virtues. For as charity may be called a general virtue, inasmuch as it directs the acts of all the other virtues to the good that is in God; so may legal justice also be called general, as it directs the acts of all the virtues to the good of the commonwealth. As then charity is a special virtue in its essence, regarding as its proper object the good that is in God; so also is legal justice a special virtue in its essence, and regards as its special object the good of the commonwealth. And thus legal justice is in the sovereign *principally and after the manner of a master-craft,* but *secondarily and subordinately* in the subject. Legal justice then is a virtue, special in its essence, general in its efficacy.

Any virtue however, inasmuch as it is directed thereby to the good of the commonwealth, may be called *legal justice;* and in this wide sense legal justice is identical in essence with all virtue, but differs in the consideration of the mind.[1]

ARTICLE VII.—*Besides general, is there any particular justice?*

R. Legal justice is not essentially all virtue: but besides legal justice, that directs men immediately to the good of the commonwealth, there must be other virtues that direct them immediately in the matter of private good, touching either a man's own self or his relation to some other individual. For the right ordering of a man within himself, we require the particular virtues of temperance and

[1] See *Ethics and Natural Law,* pp. 103, 104. (Trl.)

fortitude: so also, besides legal justice, there must be some particular justice, rightly to order a man in matters that touch another private individual.

ARTICLE VIII.—*Has particular justice any special subject-matter?*

R. All things whatever that can be set right by reason, are the subject-matter of moral virtue. Now the interior passions of the soul, and exterior actions, and exterior things that come under the use of man, are all capable of being set right by reason. The rectification of a man within himself involves attention to interior passions. But the relation of one man to another is by exterior actions, and by exterior things that men can share one with another. And therefore, since justice is in relation to another, it does not embrace the whole subject-matter of moral virtue, but exterior actions only, and exterior things, inasmuch as one man thereby has dealings with another.

ARTICLE IX.—*Does justice deal with the passions?*

R. The true answer to this question is evident from two considerations; first from considering the subject of justice, which is the will, the motions of which power are not passions; only the motions of the sensitive appetite are termed passions; and therefore justice does not deal with the passions, as do temperance and fortitude, which are found in the concupiscible and irascible faculties respectively. In another way the answer appears from the consideration of the subject-matter: for the matter of justice is our dealings with our neighbour; now it is not by the passions that we are brought into immediate relation with our neighbour.[1]

ARTICLE XI.—*Is it the act of justice to render to every man his own?*

R. The subject-matter of justice is exterior conduct, inasmuch as the conduct itself, or the thing that we make use of therein, is proportioned to another person, to whom we have relations of justice. Now that is said to be every person's *own*, which is due to him on the principle of proportionate equality.[2] And therefore the proper act of justice is nothing else than to render to every one his own.

[1] Article x. repeats the doctrine of I-II. q. 64. art. 2. (Trl.)
[2] The principle of τὸ ἴσον τὸ ἀντιπεπονθός, which Aristotle (*Politics*, II. ii. 4.) says "is the saving of society."

QUESTION LIX.

OF INJUSTICE.

ARTICLE III.—*Can one suffer injustice willingly?*
R. Properly, and formally speaking, no one can do injustice otherwise than willingly, nor suffer it otherwise than unwillingly. But accidentally, and materially speaking, one may either do unwillingly, or suffer willingly, that which is of itself unjust.

QUESTION LX.

OF JUDGMENT.

ARTICLE III.—*Is judgment unlawful when it proceeds upon suspicion?*
R. Suspicion is an evil opinion entertained on slight grounds. It may arise in three ways. In one way from the evil character of him who entertains it, who conscious of his own wickedness, easily thinks ill of others; according to the text: "The fool when he walketh in the way, whereas he is himself a fool, esteemeth all men fools."[1] In another way from being ill-affected towards a neigh-

[1] Eccles. x. 3.

bour: for when you despise or hate a person, or are angry with him or envy him, you are apt to think evil of him upon slight indications, because every one easily believes that which he desires. In a third way this arises from long experience: hence the Philosopher says that "old men are particularly suspicious, because they have often had experience of others' shortcomings." Now the first two causes of suspicion manifestly argue some moral obliquity in the harbourer of the suspicion: while the third cause takes off from the essence of the suspicion, inasmuch as experience is an advance towards certainty, and certainty is essentially opposed to suspicion. Therefore suspicion involves a moral flaw in him who harbours it; and the further the suspicion goes, the greater the vice. Now there are three degrees of suspicion. The first degree consists in a man beginning to doubt of the goodness of another on slight indications. This sin is venial and light, a part of that human temptation without which this life cannot be lived. The second degree is when you make up your mind for certain as to the wickedness of another on slight indications; and if this be on any grave matter, it is a mortal sin, inasmuch as it is not without contempt of your neighbour. Hence the gloss says: "If we cannot avoid suspicions, because we are men; at least we ought to refrain from judgments, that is, from definitive and fixed pronouncements." The third degree is when a judge proceeds to condemn a man on suspicion; and this is a direct act of injustice, and consequently a mortal sin.

ARTICLE IV.—*Is a favourable construction to be put on dubious proceedings?*

R. By having a bad opinion of another without sufficient cause, you do him an injury and contemn him. Now none ought to contemn another, or do him any hurt, without cogent reason. And therefore, where no clear indications appear of another's wickedness, we ought to hold him to be good, putting a favourable construction on what is doubtful.

§ 2. It is one thing to judge of things, another of persons. In judging of things, there is no question of any good or evil to accrue to the thing that we judge of: for the thing is not hurt, however we judge of it. The only matter at stake here is the estate of him who forms the judgment—good, if he judges rightly; evil, if he judges falsely: because truth is the good of the intellect, and falsehood the evil thereof; and therefore every one ought to strive to judge of things as they are. But in judging of men, the principal matter at stake is the good or evil thereby accruing to him who is judged,—who is held to be worthy of honour in being judged to be good, and is held up to contempt, if he is judged to be a bad man. And therefore in such a judgment we should rather make a point of judging a man to be good, unless manifest reason appear to the contrary.

§ 3. A favourable or unfavourable construction may be put upon a proceeding, *hypothetically.* In that way, when we are bound to apply a remedy to evils, whether our own or other people's, it is expedient for the safer application of the remedy to suppose the worse side of the case; because the remedy that is efficacious against a greater evil is much more efficacious against a smaller evil. Or the construction may be put *definitively* or *peremptorily;* and in that way, in judging of *things,* we ought to strive to interpret each thing according as it is; but in judging of *persons,* to lean in our interpretation to the better side.

ARTICLE VI.—*Does usurpation make judgment void?*

R. He who pronounces judgment, interprets the utterance of the law, applying it to a particular case. Now it belongs to the same authority to enact a law and to interpret it. A law cannot be enacted, nor a judgment passed, except by public authority. And thus, as it would be unjust to compel a man to observe a law that was not enacted by public authority, so also is it unjust to compel a man to submit to a sentence that is not passed by public authority.[1]

[1] This is the condemnation of *imperium in imperio,* that is, of two authorities *in the same order* in one State. (Trl.)

QUESTION LXI.

OF THE PARTS OF JUSTICE.

ARTICLE I.—*Is it proper to assign two species of justice, commutative and distributive?*

R. Particular justice is in relation to some private person, who stands to the community as a part to the whole. Now to a part we may either have another part related; and that expresses the relation of one private person to another, which relation is regulated by *commutative justice*, or the justice that is concerned with the mutual dealings of two private persons one with another: or again, we have the relation of the whole to the part; and such is the relation of the community to the individual, which relation is presided over by *distributive justice*, or the justice that distributes the goods of the common stock according to proportion. And therefore there are two species of justice, *distributive* and *commutative*.

§ 3. The act of distribution of the goods of the common stock belongs to him alone who presides over the common stock. Nevertheless distributive justice is found also in the subjects to whom the distribution is made, inasmuch as they are content with a just distribution.

ARTICLE II.—*Is the mean taken in the same way in distributive as in commutative justice?*

R. In distributive justice the mean is not taken according to equality of thing to thing, but according to the proportion of things to persons, so that in proportion as one person exceeds another, so also the thing that is given to the one person exceeds the thing that is given to the other. But in exchanges we must equalize thing to thing, so that whatever excess one party gets, over and above what is his own, of what belongs to another, so much exactly he should restore to the party to whom it belongs.

ARTICLE III.—*Is the matter of each of these two species of justice the same?*

R. Justice is conversant with the exterior acts of distribution and exchange. These are acts of disposing of exterior objects, either *things*, or *persons*, or *services*: *things*, as when one takes away from or restores to another the thing that is his; *persons*, as when one does wrong to the corporal presence of a man, striking him, or using insulting language to him, or again, when one shows him reverence; *services*, as when one justly exacts some service of another, or renders him some service due. If, therefore, we take as the matter of both species of justice the objects that we act upon and use, the matter of distributive and commutative justice is the same; for things can be distributed from the common store to individuals, and also exchanged between one individual and another: and there is also a distribution of laborious services, and a recompensing of the same. But if we take as the matter of the two species of justice the principal actions themselves by which we make use of persons, things, and services, at that rate we find different subject-matter in the two species. For distributive justice presides over distributions, while commutative justice presides over the exchanges that may have place between two individuals. Of these exchanges some are *involuntary*, some *voluntary*. Those are *involuntary*, in which one uses the thing, or person, or service of another against his will.[1] This is done sometimes by fraud, sometimes by open violence. Both the one and the other have place either touching your neighbour's *thing*, or touching his *person*, or touching *some person related* to him. Touching a *thing*, if one takes the thing of another secretly, it is called *theft*; if openly, it is called *robbery*. The involuntary exchange touches the *person* of your neighbour either in its *substance* or in its *dignity*. In the *substance* of his person, a neighbour is injured *secretly* by *assassination*, or by *poison*; *openly* by open *murder*, or by *imprisonment*, or by *beating*, or by *maiming*. In the *dignity* of his person, a neighbour is injured *secretly* by *false witness* or *detraction*; *openly*, by a *judicial accusation*, or by *abusive language* addressed to him. Touching a *person related* to him, a man is injured in his wife by *adultery*, and that *secretly* for the most part.

 Voluntary exchanges, as they are called, are when

[1] *Ethics and Natural Law*, pp. 106 foot, 107. (Trl.)

one voluntarily transfers the thing that is his to another. If the transference is absolute without its being due, as in a gift, that is not an act of justice, but of liberality. A voluntary transference is a matter of justice, then when it bears some character of being due. And this character may be borne in many ways. One way is when a person absolutely transfers the thing that is his to another, to receive compensation in something else, as in *buying and selling*. Another way is when one hands over the thing that is his to another, granting him the use of the thing, but reserving a claim to the recovery of the thing. If he grants the use of the thing gratis, it is called *usufruct* in things that fructify, *loan* or *lending* in things that do not fructify. If not even the use is granted gratis, it is called *letting* and *hiring*. In a third way a man hands over the thing that is his, making it returnable to himself, and bargaining that the receiver shall not use it in the meanwhile, but shall merely hold it in safe-keeping, as a *deposit* or a *pledge*.

In all transactions such as these enumerated, whether voluntary or involuntary, the same principle holds of fixing the mean according to an even balance of *give* and *take*. And therefore the said transactions all belong to one species of justice, namely, commutative.

QUESTION LXII.

OF RESTITUTION.

ARTICLE I.—*Is restitution an act of commutative justice?*

R. To *restore* is nothing else than to re-establish a man in the possession or ownership of that which is his; and thus in restitution the equality of justice is obtained by weighing *thing* against *thing;* which is characteristic of commutative justice. And therefore restitution is an act of commutative justice, and has place when the thing belonging to one man is held by another, whether by the will of the owner, as in a case of loan or deposit, or against his will, as in robbery or theft.

ARTICLE II.

§ 2. There are three ways of taking away another's character. One is by telling the truth in due order of justice; and then no obligation of restitution exists. Another way is by telling a falsehood contrary to justice; and then the party is bound to restore his neighbour's character by confessing that what he said was false. The third way consists in telling the truth, but unjustly, as when in violation of due order one reveals the crime of another; in which case he is bound to restore that other's character, so far as he can without lying, as by saying that he has spoken amiss, or has defamed him unjustly; or if he cannot restore his character, he is bound to make it up to him in some other way.

ARTICLE III.—*Is it enough to restore the simple amount that has been unjustly taken away?*

R. There are two things to consider in a case of one man taking that which belongs to another. There is first the disturbance of equilibrium of possession, which disturbance may be without injustice, as in loans. Then there is the crime of injustice, which may exist even where equilibrium of possession is undisturbed, as when one seeks to do violence but prevails not. On the first count a remedy is applied by restitution, whereby the equilibrium is restored; and for this it suffices to restore the exact amount that we have taken of another's property. But to the crime a remedy is applied by a penalty, which it is the judge's office to inflict. And therefore, before the culprit is condemned by the judge, he is not bound to restore more than he has taken; but after he is condemned, he is bound to pay the penalty.

ARTICLE IV.—*Is any one bound to restore what he has not taken away?*

R. Whatever causes loss to another may be considered to take away from him so much as the loss amounts to; for according to the Philosopher, *loss* means some one having *less* than he ought to have.[1] And therefore a man is bound to restore the amount of loss that he has caused. But there are two ways of suffering loss. One way is by a person being deprived of what he actually had; and such loss must always be made good by paying back an equal amount. Thus if one pulls down another man's house, he is bound to restitution to the extent of the value of the house. Another way of causing loss to a neighbour is by hindering him from attaining what he was in the way of having. Such loss need not be made good by the payment of an equal amount, because the potential having of a thing is less than the actual having; and he who is in the way of attaining has the thing only virtually or potentially; and therefore, if restitution were so made to him as that he should have the thing in act and present reality, he would have that which was taken away restored to him, not simply, but with advantages, which is not necessary to perfect restitution. But he who took it away is bound to make some restitution according to the condition of persons and affairs.

§ 1. He who has sown seed in his land has not yet got the harvest actually, but only virtually; and in like manner [§ 2] he who has money has not yet got gain actually, but only virtually; and both

---

[1] *Loss, less; damnum, minus.* The etymology, if any is intended, is more apparent in the English than in the Latin. Aristotle (*Ethics*, V. iv. 13) says simply, τὸ ἔλαττον τῶν ἐξ ἀρχῆς ἔχειν—"Loss is having less than one had to start with." (Trl.)

the one and the other acquisition may in many ways be hindered.[1]

ARTICLE V.—*Is restitution always to be made to the person from whom the thing was taken?*

R. By restitution a return is made to the equality of commutative justice, which consists in an equilibrium of possessions. Such equilibrium would be impossible, unless the deficiency were made up to him who has got less than of right belongs to him. In order to make up this deficiency, restitution must be made to him from whom the thing was taken away.

§ 1. When the thing to be restored is evidently grievously hurtful to the party to whom restitution is due, or to another party, then restitution ought not to be made to him, because the end of restitution is the utility of him who receives it; for all articles of possession fall under the category of the useful. Still the retainer of another man's goods ought not to appropriate them to himself, but either preserve them for restitution at a fit time, or hand them over to another for safer custody.

§ 2. There are two sorts of unlawful giving. In one the giving itself is unlawful and illegal, as in the case of simony. The giver there deserves

---

[1] Might be hindered, that is to say, in the thirteenth century. St. Thomas was reluctant to recognize a principle that he saw would go to justify the taking of interest on money lent. We have in fact here the title of interest known as *lucrum cessans*, a title that has been generally validated by circumstances which have arisen since St. Thomas wrote. See *Ethics and Natural Law*, pp. 260, 261. (Trl.)

to lose his gift : hence restitution ought not to be made to him. And because the receiver also has broken the law in receiving, he ought not to keep the money for himself, but to turn it to pious uses. The other sort of unlawful giving is giving for a service that is unlawful, though the giving itself is not unlawful, as when one gives to a prostitute her hire. Hence such a woman can keep what is given her: but if she had extorted anything in excess by fraud or guile, she would be bound to make restitution to the party of whom she had it.

§ 3. If no trace can be found of the person to whom restitution is due, the other party is bound to restore so far as he can, by giving alms for his good estate, alive or dead, but not before diligent inquiry made after the person. If the party is dead, restitution is due to his heir, who counts as one person with him. If he is far distant, what is due should be forwarded to him, especially if it is a thing of great value, and can be forwarded easily : otherwise it should be deposited in some safe place to keep for him, and notification thereof sent to the owner.

ARTICLE VI.—*Is he always bound to restitution, who has taken the thing?*

R. There are two matters to consider, the thing itself taken, and the taking of it. Now on the score of the thing taken, a party is bound to restitution so long as he has the thing in his possession : because what he has over and above his own, ought to be withdrawn from him and given to the person to whom it is missing, according to the form of commutative justice. But the act itself of taking the thing that is another's may assume three several shapes. Sometimes it is wrongful, being done against the will of the owner, as in theft or robbery; and then the taker is bound to restitution, not only on the score of the thing, but also on the score of the wrongful act, even though the thing does not remain in his possession. For as he who strikes another is bound to make compensation for the injury to the sufferer, although nothing remains in his possession: so whoever robs or steals is bound to compensate the loss inflicted, even though he have no profit therefrom; and he ought further to be punished for the wrong done. In another way one takes the thing of another to his own benefit without wrong-doing, that is, with the consent of the owner, as in loans; and then the taker is bound to restitution of the thing taken, not only on the score of the thing, but also on the score of the taking, even though he has lost the thing: for he is bound to recompense him who has done him a favour, which will not be recompensed if the benefactor loses by the transaction. In a third way one takes the thing of another without wrong-doing, but without any benefit to himself; such is the case of a deposit; and he who thus takes a thing is nowise bound on the score of the taking,—nay, by taking he renders a service; but he is bound on the score of the thing taken. And therefore, if the thing passes from him without his own fault, he is not bound to restitution. It would be a different case, if he lost the deposit through his own great fault.

ARTICLE VII.—*Are they bound to restitution, who have not taken the thing?*

R. There is an obligation of restitution, not only on the score of the thing taken, belonging to another, but also on the score of wrongful taking. And therefore whoever is a cause of wrongful taking, is bound to restitution. And this has place in two ways, *directly* and *indirectly*.[1] *Directly,* when one induces another to take a thing, either by express precept, counsel, or consent, moving him to take, or by praising him as a man of spirit for having taken, or by harbouring him, or by lending a hand in his crime of theft or robbery. *Indirectly,* when one does not hinder it, having the power and the duty to hinder it, or when one keeps back a command or an admonition that would hinder the theft or robbery, or withholds his own assistance whereby he could prevent it, or conceals the deed after it is done. We must know however that five only of the above connections always bind to restitution. First, *command*, because whoever commands is the prime mover: hence he is primarily bound to restore. Second, *consent*, in the case of him without whose consent the robbery could not be committed. Third, *harbouring*, when one is a harbourer and patron of robbers. Fourth, *partaking* in the crime and in the booty. Fifth, *non-intervention*, when you are bound to intervene; as princes, who are bound to maintain justice in the land, are bound to restitution, if by their shortcoming robbers increase; because the revenues that they have are a sort of pay

---

[1] We should say, *positively* and *negatively*. (Tri.)

regularly given to this end, that they may maintain justice. But in the other cases enumerated there is not always an obligation of restitution; for *counsel*, or *flattery*, or the like, is not always an efficacious cause of robbery. Hence the adviser or flatterer is then only bound to restitution, when there is room for a probable estimate that the unjust taking followed on such causation.

§ 3. He who does not inform against a robber, or who stands not in his way, or reproves him not, is not always bound to restitution, but only when he has an official duty to do these things, as rulers of the land have, who are not much endangered by doing so: for it is to this effect that they hold office, that they may be the guardians of justice.[1]

[1] It is not enough that you have sinned anyhow, say, against charity, in allowing your neighbour to sin against justice; but your connivance at his act must amount to a breach of commutative justice in you, before you are bound to restitution in default of his making it. See *Ethics and Natural Law*, pp. 107, 108, 244. (Tr.)

QUESTION LXIII.

OF THE RESPECTING OF PERSONS.

ARTICLE I.—*Is the respecting of persons a sin?*

R. The respecting of persons[1] is opposed to distributive justice. For the equality of distributive justice consists in this, that to different persons different things are assigned in proportion to their several dignities and deserts. If therefore one has regard to that attribute in a person, which makes the thing conferred due to him, that is no respecting of the person but a regard for the cause. For instance, if one promotes a person to the degree of master on account of his sufficiency of learning, there the cause of the thing being due[2] is regarded, not the person. But if in the person on whom you bestow some emolument you consider, not the reason that makes the bestowal appropriate or due to him, but only the fact of his being this man, Peter, or Martin, that is a respecting of persons, because the honour is awarded, not for any cause that makes the receiver worthy, but it is awarded simply to the person. That consideration must be held to be a purely personal consideration, which is not in respect of any cause rendering the party

---

[1] Deut. i. 17.   [2] Read *causa debiti*. (Trl.)

worthy of the gift in question. Thus if one promotes another to a prelacy, or to a master's degree, because he is rich, or because he is a relation of his, that is a respecting of the person.

§ 3. There are two manners of giving: one appertaining to justice, whereby one gives to another what is due to him; and about such gifts the respecting of persons has place. There is another manner of giving appertaining to liberality, whereby that is given gratuitously to another which is not due to him. Such is the bestowal of the gifts of grace, by which sinners are taken into favour by God. In this bestowal the respecting of persons has no place, because without injustice every one may give of his own as much as he wills, and to whom he wills, according to the text: "Is it not lawful for me to do what I will? Take what is thine and go thy way."[1]

ARTICLE II.—*Is there room for the respecting of persons in the dispensation of spiritualities?*

R. Seeing that it is a respecting of persons when something is assigned to a person beyond the proportion in which he is worthy, we may observe that the worthiness of a person may be determined from two points of view. One way it may be determined *absolutely and in itself;* and in that way he is the more worthy, who abounds more in spiritual gifts of grace. Another way is in reference to the common good; for sometimes the less holy and the less learned may be more available for the common

[1] St. Matt. xx. 14, 15.

good, by reason of worldly ability or business capacity, or some other such advantage. And because the dispensing of spiritualities has place principally in view the profit of the community, according to the text: "The manifestation of the Spirit is given to every man unto profit:"[1] therefore at times, without any respecting of persons, the absolutely less good are preferred to the better in the dispensation of spiritualities,[2] as also God at times grants to the less good the graces that are *graciously given.*[3]

§ 1. Concerning a Prelate's kindred a distinction must be drawn. For sometimes they are less worthy both absolutely and in regard of the common good; and in that case, if they are preferred to others more worthy, it is a sin of respect-

---

[1] 1 Cor. xii. 7.

[2] An example of the holier as distinguished from the more capable Pontiff, might perhaps be found in Celestine V. (St. Peter Celestine), in comparison with his successor, Boniface VIII. (Trl.)

[3] The priestly powers of absolving, consecrating, &c., are called by theologians *graces graciously given.* "There is one grace whereby the man himself is united to God, which is called *grace making gracious*: another grace by which one man co-operates with another to the end that the latter may be brought under God. Such a gift is called a *grace graciously given,* because it is granted above the power of nature and above the merit of the person. But because it is not given to the end that the man himself may be justified by it, but rather that he may co-operate towards the justification of another, therefore it is not called *making gracious.*" I-II. q. 111. art. 1. (not translated).

In other words, *grace making gracious* is mainly intended for the sanctification of the receiver, and makes him dear or acceptable to God. *Grace graciously given* is mainly given for the sanctification of others, and is so called because, being given gratuitously, it should be administered gratuitously. (Trl.)

ing of persons in the dispensing of spiritual goods, goods of which the Prelate is not master, to be able to give them as he likes, but only dispenser.[1] Sometimes on the other hand the Prelate's kindred are equally worthy with the rest; and in that case he may lawfully prefer his kindred without respecting of persons; because in this at least they are superior, that he can trust them more to be of one mind with him in the handling of ecclesiastical affairs. Still this advantage should be foregone on the ground of scandal, if others would take example thence of giving the goods of the Church to their kinsmen even apart from worthiness.

§ 3. For the election to be unexceptionable before a judicial tribunal, it is enough to choose a good man, and there is no need to choose the better man; otherwise every election would be open to cavil. But for the conscience of the elector it is necessary to choose him who is the better man, either absolutely, or in respect of the common good. The reason is, because if a more fit and proper person can be found for the dignity, and another is preferred to it, this must be for some cause: now if that cause be germane to the matter, then the more fit and proper person will be the person elected; but if it be not germane to the matter, that which is had in view as the cause will be manifestly a respecting of persons.

§ 4. He who is taken from the bosom of the local church to which he is appointed, usually proves more useful for the common good, because he has

[1] 1 Cor. iv. 1.

a greater love for the church in which he has been brought up. And therefore the command is given, "Thou shalt not make a man of another nation king, that is not thy brother."[1]

ARTICLE III.—*Has the sin of respecting of persons any place in the showing of honour and reverence?*

R. Honour is a testimony to the virtue of him who is honoured; and therefore virtue alone is a due cause of honour. But it must be observed that a person must be honoured, not only for his own virtue, but also for the virtue of another; as Princes and Prelates are honoured, though they be of evil life, inasmuch as they bear the person of God, and of the community over whom they are set, according to the text: "As he that casteth a stone into the heap of Mercury,[2] so is he that giveth honour to a fool."[3] For because the Gentiles assigned the keeping of accounts to Mercury, *a heap of Mercury* means *a heap of pebbles used for keeping accounts*, in which a merchant sometimes puts one pebble or counter in place of a hundred dollars. Thus also the fool is honoured, who is set in place of God and in place of the whole community.

[1] Deut. xvii. 15.
[2] The Anglican version of this obscure text is, "As he that bindeth a stone in a sling:" which is taken to mean that, as the stone cast from a sling is lost, so the honour paid to a fool is thrown away. (Trl.)
[3] Prov. xxvi. 8.

QUESTION LXIV.

OF HOMICIDE.

ARTICLE I.—*Is the killing of living creatures in all cases an unlawful act?*

R. No one does wrong in using a thing for the purpose for which it exists. Now in the order of being, less perfect things exist for the sake of the more perfect, as in the way of generation nature proceeds from imperfect to perfect things. Hence it is that as in the generation of man there is first the living thing, then the animal, and lastly the man; so also the things that merely live, as plants, exist generally for the sake of animals; and all animals exist for the sake of man. And therefore if man uses plants for the benefit of animals, and animals for the benefit of mankind, it is not unlawful. But of all uses the most necessary seems to be that animals should use plants for food, and men animals, which cannot be without putting them to death. And therefore it is lawful to do plants to death for the use of animals, and animals to death for the use of men. For it is said: "Behold I have given you every herb and all trees to be your meat, and to all beasts of the earth;"[1] and, "Everything that moveth and liveth shall be meat for you."[2]

[1] Genesis i. 29.   [2] Genesis ix. 3.

§ 1. By divine ordinance the life of animals and plants is preserved, not for their own sakes, but for the sake of man. Hence as Augustine says, "both their life and their death are subject to our uses."

§ 2. Dumb animals and plants have no rational life, thereby to be led of themselves; but they are always led as it were of another, by natural impulse; and this is a sign that they are *naturally slaves*,[1] and suited to serve the uses of others.

ARTICLE II.—*Is it lawful to slay sinners?*

R. Every part is referred to the whole as the imperfect to the perfect; and therefore every part naturally exists for the whole. And therefore we see that if it be expedient for the welfare of the whole human body that some member should be amputated, as being rotten and corrupting the other members, the amputation is praiseworthy and wholesome. But every individual stands to the whole community as the part to the whole. Therefore, if any man be dangerous to the community, and be corrupting it by any sin, the killing of him for the common good is praiseworthy and wholesome. For "a little leaven corrupteth the whole lump."[2]

§ 1. To preserve the wheat, that is, the good, our Lord has commanded us to abstain from rooting out the cockle,[3] teaching us rather to let the wicked

---

[1] A celebrated phrase of Aristotle, *Politics*, i. 5. (Trl.)

[2] 1 Cor. v. 6. On the way in which this corruption works, cf. *Ethics and Natural Law*, p. 348. St. Thomas puts the abstract lawfulness of slaying sinners first, and the practical limitations to it afterwards. (Trl.)

[3] St. Matt. xiii. 29.

live than to let the good be slain with them. But when from the slaying of the wicked there arises no danger to the good, but rather protection and deliverance, then the wicked may be lawfully slain.

§ 2. God, according to the order of His wisdom, sometimes punishes sinners on the spot for the deliverance of the good; sometimes again He leaves them time to repent, according as He knows to be expedient for His elect. And this method of procedure human justice imitates to the best of its power: for those who are ruinous to others it slays; but those who sin without grievous hurt to others, it reserves to repentance.

§ 3. Man by sinning withdraws from the order of reason, and thereby falls from human dignity, so far as that consists in man being naturally free and existent for his own sake; and falls in a manner into the state of servitude proper to beasts, according to that of the Psalm: "Man when he was in honour did not understand: he hath matched himself with senseless beasts and become like unto them;"[1] and, "The fool shall serve the wise."[2] And therefore, though to kill a man, while he abides in his native dignity, be a thing of itself evil, yet to kill a man who is a sinner may be good, as to kill a beast. For worse is an evil man than a beast, and more noxious, as the Philosopher says.[3]

[1] Psalm xlviii. 15.   [2] Prov. xi. 9.
[3] On the importance of this remark, see *Ethics and Natural Law*, p. 350. (Trl.)

ARTICLE III.—*Is it lawful for a private person to slay a sinner?*

R. The slaying of an evil-doer is lawful inasmuch as it is directed to the welfare of the whole community, and therefore appertains to him alone who has the charge of the preservation of the community; as the amputation of an unsound limb belongs to the surgeon, when the care of the welfare of the whole body has been entrusted to him. Now the care of the common good is entrusted to rulers having public authority; and therefore to them is it lawful to slay evil-doers, not to private individuals.

§ 2. A beast is naturally distinguishable from a man: hence on this point there is no need of judgment whether it ought to be slain, if it is in the wild state; but if it is domesticated, judgment is required, not on the creature's own account, but for the owner's loss. But a sinner is not naturally distinguishable from just men; and therefore he needs a public judgment to make him out, and determine whether he ought to be slain for the benefit of the common weal.

§ 3. To do a thing for the public benefit that hurts no man, is lawful to any private person: but if the doing be with the hurt of another, it ought not to be done, except according to the judgment of him to whom it belongs to estimate what is to be withdrawn from the parts for the well-being of the whole.

ARTICLE V.—*Is it lawful for any man to kill himself?*

R. To kill oneself is altogether unlawful, for

three reasons. First, because naturally everything loves itself, and consequently everything naturally preserves itself in being, and resists destroying agencies as much as it can. And therefore for any one to kill himself is against a natural inclination, and against the charity wherewith he ought to love himself. And therefore the killing of oneself is always a mortal sin, as being against natural law and against charity. Secondly, because all that any part is, is of the whole. But every man is of the community; and so what he is, is of the community: hence in killing himself he does an injury to the community. Thirdly, because life is a gift divinely bestowed on man, and subject to His power who "killeth and maketh alive."[1] And therefore he who takes his own life sins against God; as he who kills another man's slave sins against the master to whom the slave belongs; and as he sins who usurps the office of judge on a point not referred to him. For to God alone belongs judgment of life and death, according to the text: "I will kill and I will make to live."[2]

§ 1. Homicide[3] is a sin, not only as being contrary to justice, but also as being contrary to the charity which a man ought to bear towards himself; and in this respect suicide is a sin in regard to oneself. But in regard to one's neighbour and to God, it has the character of a sin even against justice.

[1] 1 Kings ii. 6.   [2] Deut. xxxii. 39.
[3] That is to say, suicide. *Suicidium* does not disfigure the pages of St. Thomas. The word is not in any Latin Dictionary, not even Du Cange's Glossary. (Trl.)

§ 2. He who holds public authority may lawfully put a malefactor to death, by the fact that he is empowered to judge him. But no one is judge in his own cause. Therefore the holder of public authority is not allowed to put himself to death for any sin; he may however submit himself to the judgment of others.

§ 3. Man is made his own master by free-will; and therefore man may lawfully dispose of himself in things that relate to this life, which is ruled by the free-will of man. But the passage from this life to another and happier one is not subject to the free-will of man, but to the divine power; and therefore it is not lawful for a man to kill himself to pass to a happier life. Neither must he do so to escape any evils of the present life, because the extremest and most terrible of the evils of this life is death, as appears from the Philosopher; and therefore to compass one's own death in order to avoid the other miseries of this life, is to take the greater evil to escape the less.[1] In like manner again it is not lawful to kill yourself for any sin that you have committed, both because thereby you do yourself the direst mischief, taking away from yourself the time necessary for repentance, and also because it is not lawful to put an evil-doer to death except by the judgment of public authority. Nor again is it lawful for a woman to kill herself to save her honour: because she ought not to commit on her own person the greatest crime, which is suicide, to avoid a less crime to be committed by another:

[1] See *Ethics and Natural Law*, pp. 216, 217, 94, 95. (Trl.)

for it is no crime of a woman to be ravished by force, if there is no consent of hers; because the body is not defiled except by the consent of the mind, as St. Lucy said. But it is certain that fornication or adultery is a less sin than murder, and especially self-murder, which is the most grievous thing of all, because you harm yourself, whom you are most bound to love; and again the most dangerous thing of all, because no time is left to expiate it by repentance. Again, it is lawful to no one to kill himself for fear of consenting to sin, because evil must not be done that good may come of it,[1] or that evil may be escaped, especially less evil and less certain; for it is uncertain whether one will consent to sin in the future, seeing that God is able to deliver a man from sin, no matter what temptation supervenes.

§ 5. It is a point of fortitude not to shrink from being put to death by another for the good gift that virtue is, and for the avoidance of sin; but for a man to put himself to death to escape penal inflictions, has indeed a certain appearance of fortitude, but it is not true fortitude: rather it is a sort of flabbiness of mind unable to endure penal ills, as appears by the Philosopher.[2]

[1] *Evil must not be done that good may come of it.* This express declaration of St. Thomas is, in so many words, the contradiction of what is so constantly alleged by Protestants to be the teaching of Catholic moralists. See also I-II. q. 20. art. 2. (Trl.)

[2] For the arguments against suicide, cf. *Ethics and Natural Law*, pp. 213—219. It is rash to discard the first of the three arguments that St. Thomas gives. (p. 43.) It is perhaps the best of the three: certainly a very solid and sufficient argument, technically viewed. (Trl.)

ARTICLE VI.—*Is there any case in which it is lawful to kill an innocent man?*

R. A man may be looked at in two ways, in himself, and in reference to some other being. Looked at in himself, it is lawful to slay no man; because in every man, even in the sinner, we ought to love the nature which God has made, and which is destroyed by killing. But the slaying of the sinner becomes lawful in reference to the good of the community that is destroyed by sin. On the other hand, the life of the just makes for the preservation and promotion of the good of the community, seeing that they are the chiefer part of the people. And therefore it is nowise lawful to slay the innocent.

§ 3. If a judge knows that a party is innocent, whose guilt is being evidenced by false witnesses, he ought to examine the witnesses more diligently, to find occasion of discharging the unoffending party, as Daniel did. If he cannot do that, he ought to leave him to the judgment of a higher court. If he cannot do that either, he does not sin by passing sentence according to the evidence before him; because it is not he that slays the innocent, but they who assert him to be guilty. But whoever is charged to carry out the sentence of a judge that condemns the innocent, ought not to obey, if the sentence contains intolerable error; otherwise the executioners who put the martyrs to death would be excused. But if the sentence does not involve manifest injustice, he does not sin in doing as he is bid: because it is not his business to discuss the sentence of his superior; nor is it he that slays the innocent, but the judge whose officer he is.[1]

ARTICLE VII.—*Is it lawful to slay a man in self-defence?*

R. There is nothing to hinder one act having two effects, of which one only is in the intention of the agent, while the other is beside his intention. But moral acts receive their species from what is intended, not from what is beside the intention, as that is accidental. From the act therefore of one defending himself a twofold effect may follow, one the preservation of his own life, the other the killing of the aggressor. Now such an act, in so far as the preservation of the doer's own life is intended, has no taint of evil about it, seeing that it is natural to everything to preserve itself in being as much as it can. Nevertheless, an act coming of a good intention may be rendered unlawful, if it be not in proportion to the end in view. And therefore, if any one uses greater violence than is necessary for the defence of his life, it will be unlawful. But if he repels the violence in a moderate way, it will be a lawful defence: for according to the Civil and Canon Laws it is allowable "to repel force by force with the moderation of a blameless defence." Nor is it necessary to salvation for a man to omit the act of moderate defence in order to avoid the killing of another; because man is more bound to take thought for his own life than for the life of his

[1] See further, II-II. q. 67. art. 2. (Trl.)

neighbour. But because to kill a man is not allowable except by act of public authority for the common good, it is unlawful for a man to intend to kill another man in order to defend himself, unless he be one who has public authority, who intending to kill a man in order to his own defence, refers this to the public good, as does a soldier fighting against the enemy, or an officer of justice fighting against robbers, though these two sin if they are moved by lust of private vengeance.[1]

ARTICLE VIII.—*Is the guilt of homicide incurred by killing a man accidentally?*

R. According to the Philosopher, chance is a cause that acts beside the intention. And therefore the events of chance, absolutely speaking, are not intended nor voluntary. And because every sin is voluntary, consequently the events of chance, as such, are not sins. Sometimes however what is not actually and in itself willed or intended, is willed or intended incidentally, inasmuch as what removes an obstacle is called an *incidental cause*. Hence he who does not remove the conditions from which homicide follows, supposing it to be his duty to remove them, incurs in a manner the guilt of wilful homicide; and this in two ways: in one way when, being engaged upon unlawful actions which he ought to avoid, he incurs homicide; in another way when he does not observe due precaution. And therefore, according to the Civil and Canon Laws,

[1] For a vindication of the argument of this important Article, see *Ethics and Natural Law*, pp. 208—213; also p. 353. (Trl.)

if one is engaged upon a lawful action, taking due care therein, and homicide follows from it, he does not incur the guilt of homicide. But if he is engaged upon an unlawful action, or, being engaged upon a lawful one, neglects to observe due precaution therein, he does not escape the charge of homicide, if the death of a man follows from his doing.

QUESTION LXV.

OF MUTILATION OF MEMBERS.

ARTICLE I.—*Can mutilation in any case be lawful?*
R. As by public authority one is lawfully deprived of life altogether for certain graver offences, so is he deprived of a member for lesser transgressions. This however is not lawful to any private person, even with the consent of the party whose member it is: because thereby an injury is done to the community, to whom the man belongs and all parts of him. But if a member by its unsoundness is in a way to corrupt the whole body, then it is lawful, at the wish of him whose member it is, to amputate the unsound member for the preservation of the body as a whole: for to every man is committed the care of his own preservation.

§ 1. There is no reason why what is against a particular nature may not be according to universal nature; as death and corruption in natural things are against the particular nature of the organism that is corrupted, but accord well with universal nature. And so to mutilate a man of a member, though it be against the particular nature of the body that suffers mutilation, is still according to natural reason in view of the common good.

§ 3. A member is not to be cut off for the bodily welfare of the person as a whole, except when there is no other way of succouring the body as a whole. But for spiritual welfare succour is always at hand by other means than by the cutting off of a member, seeing that sin is subject to the will. And therefore in no case is it lawful to cut off a member for the avoidance of any sin whatever. Hence Chrysostom says: "Not by cutting off of members, but by the breaking off of evil thoughts: for he is under a curse who cuts off the member: murderers they are who venture on such things."

ARTICLE II.—*Is it lawful for fathers to flog their sons?*

R. By flogging hurt is done to the body of the person flogged, otherwise however than in the case of mutilation: for mutilation takes away the integrity of the person, but flogging merely gives pain to the sense. It is lawful to no one to do any hurt to another otherwise than by way of punishment for justice' sake. But no one justly punishes another, unless he be subject to his jurisdiction. And therefore it is not lawful to beat another, except in him who has some authority over the person beaten. And because the son is subject to the authority of his father, the father may lawfully flog his son.

§ 1. Anger being a desire of vengeance, the passion is especially excited when a sufferer thinks himself ill-treated unjustly. And therefore the prohibition addressed to fathers,[1] that they should not provoke their children to anger, does not forbid their flogging their sons by way of maintenance of discipline, but only forbids excessive floggings.

§ 2. The greater authority ought to have the greater power of coercion. Now as a State is a perfect community, so the ruler of the State has perfect coercive power; and therefore he can inflict the irreparable penalties of death or mutilation. But a father, being the head of a family, which is an imperfect community, has an imperfect power of coercion in the way of lighter penalties, which do no irreparable hurt; and such is flogging.

§ 3. To render discipline to one willing to receive it, is lawful to any man. But to apply discipline to an unwilling subject, belongs to him alone who has another entrusted to his charge.

ARTICLE III.—*Is it lawful to put a man in prison?*

R. Among goods of the body three are discernible in order. The first is the *wholeness of the person*, which is impaired by killing or mutilation. The second is *pleasure*, or *repose of sense*, with which repose beating, or anything that gives pain to sense, is inconsistent. The third is the *movement and use of the limbs*, which is hindered by bonds, or prison, or any detention. And therefore to imprison any one, or otherwise detain him, is unlawful except it

[1] Ephes. vi. 4.

be done in course of justice, either as a punishment, or as a precaution for the avoidance of some evil.

§ 1. A man who abuses the power given him, deserves to lose it; and therefore the man who has sinfully abused the free use of his limbs, is a suitable subject for imprisonment.

§ 3. It is lawful for any one to hold back a man for a time from doing there and then an unlawful act; as when one holds back another from casting himself headlong, or from committing assault. But absolutely to lock a man up, or put him in fetters, belongs to him alone who has general control over the life and actions of another: because thereby the party is hindered, not only from doing evil, but also from doing good.

QUESTION LXVI.

OF THEFT AND ROBBERY.

ARTICLE I.—*Is the possession of exterior things natural to man?*

R. An exterior thing may be considered in two ways; in one way in respect of its nature, which is not subject to human control, but only to the control of God, whose slightest command all things obey: in another way as regards the use of the thing; and in this way man has natural dominion over exterior things, because by reason and will he can use exterior things to his own profit, as things made for him; for the less perfect is ever for the more perfect. This natural dominion over other creatures attaches to man in virtue of his reason, whereby he is the image of God, as appears from the account of creation: "Let us make man to our image and likeness, and let him have dominion over the fishes of the sea," &c.[1]

ARTICLE II.—*Is it lawful for any one to possess anything as his own?*

R. Two things are competent to man regarding any exterior good. The one is the power of *manag-*

[1] Genesis i. 26.

ing and *dispensing* it; and so far as that goes, it is lawful for a man to have property of his own. It is also necessary to human life for three reasons: first, because every one is more careful to look after a thing that is his own private concern than after what is common to all or many: since every one avoids labour, and leaves to another to do the duty that belongs to a number of persons in common, as happens where there are many persons to wait on you. The same appears in another way, because human affairs are handled in more orderly fashion, where every individual has his own care of something to look to: whereas there would be confusion if every one indiscriminately took the management of anything he pleased. Thirdly, because a peaceful state of society is thus better ensured, every one being contented with his own lot. Hence we see that disputes arise not uncommonly among those who have any possession in joint stock.

Another thing within the reach of man regarding exterior goods is the *use* of them. In that respect a man ought not to hold exterior goods as exclusively his own, but as common possessions, so as readily to share them with others in their need. Hence the Apostle says: "Charge the rich of this world to give easily, to communicate to others."[1]

§ 1. Community of goods is set down as a point of natural law, not as though it were a dictate of natural law that all things should be possessed in common, and that there should be no private property: but because the marking off of separate

[1] 1 Timothy vi. 17, 18.

possessions is not done according to natural law, but rather according to human convention, which belongs to positive law. Hence private property is not against natural law, but is an institution supplementary to natural law invented by human reason.[1]

§ 2. He who coming first to a public spectacle should prepare the way for others, would not act unlawfully; but it is then that a person acts unlawfully, when he prevents others from seeing. In like manner a rich man does not act unlawfully, if he seizes possession beforehand of a thing that was common to start with,[2] and then shares it with others: but he does sin if he keeps out everybody else without distinction from using the thing.

ARTICLE III.—*Does the essence of theft consist in the secret taking of the property of another?*

R. To the notion of theft three elements concur. The first is contrariety to justice, the virtue that gives to every one his own: hence the description applies to theft, that it is a seizing upon *what is another's.* The second element belongs to theft as distinguished from sins committed on the person, like murder and

---

[1] See *Ethics and Natural Law*, pp. 280, 281, n. 4. For St. Thomas's concept of *natural law* see I-II. q. 94. art. 2. Here he seems almost to take it in the sense of the Roman lawyer, whom he quotes, II-II. q. 57. art. 3 : "that law which is common to all animals." Cf. I-II. q. 94. art. 5. § 3.

[2] Understand, *negatively* common, like the diamonds in the earth at Johannisberg, *Ethics and Natural Law*, p. 280. St. Thomas, however, is not thinking of diamonds, but of waste land, that is no man's land, and not, as the *commons* are or were in England, the property of a specified community (Trl.)

adultery; and thus it applies to theft to say that it is about an article of *property:* for it is not exactly theft to take that which is another's, not as property, but as either part of the person, as a limb; or a personal connection, as daughter or wife. The third distinguishing feature that completes the notion of theft, is that the seizure of what is another's is made *secretly.* Thus the proper essence of theft is a secret taking of another's property.

ARTICLE V.

§ 3. Whoever takes by stealth his own property from another, in whose hands it is unjustly detained, sins, not for any annoyance he gives the holder —hence he is not bound to any restitution or compensation; but he sins against general justice, usurping the office of judge in his own cause, in disregard of the due course of law. And therefore he is bound to make satisfaction to God, and to appease any scandal of his neighbours that may have arisen from his proceeding.[1]

ARTICLE VI.—*Is theft a mortal sin?*

R. A mortal sin is what is contrary to charity, the spiritual life of the soul. Now charity consists principally in the love of God; secondarily, in the love of our neighbour, the office of which love is to wish and do good to our neighbour. But by theft a man injures his neighbour in his property; and if

---

[1] This doctrine puts some restraint on the working of the principle, *res clamat domino,* at least in a civilised community, where " due course of law " is open—and inexpensive. (Trl.)

all men promiscuously were to steal, human society would be lost. Hence theft is a mortal sin, as being contrary to charity.

§ 2. The punishments of the present life are rather medicinal than retributive: for retribution is reserved to the judgment of God, which falls upon sinners according to truth. And therefore in the judicial procedure of the present life the punishment of death is not inflicted for every mortal sin, but only for those that do irreparable mischief, or are marked by circumstances of horrible atrocity. And therefore for theft, which does not do irreparable mischief, the punishment of death is not inflicted in our present courts of law, unless the theft be aggravated by some grave circumstance, as in sacrilege, peculation, and kidnapping.

§ 3. A small quantity counts as nothing. And therefore a man does not reckon himself aggrieved in very small things; and he who takes such things may presume that it is not against the will of the owner. And thus far forth the pilfering of such very small things may be excused from mortal sin.[1]

ARTICLE VII.—*Is it lawful to steal on the plea of necessity?*

R. The institutions of human law cannot derogate from natural law or divine law. But according to the natural order established by Divine Providence, inferior things are ordained to

[1] It is excused from all sin, if the thing is literally of no value; and from mortal sin, but not from venial, on the ground of *parvity of matter*, if the value is very small. (Trl.)

the end that out of them the needs of men may be relieved. And therefore the division and appropriation of goods, that proceeds from human law, cannot come in the way of a man's need being relieved out of such goods. And therefore the things that some men have in superabundance, are claimed by natural law for the support of the poor. Hence Ambrose says: "It is the bread of the hungry that you hold back: the clothing of the naked that you keep in store: the ransom and deliverance of the unfortunate is contained in the money that you bury in the earth." But because there are many sufferers in need, and all cannot be relieved out of the same goods, there is entrusted to the discretion of every proprietor the disbursement of his own substance, that out of it he may relieve the needy. If however a need be so plain and pressing, that clearly the urgent necessity has to be relieved from whatever comes to hand, as when danger is threatening a person and there is no other means of succouring him, then the man may lawfully relieve his distress out of the property of another, taking it either openly or secretly; nor does this proceeding properly bear the stamp of either theft or robbery.[1]

§ 2. To use the property of another, taking it secretly, in a case of extreme need, cannot properly

[1] What St. Thomas contemplates is the case of starving people seizing upon the primary necessaries of life to stave off instant death. He is eminently *not* thinking of a clerk, when he is "hard up," taking his employer's money. When the clerk accepted his situation, he virtually contracted with his employer to do nothing of the kind. For the supposed communism of this article, see *Ethics and Natural Law*, p. 281, n. 5. (Trl.)

speaking be characterized as theft, because what one takes for the support of his life is made his by such necessity.

ARTICLE VIII.—*Can robbery be committed without sin?*

R. Robbery involves a certain amount of violence and constraint, whereby a man's own is taken away from him contrary to justice. But in human society no one has the right of coercion otherwise than by public authority; and therefore whoever, being a private person, and not using public authority, forcibly takes away anything from another, acts unlawfully, and commits robbery, as highwaymen do. To rulers public authority is entrusted to the end that they may be guardians of justice; and therefore it is not lawful for them to use force and coercion except according to the tenor of justice, either fighting against foreign enemies, or against citizens, punishing evil-doers;[1] and what is taken away by such use of force cannot be said to be carried off by robbery, seeing there is no violation of justice.

§ 3. If rulers exact from their subjects what is due in justice for the maintenance of the common weal, that is not robbery, even though force be used over it: but if they extort anything by use of force against justice, it is robbery like the doings of highwaymen. Hence Augustine says: "Justice apart, what are kingdoms but organized brigandage?"

[1] War and punishment however are not in the same category. See *Ethics and Natural Law*, pp. 351—353. (Trl.)

ARTICLE IX.—*Is theft a more grievous sin than robbery?*

R. Robbery is a more grievous sin than theft, because violence is more directly opposed to the will than ignorance. There is also another reason: because by robbery not only is loss inflicted on another in his property, but there is also something of personal insult or injury enacted.

QUESTION LXVII.

OF INJUSTICE IN A JUDGE.

ARTICLE I.—*Can it be just to sit in judgment on one who is not a subject of the court?*

R. The sentence of a judge is a sort of private law made on occasion of some individual act. And therefore as a general law ought to be fraught with coercive power, so also should a judge's sentence be fraught with coercive power, whereby both parties may be bound to observe the sentence of the judge: otherwise the judgment would not be effectual. Now coercive power is not lawfully wielded in society except in the hands of public authority. They who bear such authority count as superiors in respect of those over whom they have received authority, whether ordinary or delegated. And therefore no one can sit as judge except over one who is in some way his subject, whether by delegation or by ordinary authority.

§ 3. The Bishop in whose diocese a person commits an offence, is rendered his superior by reason of the offence, even though the offender be an exempt religious, unless he happen to offend in some exempt matter, as in the administration of the goods of an exempt monastery. But if any exempt religious commits theft, or murder, or any crime of that sort, he may justly be condemned by the Ordinary.

ARTICLE II.—*Is it lawful for a judge to give sentence against what is to him the known truth, on the ground of the evidence that is brought forward to the contrary?*

R. To give sentence is the office of the judge inasmuch as he bears a public commission; and therefore in passing sentence he ought to be informed, not by what he knows himself as a private individual, but by what comes to his knowledge as a public person. Knowledge comes to him in that capacity both in general and in particular: in general by the public laws, whether divine or human, against which he ought to admit no pleas; in the particular business on hand by deeds and witnesses and other such lawful informations; and these he ought to follow in giving sentence rather than what he himself knows as a private individual. By this latter source of information however he may be aided in making a severer examination of the evidence alleged, so as to trace out where it is wanting. But if he cannot lawfully set it aside, he ought to follow it in giving sentence.

§ 4. In what belongs to his own person, a man ought to form his conscience by his own knowledge: but in what belongs to public authority, a man must form his conscience according to what can be known in a public court of law.

ARTICLE III.—*Can a judge condemn where there is no accuser?*

R. In criminal cases a judge cannot pass sentence on any one unless he has an accuser, according to that: "It is not the custom of the Romans to condemn any man, before that he who is accused have his accusers present, and have liberty to make his answer, to clear himself of the things laid to his charge." [1]

§ 2. In denunciation [2] there is intended, not the punishment of the offender, but his amendment; and therefore nothing is done against him whose sin is denounced, but for him; and therefore no accuser is necessary there.

ARTICLE IV.—*Can a judge lawfully remit the penalty?*

R. There are two things to observe about a judge: on the one hand, he has to judge between accuser and accused; on the other, he does not pass a judicial sentence of his own, but by public authority. And therefore there are two reasons to

---

[1] Acts xxv. 16.
[2] As practised in Religious Orders. See Suarez, *On the Religious State*, translated by Humphrey, vol. iii. pp. 352, seq. Also II-II. q. 33. art. 7; q. 68. art. 1; q. 68. art. 2. § 3.

hinder a judge from letting a guilty person off his punishment: first, on the part of the accuser, to whose right it sometimes appertains to have the accused punished, as for some wrong done him which it is not in the judge's power to condone, because every judge is bound to render to every man his own. In another way, he is hindered on the part of the commonwealth, whose authority he wields; since it concerns the good of the commonwealth that wrong-doers be punished. Nevertheless on this point there is a difference between inferior judges and the Supreme Judge, or Sovereign, to whom the plenitude of civil authority is entrusted. For an inferior judge has no power to let a guilty party go scot-free, against the laws laid down for his guidance by higher authority. But if the person who has suffered the injury is willing to pardon it, the Sovereign, having full power in the State, can lawfully discharge the guilty party, if he sees that course to be not prejudicial to the public interest.

QUESTION LXVIII.

OF WHAT RELATES TO AN UNJUST ACCUSATION.

ARTICLE I.—*Is accusation a duty?*

R. This is the difference between denunciation and accusation, that in denunciation the object is the amendment of a brother, but in accusation the punishment of a crime. Now the punishments of the present life are not ends in themselves, because the final time and place of retribution is not here; but punishments as at present inflicted are things medicinal, tending either to the amendment of the offender or to the good of the commonwealth, the peace whereof is procured by the punishment of offenders. The former of these objects is aimed at in denunciation; the latter properly belongs to accusation. And therefore if the crime has been such as to tend to injure the commonwealth, a man is bound to accusation, provided he can furnish sufficient proof, as belongs to the office of an accuser. But if the crime has not been such as to affect the community at large, or if he cannot furnish sufficient proof, he is not bound to lay an accusation, because no one is bound to that which he cannot duly go through with.

§ 3. To reveal secrets to the evil of an individual is against fidelity, but not if they are revealed for the sake of the public good, which is always to be preferred to private good. And therefore it is not lawful to accept any communication as secret, contrary to the public good.[1] However that is not altogether a secret, which is capable of proof by sufficient witness.

ARTICLE II.

§ 1. It is difficult to remember a statement word for word on account of the multitude and variety of words. A number of persons hearing the same words would not repeat them alike even after a short interval. And since a slight difference of words alters the sense, therefore, although the judge's sentence has to be pronounced almost forthwith, still the sentence gains in exactitude and reliability by the accusation being drawn up in writing.[2]

§ 3. A denouncer does not bind himself to proof: hence neither is he punished, if he fail to prove what he has said. And therefore in denunciation no writing is needed, but it is enough if one verbally denounces the matter to the Church, who according to her office will take steps for the amendment of the erring brother.

---

[1] See *Ethics and Natural Law*, p. 232 (Trl.)

[2] The absence of written testimonies and oaths in an ordinary domestic quarrel, renders it impossible for inquiry to make certain what the aggrieved and aggrieving parties have severally said and done. (Trl.)

Article III.

§ 1. A man ought not to proceed to accusation except upon a point that he is altogether sure of, so that ignorance of fact can have no place there. Still it is not every one that falsely imputes a crime to another that is a malicious accuser, but he only who breaks out into false accusation from malice. For sometimes one proceeds to accusation from mere levity of mind, too easily believing what one hears, and that is rashness. Sometimes again one is moved to accuse by a justifiable error. All these several cases should be distinguished according to the prudence of the judge, so that he should not pronounce him guilty of malicious accusation, who has broken out into false accusation from levity of mind or from justifiable error.

QUESTION LXIX.

OF SINS AGAINST JUSTICE ON THE PART OF THE ACCUSED.

ARTICLE I.—*Is an accused party guiltless of mortal sin, in denying the truth that would lead to his condemnation?*

R. Whoever acts against a duty binding in justice, sins mortally.[1] But the duty of obedience to a superior in matters to which the right of his superiority extends, is a duty binding in justice.[2] Now a judge is superior over him who is judged. And therefore the accused is in duty bound to declare to the judge the truth that is required of him according to form of law; and if he will not confess the truth that he is bound to tell, or gives a lying denial of it, he sins mortally. But if the judge asks a question that he cannot ask according to order of law, the accused is not bound to answer him, but may evade the question by appeal, or

---

[1] That is to say, the sin is *mortal of its kind*, for the meaning of which phrase see I-II. q. 88. art. 2. with note. (Trl.)

[2] In *legal* justice (*Ethics and Natural Law*, p. 103, n. 3), the violation of which is mortal, where the matter is of consequence. (Trl.)

by any other lawful subterfuge. A lie however he is not allowed to tell.[1]

ARTICLE II.—*Is it lawful for an accused party to set up a fraudulent defence?*

R. Suppression of truth is one thing; the putting forward of falsehood another. The former is in some cases lawful: for an accused is not bound to confess the whole truth, but that only which the judge can ask and ought to ask of him according to the order of law: that is, when there has been an antecedent evil report commonly current about the man, pointing to some crime; or when some express indications have appeared; or when some semi-complete proof has gone before.[2] But in no case is it lawful for any one to plead what is false. Now to a lawful end a man may proceed either by lawful ways, and ways suitable to the end intended, which method is the part of prudence; or by unlawful ways, and ways out of keeping with the end in view, which is the part of cunning, fraud, and guile. Thus then it is lawful for the accused party to adopt any suitable methods, as not answering, to conceal such part of the truth as he is not bound to confess. This is not a fraudulent defence, but

[1] See note to Article following This Article has its bearing on the matter of Lying and Mental Reservation; also on those interrogatories that may be put by parent to child, or by one who holds the place of a parent. It is important in such interrogations to make quite sure whether the question, as you put it, is "according to form of law," or within the bounds of your parental right. (Trl.)

[2] These were the conditions under which the Roman Law prescribed that a prisoner should be judicially interrogated as to his guilt, and expected him to incriminate himself. (Trl.)

a prudent evasion. But it is not lawful for him either to tell a falsehood, or to conceal the truth which he is bound to confess, nor again to employ any trickery or fraud, because trickery and fraud are equivalent to a lie; and this is the meaning of a fraudulent defence.

ARTICLE III.—*Is it lawful to escape sentence by an appeal?*
R. There are two motives that may move a man to appeal. One is confidence in the justice of his cause; and on that motive it is lawful to appeal. Another is desire to throw delays in the way of a just sentence being pronounced against him; and that is a fraudulent defence, which is unlawful: for it wrongs both the judge, whose office it impedes, and the adversary, whose just claim it does its best to upset. And therefore, as is said, "by all means he is to be punished, whose appeal is pronounced unjust."

ARTICLE IV.—*Is it lawful for a condemned criminal to take what steps he can in the way of self-defence?*
R. It is not lawful for one justly condemned to death to defend himself, for it is lawful to the judge to use armed force to overcome his resistance; hence it remains that on the criminal's part the conflict is unjust: hence undoubtedly he sins. But an unjust condemnation is like the violence of robbers. And therefore it is lawful in such a case to resist, except haply for the avoidance of scandal,

when grave disturbance might be apprehended from such resistance.

§ 1. For this purpose is reason given to man, that he may fulfil the things to which nature inclines him, not indiscriminately, but according to the order of reason. And therefore not every self-defence is lawful, but that defence only which has place with due moderation.

§ 2. The tenor of no man's sentence is that he should put himself to death, but that he should suffer death; and therefore a criminal is not bound to do that whence death is apt to follow, namely, remain in a place whence he is to be led to death; though he is bound not to use resistance to escape what is just for him to suffer. Thus if one is condemned to die by starvation, he does not sin in taking food secretly supplied to him; for not to take it would be to kill himself.

QUESTION LXX.

OF INJUSTICE IN THE PERSON OF THE WITNESS.

ARTICLE I.—*Is it a duty to give evidence?*

R. Sometimes a man's evidence is called for, sometimes not. If a subject's evidence is called for by the authority of a superior whom he is bound to obey in matters of justice, beyond doubt he is bound to give evidence upon those points on which his evidence is taken according to order of law; but if his evidence is asked for on other points, he is not bound to give it. If however his evidence is not called for by any superior authority, then if his evidence is required to deliver a man from any unjust punishment whatever, he is bound to give it; but he is not bound to give evidence tending to the condemnation of a man, unless compelled by superior authority according to order of law. The reason is, because no special loss accrues to any one from the concealment of the truth in this case; or if there be a danger to the accuser, that is not to be regarded, because he has voluntarily thrust himself into the danger. It is otherwise with the accused, who is in danger against his will.

§ 2. Of the things that are entrusted to a man under the secret of confession, he ought on no account to give evidence, because such things he knows not as man, but as the minister of God; and the bond of the sacrament is stronger than any command of man. As regards other things entrusted to a man under secret, a distinction must be drawn. For sometimes they are such that as soon as they come to a man's knowledge he is bound to manifest them; that is, when they make to the spiritual or corporal undoing of the people, or to the grave detriment of an individual, or are aught else of a nature that a person is bound to make known either by testimony or by denunciation. Against this duty you cannot be bound by any obligation of secret entrusted to you, because that would be a breach of the good faith that you owe to a third party.[1] Sometimes, on the other hand, the matter of the secret is such as the person hearing it is not bound to publish. You are capable in such a case of having an obligation imposed upon you by the fact of the matter being confided to you under secret: then you ought on no account to betray the secret, not even under the precept of a superior: because to keep one's word is an obligation of natural law, and nothing can be commanded a man against an obligation of natural law.

---

[1] Sometimes however you are bound to keep secret some matter committed to you for your advice, which, if you had yourself discovered it, you would have been bound to make known. The chief thing to look to, is whether there is danger to a third person from the obstinate malice of the owner of the secret. See *Ethics and Natural Law*, p. 232. In practice here cases arise of great delicacy and difficulty. (Trl.)

Article II.

§ 2. Evidence is invalidated by a discrepancy of witnesses on primary points, involving variation of the substance of the fact, as on time, or place, or principal agents; because if the witnesses disagree on such points, they seem to stand severally alone in their evidence, and to speak of different events. Thus if one says it happened at such a time and place, another at another time and place, they do not seem to be speaking of the same event. But it is no prejudice to the evidence, if one witness says that he does not remember, while another asserts a definite time or place. In a case of total discrepancy between the witnesses for the prosecution and those for the defence, if the witnesses are equal in number and alike in respectability, the case goes in favour of the defendant, because the judge ought to be more forward to acquit than to condemn; except it be in a case where the favour of the law rests with the other side, as in action brought to establish a claim to personal liberty. But if the witnesses on the same side disagree, the judge must work his own wits to find out which side he should prefer, either from the number of the witnesses, or from their respectability, or from the favourable light in which the law views the suit, or from the general posture of the case. Much more is the evidence of one man rejected, if he disagrees with himself when asked what he has seen and knows; but not when he is asked as to what he thinks and has heard said, because he may be prompted to different answers according to different things that he has seen and heard. But if there be a discrepancy of evidence on points that leave untouched the substance of the fact, for instance, as to the weather being cloudy or fine, the house painted or not, such a discrepancy does not prejudice the evidence; because men generally do not trouble themselves much on such points, which therefore easily slip their memory. Nay, a certain disagreement on such matters makes the evidence more credible; because if they agreed on all points, even the smallest, they might seem to be telling the same story by previous arrangement. This however is left to the judge's prudence to discern.

ARTICLE IV.—*Is false witness always a mortal sin?*

R. False witness has a triple deformity: one from perjury, because witnesses are not admitted except on oath, and this deformity is always a mortal sin; one from the violation of justice,—and this is always a mortal sin in its kind, as every other form of injustice; a third from the falsehood itself, inasmuch as every lie is a sin,—and on this head false witness has not the character of being always a mortal sin.[1]

§ 3. Men most abhor the sins that are against God, as being the most grievous; of the number of which is perjury. But they do not stand in so much horror of sins against their neighbour. And therefore, for the greater certainty of the evidence, the witness's oath is required.

[1] An untruth, simply as an untruth, apart from injury done, scandal given, or other circumstances, is always sinful, never a mortal sin. Cf. below, q. 110. art. 4. (Trl.)

QUESTION LXXI.

OF INJUSTICE ON THE PART OF COUNSEL AT LAW.

ARTICLE I.—*Is counsel bound to take up the case of poor clients?*

R. Taking up the case of poor clients is a work of mercy, and we must speak of it as of other works of mercy. Now no one has it in his power to do works of mercy to all the needy. And therefore, as Augustine says, "Since you cannot help all, you should look to those especially who are as it were allotted to you, and bound to you by time, place, or other circumstance bringing them in your way." He mentions *place*, because a man is not bound to traverse the earth seeking needy people to help; but it is enough if he does the work of mercy to those who come in his way. He further mentions *time*, because a man is not bound to provide for another's future need, but it is enough if he relieves his present necessity. He adds the mention of *other circumstances*, because a man ought especially to bestow his care on those who are related to him by any tie of kindred. Still, when these conditions concur, it further remains to be considered, whether the necessity that the distressed party is in be such as not to admit of ready apparent relief from any other quarter: if such it be, you are bound to do the work of mercy to him. Otherwise, if there is an appearance of possible relief for him, either by his own exertions, or by some other person more closely tied to him than you are, or better able, you are not absolutely bound under pain of sin to relieve his distress; though if you do relieve him without such absolute obligation, your generosity is to be commended. Hence counsel is not always bound to take up the case of the poor, but only when there is a concurrence of the aforesaid conditions: otherwise a man would have to drop all other business, and spend all his energies on helping out poor men's cases. The same is to be said of a doctor as regards his attendance upon the poor.

ARTICLE III.—*Does a lawyer sin by defending an unjust cause?*

R. It is unlawful for any one to co-operate in the doing of evil, whether by counsel or aid or any manner of consent, because he who lends counsel and aid is in a manner the doer; and the Apostle says: "They are worthy of death, not only that do evil, but also that consent to them that do it."[1] Hence all such persons are bound to restitution. But clearly a lawyer lends both aid and counsel to him whose cause he takes up. Hence if he knowingly defends an unjust cause, without doubt he sins grievously, and is bound to restitution of the loss that the other side incurs unjustly through his aid. But if he defends an unjust cause in ignorance,

[1] Romans i. 32.

thinking it to be just, he is excused to the extent that ignorance is excusable.

§ 2. If a lawyer in the beginning has believed a cause to be just, and afterwards as the procedure goes on it comes out to be clearly unjust, he ought not to betray the cause; that is, he ought not to help the other side, or reveal to the other the secrets of his own client. But he can throw up the case, and ought to do so, or induce his client to yield, or to compromise the matter without loss to the other party.[1]

ARTICLE IV.—*Is it lawful for a lawyer to take money for his pleading?*[2]

R. A man may justly take a fee for services that he is not bound to render. Now a lawyer is not always bound to plead or give advice in other men's causes. And therefore if he sells his pleading or advice, he does not act against justice. And the case is the same with a doctor giving his aid to a

---

[1] (1) A *criminal* cause, where the client is guilty, is not an unjust cause.

(2) A *civil* cause that is not certainly unjust, may be defended, observing the doctrine of II-II. q. 69. art. 2.

(3) The complexity of law and fact together is such, that a cause certainly unjust, to one who is not in the position of a judge, is a comparatively rare occurrence.

(4) Whatever evidence of injustice comes out in court during the trial, the court may be expected to rule according to that evidence, if it is not rebutted mendaciously and fraudulently. In this an unjust suit differs from an unjust war. In war the battle commonly is to the strong, but in an English court of justice right is might. (Trl.)

[2] There was a notion once current, that to sell the fruit of the mind, being the sale of a spiritual thing, was simony. (Trl.)

patient, and with all such personages, provided their fees are moderate, considering the condition of persons and affairs and labour, and the custom of the country.

§ 2. Though legal knowledge is a spiritual gift, yet use of it is made by bodily work; and therefore it is lawful to take money in return for it: otherwise no artificer could lawfully gain by his art.

QUESTION LXXII.

OF INJURIOUS LANGUAGE OUT OF COURT, AND FIRST OF CONTUMELY.

ARTICLE I.—*Does contumely consist in words?*

R. Contumely implies the dishonouring of another, which may be done in two ways. Seeing that honour follows upon excellence, one way of dishonouring another is to rob him of the excellence for which he was honoured: which is done by sins of deed. Another way is when one brings that which makes against the honour of another to the notice of the party himself and of others: which is done by signs. But as Augustine says: "Other signs are few, compared with words: for words amongst men bear the principal part in signifying all the thoughts of the mind." And therefore contumely, properly speaking, consists in words. Still because in sundry deeds also there is a certain signification, the name of *contumely* is extended also to deeds.

§ 1. It is the greater contumely, if one tells another his defect before many; and yet, if he tells it him in private it may be contumely, inasmuch as the speaker acts unjustly against the reverence due to his hearer.

ARTICLE II.—*Is contumely a mortal sin?*

R. Words as mere sounds do not hurt any, but only inasmuch as they signify something, which signification proceeds from the interior disposition of the speaker. And therefore in sins of word the great point to consider is the interior disposition with which the words are uttered. Since then contumely essentially involves a certain dishonour, if the speaker's intention is fixed on taking away the honour of the hearer by the words that he utters, this properly and in itself is to utter contumely; and that is a mortal sin no less than theft or robbery, for a man loves his honour not less than his property. But if one has spoken a word of contumely to another with no purpose of dishonouring him, but perhaps for his correction or for some other end, that is not uttering contumely formally and in itself, but incidentally and materially, inasmuch as the speaker says that which may be contumely: hence this may be sometimes a venial sin, sometimes no sin at all. Discretion however is needed in the matter to use such words moderately: because the reproach might be so severe as that the incautious utterance of it would take away the honour of the person assailed; and then a man might sin mortally, even though he did not intend the dishonour of the other; as one who striking another in jest should do him grievous hurt would not be free from blame.

§ 1. It is witty to utter some slight taunt, not to dishonour or grieve the person at whom it is levelled, but rather for amusement and joke; and this may be without sin, if due circumstances are observed. But if one shrinks not from aggrieving him at whom he levels his wit, provided only he can raise a laugh,—that is vicious.

ARTICLE III.—*Ought a man to bear the contumelies put upon him?*

R. As patience is necessary in what is done against us, so also in what is said against us. But the precepts of patience in what is done against us are to be kept "in readiness of heart," as Augustine says on the Lord's precept: "If one strike thee on thy right cheek, turn to him also the other:"[1] that is to say, a man should be prepared so to behave, if there be occasion. But he is not bound always actually to behave so; for neither did the Lord Himself do that; but when He had received a blow, He said: "Why strikest thou me?"[2] And therefore the same is also to be understood as regards contumelious words, when they are spoken to us. For we are bound to have our heart in readiness to bear contumelies, if it be expedient. Sometimes however we must rebut the contumely put upon us, for two reasons chiefly: the one is the good of him who offers the contumely, that his boldness may be

[1] St. Matt. v. 39.   [2] St. John xvii. 23.

checked and he may not try such things on again, according to the text: "Answer a fool according to his folly, lest he imagine himself to be wise;"[1] the other is for the good of the many, whose advancement is hindered by the contumelies put on us. Hence Gregory says: "They whose life is set up for an example to imitate ought, if they can, to restrain the utterances of them that disparage them, lest those who might otherwise have listened refuse now to hear their preaching, and so remain in their evil ways and scorn a good life."

§ 2. The greed of private honour is not so much to be dreaded in the repressing of contumelies offered to another as in the rebutting of what is levelled at ourselves. The former seems rather to be a course dictated by charity.

§ 3. If a man were to hold his peace on purpose to provoke his assailant to anger, that would be an act of vindictiveness; but if he holds his peace as wishing to give place to anger, it is praiseworthy. Hence it is said: "Strive not with a man that is full of tongue, and heap not wood on his fire."[2]

[1] Prov. xxvi. 5.   [2] Ecclus. viii. 4.

QUESTION LXXIII.

OF DETRACTION.

ARTICLE I.—*Is it a suitable definition of detraction, that it is a blackening of another's character by words?*

R. As there are two ways of harming another in deed, openly by robbery or any sort of violence, and secretly by theft and assassination; so in word also there are two ways of harming another, one way openly, by contumely; another way secretly, by detraction. By the fact of speaking out against a man openly and to his face you seem to make light of him, and so to dishonour him; and therefore contumely wounds the honour of him against whom it is uttered. But he who speaks against another in secret seems to fear him rather than to make light of him: hence he does not directly damage his honour but his character, inasmuch as by such secret speeches he does what in him lies to create a bad opinion of him against whom he speaks. For this the detractor seems to intend, and to bend his efforts to this, that credence may be given to his words. Clearly then detraction differs from contumely in two respects: one is the mode of utterance, because the giver of contumely speaks out against a man to his face, but the detractor in secret; the other is the end intended, or hurt done, because the giver of contumely takes away from the honour of another, the detractor from his good name.

§. A detractor is so called, not as diminishing aught of the truth, but as diminishing his neighbour's good name.

ARTICLE II.—*Is detraction a mortal sin?*

R. Sins of word are to be judged principally by the intention of the speaker. Now the essential purpose of detraction is the blackening of another's character. Hence he is properly a detractor who speaks ill of another in his absence with intent to blacken his character. Now to take away another's character is a very serious thing: because among temporal things a good name counts for a thing of particular value, as the loss of it debars a man from many avenues to success. Hence it is said: "Take care of a good name: for this shall continue with thee more than a thousand treasures precious and great."[1] And therefore detraction of itself is a mortal sin. It happens however at times that one utters some words that lessen another's good name, not with any intention of doing so, but with something else in view. This is not detraction *ordinarily* and *formally* speaking, but only *materially* and *incidentally*. And if the words by which another's good name is diminished are uttered for some necessary purpose of good, with due observance of circumstance, there is no sin at all, and that cannot be

[1] Ecclus. xli. 15.

called detraction. But if they are uttered from thoughtlessness, or from some motive not of necessity, it is not a mortal sin, unless the utterance happens to be so pregnant with serious matter as notably to damage the party's good name, particularly on the point of personal morality.

ARTICLE III.—*Does detraction stand pre-eminent above all the rest of the sins that are committed against one's neighbour?*

R. Ordinarily, sins against one's neighbour are to be weighed according to the hurt that they do him. Now a hurt is greater as the good that is taken away is greater. Of the three goods of man, that of the soul, that of the body, and that of exterior possessions, the good of the soul, which is the greatest, cannot be taken away by another otherwise than merely by giving occasion to its loss, by evil incitement, which does not amount to necessity; but the other two goods, of the body and of exterior possessions, may be violently taken away by another. But because the good of the body is preferable to the good of exterior possessions, the sins that do personal hurt are more grievous than sins against property. Hence of all the sins against one's neighbour homicide is the most grievous, whereby the life of a neighbour already in actual existence is taken away. Next to that comes adultery, which is against the due order of human generation, by which is the entry to life. After the good of the body are exterior possessions, among which a good name stands above riches, as being nigher akin to spiritual goods: hence it is said, "A good name is better than great riches."[1] And therefore detraction, of its kind, is a greater sin than theft, but less than murder or adultery. However there may be another order determined by aggravating or extenuating circumstances. But *incidentally*, the gravity of sin is measured with respect to the sinner, who sins more grievously, if he sins of set purpose, than if he sins of frailty and want of care. In this respect sins of speech have some palliation, since they arise easily by a slip of the tongue without malice prepense.

ARTICLE IV.—*Does the listener sin grievously who endures a detractor?*

R. According to the Apostle: "They are worthy of death, not only who do (what is sinful), but they also that consent."[2] Consent in one form is *direct* [positive,] when one induces another to sin, or takes pleasure in his sin. In another form it is *indirect* [negative], when one neglects to withstand the sin, being able to withstand it; and this neglect happens at times, not because one has any pleasure in the sin, but through some human respect. We must say then that if you listen to detraction without resistance, you seem to consent to, or concur with, the detractor: hence you become partaker of his sin. And if indeed you lead him on to the detraction, or at least take pleasure in the detraction through hatred of the person whose character is

[1] Prov. xxii. 1.   [2] Romans i. 32.

taken away, you sin no less than the detractor, and sometimes more. Hence Bernard says: "To detract or to listen to a detractor, I could not easily say which of these two merits the greater condemnation." But if you take no pleasure in the sin, but through fear or negligence or shyness omit to rebut the detractor, you sin indeed, but much less than the detractor, and commonly only venially.[1]

§ 1. No one hears his own detractors, because the evil things that are said of a man in his hearing are not cases of detraction but of contumely.

§ 2. You are not always bound to resist a detractor by charging him with falsehood, especially if you know that what is said is true; but you ought in words to rebuke him for his sin of detraction against his brother, or at least to show that the detraction displeases you by the sadness of your countenance, because, as it is said: "The north wind driveth away rain, as doth a sad countenance a backbiting tongue."[2]

---

[1] And often not even that, if you are much inferior in age or station, or apprehend that any contradiction on your part would only drive the detractor to say stronger things. See § 2. (Trl.)

[2] Prov. xxv. 23.

QUESTION LXXIV.

OF MISCHIEF-MAKING.

ARTICLE I.—*Is mischief-making a distinct sin from detraction?*

R. The mischief-maker and the detractor agree in the matter, and also in the form or manner of their speech, because both of them speak evil of their neighbour. But they differ in the end in view: for the detractor intends to blacken the character of his neighbour; hence he brings out particularly those evil reports about him that seem likely to destroy or at least diminish his good name; whereas the mischief-maker intends to dissolve a friendship; and therefore he brings out such evil stories of his neighbour as may move the mind of the hearer against him, according to the text: "A sinful man will trouble his friends, and bring in debate in the midst of them that are at peace."[1]

§ 1. In this the mischief-maker differs from the detractor, that he does not intend to report what is absolutely evil, but anything whatever that is likely to trouble one man's mind and set him against another, though the thing reported be

[1] Ecclus. xxviii. 2.

absolutely good, provided it appear evil, and as such annoy the person to whom it is told.

ARTICLE II.—*Is detraction a more grievous sin than mischief-making?*

R. Sin against a neighbour is more grievous, the greater the harm done to the neighbour thereby. Harm again is greater, the greater the good destroyed. Now among exterior goods friendship stands pre-eminent, since "none can live without friends," as appears by the Philosopher. Hence it is said: "Nothing can be compared to a faithful friend."[1] Nay, the good name that is destroyed by detraction is especially needed for this, that a man may be accounted fit for friendship. And therefore mischief-making is a greater sin than detraction, and even than contumely, because a friend is better than honour, and better is it to be loved than to be respected.

§ 1. The species and gravity of a sin goes rather by the end in view than by the material object; and therefore an account of the end in view mischief-making is the graver sin, though the detractor sometimes says worse things.

[1] Ecclus. vi. 15.

QUESTION LXXVI.

OF CURSING.

ARTICLE I.—*Is it lawful to curse any one?*

R. To do a thing and to wish it are two acts that wait on one another for good and evil. Hence if a man commands or wishes the evil of another man in so far as it is evil, intending the evil itself, the utterance of such a command or wish for evil will be unlawful, and this utterance is cursing, ordinarily so called. But if a man commands or wishes the evil of another under the aspect in which it is good, that is lawful; and the utterance of such a wish will not be cursing, ordinarily so called, but only incidentally, because the principal intention of the speaker tends not to evil but to good. Now evil may be uttered in the way of a command or a wish under two aspects of good. Sometimes it is under the aspect of *justice:* thus a judge lawfully dooms him on whom he orders a just punishment to be inflicted. So also the Church pronounces a curse in her anathemas; and the Prophets in Scripture imprecate evil on sinners. Therein the Prophets speak as conforming their will to the divine justice; though these imprecations may also be understood as predictions. Sometimes again evil is uttered under the aspect of *utility;* as when one wishes a sinner to suffer a sickness, or have some other obstacle thrown in his way, either for his personal improvement, or at least to keep him from hurting others.

ARTICLE III.—*Is cursing a mortal sin?*

R. By *cursing* we here understand the denouncing of evil upon another, by way either of command or wish. Now to wish or to move by command to another's evil is of itself repugnant to that charity with which we love our neighbour and wish his good; and therefore is a mortal sin of its kind, and all the more grievous, the more we are bound to love and reverence the person whom we curse. At times however the utterance of a curse is a venial sin, either from the trifling nature of the evil imprecated, or for the disposition of the utterer, who says such things with small animus, or in jest, or by surprise. For sins of word are weighed principally according to the disposition in which they are uttered.

QUESTION LXXVII.

OF FRAUDULENT DEALING IN BUYING AND SELLING.

ARTICLE I.—*May one lawfully sell a thing for more than it is worth?*

R. To use fraud to sell a thing above its just price is a downright sin, being the deceiving of another to his loss. Fraud apart, we may speak of buying and selling in two ways. In one way *ordinarily;* and in that way we see that the institution of buying and selling is for the common good of both parties, each party wanting what the other has got. Now a transaction designed for the common advantage of both, should not bear harder upon the one party than upon the other; and therefore the contract between them should proceed on the principle of equality of thing to thing. Now the quantity of a thing that serves human use is measured according to the price given for it; for which purpose we have the invention of money. And therefore, if either the price exceeds the quantity of the value of the thing, or conversely the thing exceeds the price, the equality of justice will be destroyed. And therefore to sell a thing dearer or buy it cheaper than it is worth, is a proceeding in itself unjust and unlawful.

In another way we may speak of buying and selling, inasmuch as *incidentally* the transaction tends to the utility of one party and to the detriment of the other, as when one has great need to have a thing and the other suffers by parting with it. In such a case the just price will be arrived at by regarding not only the thing that is sold, but also the loss which the seller incurs by the sale. And thus there will be an opening for the thing being lawfully sold for more than it is worth ordinarily and in itself, though not for more than it is worth to its possessor.[1] But if one party is much benefited by the commodity which he receives of the other, while the other, the seller, is not a loser by going without the article, no extra price must be put on. The reason is, because the profit that accrues to the one party is not from the seller, but from the condition of the buyer. Now no one ought to sell to another that which is not his, though he may sell the loss that he suffers. He however who is much benefited by the commodity which he receives of another, may spontaneously bestow some extra recompense on the seller; that is the part of one who has the feelings of a gentleman.[2]

---

[1] We should phrase it, for more than its *market-value*, though not for more than its *use-value* to the seller in this instance. The counter-principle next laid down by St. Thomas, that no charge beyond the market-value must be made for any special use-value that the article has to the purchaser, is the principle that fixes the guilt of usury. It is a principle of prime importance in commercial morality. (Trl.)

[2] It would be a different thing, if not one solitary individual, but a whole community were in special need of, or had set up a special

ARTICLE II.—*Is a sale rendered unlawful by a defect in the thing sold?*

R. We may consider three defects in a thing that is sold. One in *kind*. Such a defect, if known to the vendor, amounts to a fraud in the sale, and renders the sale unlawful. And this is what is said against certain persons: "Thy silver is turned into dross, thy wine is mingled with water;"[1] for what is mingled with anything else suffers a defect in kind. Another defect is in *quantity*, which is known by measure. And therefore if one knowingly uses short measure in selling, he commits a fraud, and the sale is unlawful. Hence it is said: "Thou shalt not have divers weights in thy bag, a greater and a less."[2] The third defect is in *quality*, as if one were to sell a sickly animal for a healthy one. If one knowingly does this, he commits a fraud that renders the sale unlawful. And in all such cases the vendor not only sins by effecting an unjust sale, but is bound to restitution. But if any of the aforementioned defects be in the article sold without the seller knowing of it, he is guiltless of sin; because, though what he does is unjust materially, yet his doing of it is not unjust: at the same time he is bound, when the fact comes to his knowledge, to make up the loss to the buyer. And what is said of the seller, is to be understood of the buyer also. For sometimes the seller believes his article to be

demand for, the commodity. That would raise its market-value: and so far as mere justice goes, you may always sell at market-value. See below, art. iii. § 4. (Trl.)

[1] Isaias i. 22. [2] Deut. xxv. 13.

less precious in *kind* than it really is, as when one sells gold for brass; and then the buyer, if he observes it, buys unjustly, and is bound to restitution. And the same of defects of *quality* and *quantity*.

ARTICLE III.—*Is the seller bound to mention any flaw there is in the thing sold?*

R. It is always unlawful to furnish to another an occasion of *danger* or *loss*, albeit it is not necessary for a man always to lend his aid or advice to the advantage of his neighbour. That is necessary only in definite cases, when you have the person under your care, or when relief for him is impossible otherwise than through you. Now the seller furnishes the buyer with an occasion of *loss* or *danger* by the fact of offering him a spoilt article: of *loss*, if the article offered for sale is of less value on account of such a flaw, while he abates nothing of the price on that account: of *danger*, if the flaw renders the use of the thing awkward or hurtful. Hence if there are secret flaws of this nature, and the vendor does not reveal them, he drives an unlawful and treacherous bargain, and is bound to compensate the purchaser for his loss. But if the flaw is manifest, as when a horse has only got one eye, or when the use of the thing, though not available to the vendor, is still available for others; and when the vendor in his price makes due abatement for the flaw; then he is not bound to declare the flaw, because on account of it perhaps the buyer would wish more to be taken off from the price than ought to be taken off: hence the seller can lawfully provide for his own indemnity by reticence as to the flaw in the article.

§ 1. A judgment cannot be made except of a manifest case: for every man judges according as he knows. Hence if the flaws in a thing exposed for sale are secret, judgment is not sufficiently left to the purchaser unless they are declared to him. The case would be otherwise if the flaws were manifest of themselves.

§ 2. To the objection taken from Cicero: "What so absurd as for the auctioneer to give out by command of the owner, *Insanitary house for sale?*"—it is to be said that a man need not make known the flaw in his wares by means of the auctioneer, because by such an announcement purchasers would be deterred from buying, not knowing the other points of the article, wherein it is truly good and useful. But the flaw in the thing must be told privately to the person who draws near to purchase it, when he is in a position to compare all the points of the thing together, good and bad. For what is faulty on one point may be useful on many others.

§ 4. To the objection, that a seller carrying corn to a place where there is a scarcity of corn, though he knows that many are coming after him similarly freighted, still is not bound to tell,—it is to be said that a flaw in a thing makes the thing here and now of less value than it appears; but in the case above mentioned the fall in value looked for is a matter of futurity: hence the seller who sells the thing according to the price that he finds, does not seem to be acting against justice in making no statement as to the future. If however he were to make a statement, or to abate something of the price, he would show a more exuberant virtue, though he does not seem to be bound thereto by any duty of justice.

ARTICLE IV.—*Is it lawful in trade to sell an article at more than cost price?*

R. It belongs to traders to be occupied with the exchange of commodities. But exchange is twofold: one form natural and necessary, either an exchange in kind, of commodity for commodity, or an exchange of a commodity for money, but in any case having for motive the necessity of living; and such an exchange does not belong to trade, but to domestic economy or to statesmanship, to the art in fact of providing a family or a State with the necessaries of life. There is another species of exchange, either of money for money, or of any sort of goods for money, the object here being not the necessaries of life, but gain; and this trade seems properly to belong to traders. Now the former exchange is praiseworthy, as ministering to a natural want: but the latter is justly blamed, because so far as in it lies it ministers to the greed of gain, which knows no bounds, but tends to go to all lengths. And therefore trade, considered in itself, contains a certain unseemliness, inasmuch as it does not essentially involve any honourable or necessary end. Still though gain, which is the end of trade, does not essentially involve anything honourable or necessary, neither does it essentially involve any element of vice, or aught that is opposed to virtue. Hence there is nothing to hinder gain from being referred to an end necessary or even honourable. And thus trade will be rendered lawful: as when one refers the moderate gain that he seeks from trade to the sustenance of his family, or to the relief of the distressed; or once more, when one applies to trade on behalf of the public interest, that the necessaries of life may not be wanting to his country, and seeks gain, not as an end, but as the wages of his labour.[1]

§ 2. It is not every one that sells a thing for more than he bought it for that trades, but he only who buys on purpose to sell dearer. But if one buys a thing, not to sell but to keep, and afterwards for some reason wishes to sell it, that is not trading, although he sells it dearer. For he may lawfully do this, either because he has improved the thing in some respect, or because the price of the thing has changed by diversity of place or time, or on account of the risk to which he exposes himself in carrying the thing from place to place, or causing it to be carried. And in this way neither the purchase nor the sale is unjust.

§ 3. Clerics ought to abstain, not only from things in themselves evil, but also from things that

[1] In this very lukewarm appreciation of the benefits of trade St. Thomas is inspired by Aristotle, *Politics*, I. 9. The upshot after all seems to come to no more than this, that a man in business ought not to make it his supreme and sovereign aim to secure "a pot of money" for himself; but should be accessible to considerations of the good of humanity, and of the civic community to which he belongs; a doctrine surely which needs inculcating even more now than in the days of St. Thomas. (Trl.)

have the appearance of evil. And this observation applies to trade, both because it refers to earthly gain, of which the clergy ought to be despisers, as also because of the vices frequently found in persons engaged in trade, because "a merchant is hardly free from sins of the lips.[1] There is also another reason, because trade too much entangles the soul in secular cares, and withdraws from spirituality; hence the Apostle says: "No man being a soldier to God, entangleth himself with secular business."[2]

QUESTION LXXVIII.

OF THE SIN OF USURY THAT IS COMMITTED IN LOANS.[3]

ARTICLE I.—*Is it a sin to take usury for the lending of money?*

R. To take usury for the lending of money is in itself unjust, because it is a case of selling what is non-existent; and that is manifestly the setting up of an inequality contrary to justice. In evidence of this we must observe that there are certain things, the use of which is the consumption of the thing; as we consume wine by using it to drink, and we consume wheat by using it for food. Hence in such things the use of the thing ought not to be reckoned apart from the thing itself; but whosoever has the

---
[1] Ecclus. xxvi. 28.   [2] 2 Timothy ii. 4.
[3] See the doctrine of this Question explained and adapted to modern times, *Ethics and Natural Law*, pp. 255—263. (Trl.)

use granted to him, has thereby granted to him the thing; and therefore in such things lending means the transference of ownership. If therefore any vendor wanted to make two separate sales, one of the wine and the other of the use of the wine, he would be selling the same thing twice over, or selling the non-existent: hence clearly he would be committing the sin of injustice. And in like manner he commits injustice, who lends wine or wheat, asking a double recompense to be given him, one a return of an equal commodity, another a price for the use of the commodity, which price of use is called *usury*. But there are things the use of which is not the consuming of the thing: thus the use of a house is inhabiting it, not destroying it. In such things ownership and use may be made the matter of separate grants. Thus one may grant to another the ownership of a house, reserving to himself the use of it for a time; or grant the use and reserve the ownership. And therefore a man may lawfully take a price for the use of a house, and besides demand back the house which he has lent, as we see in the hiring and letting of houses. Now according to the Philosopher, money was invented principally for the effecting of exchanges; and thus the proper and principal use of money is the consumption or disbursal of it, according as it is expended on exchanges.[1]

[1] As we saw above, q. 77. art. 4. there are two sorts of exchanges. In a society where the only exchange in vogue is the former of those two sorts, all interest on money is usury and injustice, as this argument shows. It is quite a different case where the latter form of exchange obtains, as in the modern commercial world. (Trl.)

§ 2. To the text, "Thou shalt not lend to thy brother money to usury, nor corn, nor any other thing, but to the stranger,"[1] it is to be said that from its being prohibited to the Jews to take usury from their brethren, that is, from other Jews, we are to understand that taking usury of any man is simply evil; for we ought to regard every man as a neighbour and a brother, especially in the Gospel state, to which all are called. As for their taking usury of strangers, that was not granted them as a thing lawful, but permitted for the avoidance of a greater evil, that their avarice might not lead them to take usury of Jews, the worshippers of God.

§ 5. To the objection, that a man may take a price for what he is not bound to do; but a man with money is not in every case bound to lend it,— it is to be said that he who is not bound to lend may receive compensation for what he has done in lending, but ought not to exact more. But compensation is given him according to the equality of justice, if the exact amount is returned to him that he has lent. Hence if he exacts more for the use of a thing that has no other use than the consumption of the substance, he exacts a price for that which has no existence, and so the exaction is unjust.

§ 6. The principal use of silver vessels is not the consumption of them; and so the use of them can be sold while the ownership is reserved. But the principal use of silver money is the disbursal of the money on exchanges. Hence it is not lawful to

[1] Deut. xxiii. 19, 20.

sell the use of it, while at the same time claiming to have back the original sum lent. There may be a secondary use of money, for show, or to pledge, and such a use of money a man may lawfully sell.

§ 7. To the objection, that any one may lawfully take a thing that the owner voluntarily hands over to him; and that the borrower voluntarily hands over the usury,—it is to be said that he who gives usury does not give it as an absolutely voluntary payment, but under some stress of necessity, inasmuch as he needs to borrow money, which the possessor will not lend without usury.

ARTICLE II.—*Is it lawful to ask a consideration of another kind in return for a loan of money?*

R. According to the Philosopher, everything counts for money that has a money price. And therefore whoever by agreement, tacit or express, takes for a loan of money anything else that has a money price, he sins against justice as if he had taken money. But if he takes a consideration of this nature, not as exacting it, nor on any bond, tacit or express, but as a gratuitous gift, he does not sin: because even before he had lent the money he might lawfully have taken a gratuitous gift, and his condition is not made the worse for his having lent it. But as for compensation in the shape of things that have no money price, as the good-will and love of the borrower, that he may lawfully exact.

§ 1. The lender may stipulate with the borrower without sin for compensation for his loss in being deprived of anything that he ought to have: for this is not to sell the use of the money, but to avoid loss; and it may be that the receiver of the loan escapes a greater loss than the giver incurs: in that case the receiver of the loan compensates the other's loss with profit to himself. But the lender cannot stipulate for compensation for his loss in respect of his not gaining upon the money; because he ought not to sell what he has not yet got and may in many ways be hindered from getting.[1]

§ 2. Return for a good deed done you, may be made in two ways: in one way as the discharge of a debt of justice, to which you may be bound by formal stipulation; and this debt is fixed according to the amount of the benefit received. And therefore he who has received a loan of money, or of any other like thing, the use of which is the consumption of it, is not bound to return more than the amount of the loan received: hence it is against justice if he is bound by stipulation to return more. The obligation to return a good deed done you, may exist in another way as a debt of friendship, wherein the affection with which it has been conferred is more to be considered than the amount of benefit done. Such a debt cannot be reduced to a civil contract, as that brings in an element of constraint, which renders the return no longer spontaneous.

[1] To wit, in the thirteenth century. That a man may sometimes sell what he has not yet got, is admitted by St. Thomas above, q. 62. art. 4. This admission is a recognition of the title of *lucrum cessans*, or gain forfeited, the justification of interest in modern times, which is not paid on *money* merely—that would be usury—but on *capital*. (Trl.)

§ 5. Whoever lends money, transfers the dominion of the money to the borrower. The latter therefore holds it at his own risk, and is bound to restore the sum in its entirety: wherefore the lender ought not to exact any more. But he who entrusts his money to a merchant or manufacturer in the way of partnership, does not transfer the dominion of the money to him, but it remains his: so that at his risk it is that the merchant trades with it, or the manufacturer works upon it: and therefore at that rate he may lawfully demand a share of the profits thence arising as from his own property.[1]

ARTICLE IV.—*Is it lawful to borrow money at usury?*

R. It is nowise lawful to induce a man to sin; but to use the sin of another unto good is lawful; because God also uses all sins unto some good, inasmuch as He draws some good out of every evil. And therefore Augustine, in reply to a certain Publicola, who asked him whether it was lawful to take the oath of a man that swore by false gods, writes: "He who uses, not to evil, but to good, the word of another who swears by false gods, does not join in his sin whereby he has sworn by demons, but joins in his good faith whereby he has kept his word. But he would sin if he

---

[1] And therefore if there are many merchants and manufacturers asking for such sleeping partners, at the same time holding out a fairly sure promise of profitable returns; and if, instead of putting my money into partnership with them, I lend it to some one else; I may ordinarily stipulate with the borrower that he is to pay me compensation for the *gain forfeited*. (Trl.)

were to induce him to swear by false gods." So in the case proposed we must say that it is nowise lawful to induce a man to lend at usury: it is lawful however for a good purpose, as for the relief of one's own necessity or that of another, to borrow money at usury of him who is prepared so to transact usuriously; as it is lawful for him who falls among robbers to declare the goods that he has, to escape being slain, after the example of the ten men who said to Ismahel: "Kill us not, for we have stores in the field."[1]

QUESTION LXXIX.

OF THE INTEGRAL PARTS OF JUSTICE, WHICH ARE TO DO GOOD AND TURN AWAY FROM EVIL.

ARTICLE I.—*Are turning away from evil, and doing good, parts of justice?*

R. If we speak of good and evil in general, to do good and to avoid evil are points that belong to all virtue; and at that rate they cannot be set down as parts of justice, unless perchance justice be taken in the sense in which it is identical with all virtue; though even in that sense justice regards a certain special feature of good, inasmuch as goodness is something due in order of law divine or human. But considered as a special virtue, justice regards good under the aspect of something due to

[1] Jerem. xli. 8.

our neighbour; and at that rate it belongs to the special virtue of justice to do good under the aspect of something due to our neighbour, and to avoid evil on the other hand as hurtful to our neighbour: while to the general virtue of justice it belongs to do good as something due to society and to God, and to avoid evil as the opposite of that. These two points are called parts of general or particular justice, and *integral*[1] parts, because both of them are requisite to the perfect act of justice. For it belongs to justice to establish equality in the dealings of one man with another. But here to establish and to maintain what is established are functions of the same. A man establishes the equality of justice by *doing good*, that is, by rendering to another his due: he maintains the equality of justice, once established, by *turning away from evil*, that is, by doing no hurt to his neighbour.

§ 1. Other moral virtues are in regard of the passions, in which to do good is to come to the golden mean, that is, to turn away from extremes as from evils; and so in other virtues it comes to the same thing to do good and to turn away from evil. But justice is about actions and exterior businesses, in which it is one thing to make equality, and another thing to avoid spoiling the equality made.

§ 2. Turning away from evil, as it is reckoned a part of justice, means no mere negation, or not doing evil; for that merits not the palm, but merely

[1] See above, q. 48. art. 1. (Trl.)

escapes punishment. But it means a motion of the will refusing evil, as the very name of *turning away* shows; and that is meritorious, especially when one is assailed with temptation to do evil, and resists.

ARTICLE II.—*Is transgression a special sin?*

R. The name of transgression is derived from bodily movements to moral acts. A man is said in bodily movement to *transgress* or *trespass*, in that he *passes beyond* the bounds assigned to him. Now in moral matters it is by a negative precept that bounds are assigned to a man, for him not to pass beyond. And therefore *transgression* properly means acting against a *negative* precept. It is distinguished from *omission*, which is against an *affirmative* precept.

ARTICLE III.

§ 3. Affirmative precepts do not bind *for always*, but for a specified time; and as that time comes, the sin of omission begins to have place. But it may happen that a man is unable just then to do what he ought; and if the inability is without any fault of his, he is not omitting what he ought to be doing. But if it is through his own fault going before, as when one has got drunk over-night and cannot rise for Matins as he ought, some say that the sin of omission then begins, when the man applies himself to the unlawful act that is incompatible with the act to which he is bound. But this does not seem true; for supposing that he were roused from his bed by force and went to

Matins, he would not omit them: hence it is clear that the drunkenness going before was not the omission, but the cause of the omission. Hence it is to be said that the omission begins to be imputed to him as a fault,[1] when the time for action has come; nevertheless it is by the cause going before that the omission which follows is rendered voluntary.

§ 4. More is required for a meritorious act of virtue than for the demerit of a fault: because one single defect makes evil, but good supposes the soundness of the entire case. And therefore an act is required for the merit of justice, but not for an omission.

ARTICLE IV.—*Is the sin of omission graver than the sin of transgression?*

R. A sin is grave in proportion as it is removed from virtue. Now the furthest remove is that of logical contrariety. Contrary is further removed from contrary than a simple negation of the thing, as *black* is further removed from *white* than simple *not white*. But manifestly transgression is the contrary to an act of virtue, while omission carries a mere negation with it. Thus it is a sin of omission if one does not pay due reverence to parents; but a sin of transgression, if one puts upon them contumely or any injury. Whence it is clear that,

[1] In the exterior court, doubtless. But in the interior court of conscience—supposing the man too drunk to rise—the fault of omitting Matins must be judged to have been all committed *in causa*, when the drunkenness was committed. See *Ethics and Natural Law*, p. 39, n. 17. (Trl.)

simply and absolutely speaking, transgression is a graver sin than omission; though some omission may be graver than some transgression.

QUESTION LXXX.

OF THE POTENTIAL PARTS OF JUSTICE.

ARTICLE I.—*Is the list of virtues annexed to justice duly made out?*

R. In the virtues that are annexed to any principal virtue, there are two things to consider: one, how those virtues agree in some point with the principal virtue: the other, how they fall short of the perfect notion of it. Now, since justice is *to another*, all the virtues that are in relation *to another* may be annexed to justice in point of that agreement. Now the essence of justice consists in this, that there is rendered to another his due according to equality. In two ways therefore a virtue that is *to another* comes short of the full idea of justice: in one way, as coming short of the idea of *equality;* in another way, as coming short of the idea of a thing *due.* For there are some virtues that render to another his due, but cannot return it in *equal* measure. And in the first place, whatever is rendered by man to God is due, but cannot be in equal measure: that is to say, it is impossible for man to make such a return as he ought. So the Psalm has it: " What shall I render to the

Lord for all the things that He has rendered to me?"[1] Annexed in this way to justice is *religion*. Secondly, to parents, it is impossible to make recompense according to equality of what is due to them; and thus *filial piety* is annexed to justice.

Considering justice as the observance of something *due*, there are two manners of falling short of it, answering to the two manners in which a thing may be due, namely, as a *moral* and as a *legal* debt. That debt is *legally due*, which a man is bound by law to pay: debts of this kind are the proper object of justice, a principal virtue. That debt is *morally due*, which one owes as part of the seemliness of virtue. And because the idea of a *debt* involves some necessity, there are two classes of *debts*, or things *due*. For some things are so necessary that without them the decent order of morality can hardly be maintained; and these things answer more than other things to the idea of a *debt*, or something *due*. Considering what is thus due on the part of him *of whom* it is due, we find it to be due in this way that a man should show himself to his neighbour in word and deed for such as he really is; and therefore another virtue attached to justice is *truthfulness*. Again we may consider this debt in regard of him *to whom* it is due, inasmuch as one person makes return to another according as that other has done to him; and thus there is annexed to justice *gratitude*. There are other things necessarily due in this sense, that they point to a better moral

[1] Psalm cxv. 3.

order, yet so that without them a decent order of morality can still be maintained. What is due in this way, is matter of *liberality*, *affability*, and virtues of that sort, wherein the idea of a *debt*, something *due*, only slightly appears.

QUESTION LXXXI.

OF RELIGION.

ARTICLE I.

§ 5. Though all in general who worship God may be called *religious*, the name is specially given to such as dedicate their entire lives to the worship of God, keeping aloof from worldly business; as the name of *contemplatives* is bestowed, not simply on persons who contemplate, but on such as devote their whole lives to contemplation.

ARTICLE II.

§ 3. It is a dictate of natural reason that a man should perform some acts by way of reverence to God. But that he should perform definitely these acts or those, is not a dictate of natural reason, but an institution of law, divine or human.[1]

ARTICLE III.—*Is religion one virtue?*

R. Habits are distinguished according to the different aspects of their objects. Now to religion

[1] See I-II. q. 94. art. 3. with note; *Ethics and Natural Law*, p. 197, and pp. 280, 281, n. 4. (Trl)

it belongs to show reverence to the one God under one aspect, inasmuch as He is the first principle of the creation and government of things. Hence He Himself says: "If I be a father, where is my honour?"[1] For it is the office of a father both to bring into being and to govern. And therefore religion is one virtue.

§ 3. Religious worship is not paid to images considered in themselves as things, but inasmuch as they are images leading on to the Incarnate God. And the movement of veneration to the image as such does not rest in it, but tends to that of which it is an image.

ARTICLE IV.—*Is religion a special virtue distinct from others?*

R. Since virtue is directed to good, there must be a special virtue where there is a special goodness. Now the good to which religion is directed, is to pay God due honour. Honour is due to a person by reason of his excellence. But to God a singular excellence attaches, inasmuch as He infinitely transcends all things in every manner of excellence. Hence there is due to Him a special honour; as in human society we see that different honour is given to the several excellences of several persons, one honour to a father, another to a king, and so of the rest. Hence it is manifest that religion is a special virtue.

§ 2. All acts done for the glory of God belong to religion, not as the virtue *eliciting*, but as the

[1] Malach. i. 6.

virtue *commanding* them. But those acts belong to religion as *eliciting* them, which specifically appertain to the reverencing of God.[1]

ARTICLE V.—*Is religion a theological virtue?*

R. Religion it is that offers due worship to God. There are two things then to consider in religion: one is what religion offers to God, namely, worship, and this stands as the matter and object of religion: the other is the being to whom it is offered, namely, God to whom the worship is paid: not that the acts whereby God is worshipped attain to God Himself; whereas when we believe God, in believing we do attain to God. Due worship is offered to God, by the doing of certain acts of worship, offering of sacrifice, and the like, by way of reverence to God. Hence clearly God does not stand to the virtue of religion as the matter or object of it, but as the end of it. And therefore religion is not a theological virtue, the object of which is the last end, but a moral virtue, the office whereof is to be concerned with what makes for that end.

ARTICLE VII.—*Does religion involve any external act?*

R. We pay reverence and honour to God, not for His sake, seeing that of Himself He is full of glory and can have nothing added to Him from the creature, but for our own sakes, because by reverencing and honouring God our mind is made subject to Him, and in that subjection its perfection

[1] Cf. II-II. q. 26. art. 7. note, for *eliciting* and *commanding*. Trl.)

consists. For everything is made perfect by being subjected to its superior, as the body by being animated by the soul, and the air by being illuminated by the sun. But the human mind, in order to be united to God, needs to be led as it were by the hand by the senses: because "the invisible things of Him are clearly seen, being understood by the things that are made."[1] And therefore in divine worship it is necessary to use some corporal means, that by those means as by signs the mind of man may be prompted to spiritual acts, which unite it with God. And therefore religion involves interior acts as principal exercises, of themselves belonging to religion; and external acts as secondary, subordinated to the acts which are interior.

ARTICLE VIII.—*Is religion the same as holiness?*

R. The name of *holiness* seems to denote two ideas, the one of *purity*, the other of *firmness*. Under both the one and the other signification it is proper that holiness be attributed to the things that are applied to divine worship, so that not only men, but also the temple and vessels and other such things are said to be *sanctified*, or *hallowed*, by their application to divine worship. For *purity* is necessary for the mind to be applied to God, because the human mind is sullied by being bent upon inferior things, in the same way that anything else is defiled by the intermingling of an inferior substance, as silver by being mixed with lead. But the mind must be withdrawn from inferior things

[1] Romans i. 20.

to enable it to be united with the Supreme Being; and therefore a mind without purity cannot be applied to God. Hence it is said: "Follow peace with all men, and holiness, without which no man shall see God."[1] *Firmness* likewise is requisite for the application of the mind to God: for the mind is applied to Him as to the last end and first beginning; and such principles ought to be especially immovable. Hence the Apostle said: "I am sure that neither death nor life . . . shall separate me from the love of God."[2] Thus then by *holiness* we mean that disposition of the human mind by which it applies itself and its acts to God. Hence holiness does not differ from religion in essence, but only in our way of looking at it. For it is called *religion*, inasmuch as it pays to God due service in what appertains especially to divine worship, as in sacrifices, oblations, and the like. Again it is called *holiness*, inasmuch as man not only refers these things but also the works of other virtues to God; or inasmuch as a man disposes himself by certain works to divine worship.[3]

[1] Hebrews xii. 14.   [2] Romans viii. 38, 39.
[3] A person or thing then is *holy* by being *abidingly set aside for the worship of God*, as, to begin with, all Christians are by their baptism. So in the Good Friday service the multitude of the baptized, apart from the catechumens, are prayed for as "the holy people of God." Within this "holy people" there are observable many grades of *official* holiness, according as by office or by state men are particularly set aside for the service of religion. There are also grades of *personal* holiness, discernible by God alone, according as different souls approach Him in different degrees of grace and virtue. Highest in *official* holiness, and in *personal* holiness presumably not the least of his brethren, is he who by office stands above all other men as the "man of God," *the Holy Father*. (Trl.)

QUESTION LXXXII.

OF DEVOTION.

ARTICLE I.—*Is devotion a special act?*

R. Devotion is so called from *devoting*: hence they are called *devoted*, who in some manner devote themselves to God, so as to make themselves entirely subject to Him. Wherefore among the heathen of ancient times they were said to be *devoted*, who devoted themselves to idols unto death for the preservation of their army, as Titus Livius tells of the two Decii. Hence devotion seems to be nothing else than *a will promptly to devote oneself to the things that concern the service of God*. Hence it is said that "the multitude of the children of Israel offered first-fruits to the Lord with a most ready and devout mind."[1] But it is manifest that a will promptly to do what belongs to the service of God is a special act. Therefore devotion is a special act.

ARTICLE II.—*Is devotion an act of religion?*

R. It belongs to the same virtue to do a thing and to have a prompt will for doing it; because there is the same object to both acts. Wherefore,

[1] Exodus xxxv. 20, 21.

as the Philosopher says: "Justice is that whereby men will and do just things." But it is manifest that the performance of what appertains to the divine worship or service belongs properly to religion. Therefore it belongs to the same to have a prompt will for the performance of such acts, that is, to be devout. And so evidently devotion is an act of religion.

§ 1. It appertains immediately to charity that a man should deliver himself over to God, adhering to Him by a union of spirit; but that a man should deliver himself over to God for the performance of acts of divine worship, that appertains immediately to religion, and mediately to charity, which is the principle of religion.

§ 3. The devotion that is had to the saints of God, living or dead, does not terminate in them, but passes on to God, inasmuch as we venerate God in the ministers of God. But the devotion which subjects are said to have to their temporal lords is of another kind, as also the service of temporal lords differs from the service of God.[1]

ARTICLE III.—*Is contemplation, or meditation, a cause of devotion?*

R. The extrinsic and principal cause of devotion is God, of whom Ambrose says: "God calls whom He deigns to call, and whom He wills He makes religious; and if He had willed, He would have made the Samaritans devout from being indevout."

[1] Cf. Cæsar, *De Bello Gallico*, iii. 22. "Cum DC. devotis, quos illi soldurios appellant." (Trl.)

But the intrinsic cause on our side must be meditation or contemplation. For devotion is an act of the will, to the effect of promptly giving oneself up to the divine service. Now every act of the will proceeds from some consideration, because the object of the will is good understood. Hence also Augustine says that "will arises from understanding." Meditation therefore needs must be the cause of devotion, inasmuch as by meditation it is that man gets the thought of giving himself over to the service of God. To this he is led by a twofold consideration: on the one hand, of the divine goodness and of the benefits of God, according to the text: "It is good for me to adhere to God, and to put my hope in the Lord God;"[1] and this consideration excites love, which is the proximate cause of devotion. On the other hand is the consideration of self and of one's own deficiencies, in consequence whereof one needs to lean on God, as it is said: "I have lifted up my eyes to the mountains from whence help shall come to me;"[2] and this consideration excludes that presumption, which is a hindrance to a man submitting to God, as it makes him rest on his own ability.

§ 1. To the objection, that subtle meditations on speculative matters are often a hindrance to devotion,—it is to be said that the consideration of what is naturally calculated to excite love of God, causes devotion; but the consideration of other topics, not appertaining to this, but withdrawing the mind from it, does hinder devotion.

[1] Psalm lxxii. 27. [2] Psalm cxx. 1.

§ 2. The attributes of the Divinity are of themselves most calculated to excite love, and consequently devotion, because God is to be loved above all things; but the weakness of the human mind requires to be led as it were by the hand to the knowledge and love of things divine, by aid of the things of sense that are known to us. Chief of these objects of sense is the Sacred Humanity, as is said in the Preface: " That while we contemplate God in visible form, by Him we may be caught up to the love of things invisible." And therefore what appertains to the Humanity of Christ especially causes devotion, and leads us by the hand thereto : and yet devotion principally turns upon the attributes of the Divinity.[1]

§ 3. Knowledge, and whatever else points to greatness, is an occasion to man of trusting in himself, and therefore of neglecting to give himself over entirely to God. Hence such gifts occasion hindrance to devotion : while in women and simple persons devotion abounds, and elation is suppressed. Knowledge however, and every other perfection, ministers increase to devotion in the man who perfectly lays it at the feet of God.

ARTICLE IV.—*Is joy an effect of devotion?*
R. Devotion ordinarily and in the first place causes spiritual joy in the mind, but consequently and incidentally it causes sorrow. For devotion arises in the first place from the consideration of

[1] As mercy, holiness, wisdom, power, faithfulness, shining upon us in fullest lustre from the Person of the God made Man. (Trl.)

the divine goodness: which consideration is taken from what we may call the *terminus* of the movement of the will giving itself over to God; and from this consideration there ordinarily arises delight, according to the text: "I remembered God and was delighted."[1] But incidentally this consideration causes a certain sorrow to them who do not yet fully possess God, as the text has it: "My soul hath thirsted after God the living spring;"[2] and after that: "My tears have been my bread." Secondarily, devotion is caused from the consideration of one's own defects: for this consideration is taken from the *starting-point*, from which the movement of a devout will recedes so that the man comes no longer to live in himself, but to subject himself to God. This consideration works in the reverse way to the former: for ordinarily it is calculated to cause sorrow, when a man cons over his own shortcomings; but incidentally it causes joy through the hope of divine succour. Thus it appears that delight belongs to devotion primarily and ordinarily; but secondarily and incidentally there belongs to it that "sorrow that is according to God."[3]

[1] Psalm lxxvi. 4.
[2] Psalm xli. 3, 4. St. Thomas reads *fontem vivum* for *fortem vivum*.
[3] 2 Cor. vii. 10.

QUESTION LXXXIII.

OF PRAYER.

ARTICLE II.—*Is it proper to pray?*
R. We must so lay down the utility of prayer as neither to attribute any fatality to the course of human history, subject as it is to Providence, nor again reckon the divine arrangement to be alterable. In evidence of this position we must consider that Divine Providence not only arranges what effects are to take place, but also from what causes and in what order they are to arise. Now among other causes human acts count as causes of certain effects. Hence men need to do sundry things, not that by their acts they may alter the divine plan, but that by their acts they may fulfil certain effects according to the order arranged by God. And so it is with prayer: for we do not pray to alter the divine plan, but to obtain what God has arranged to be fulfilled by prayers, "to the end that men by asking may deserve to obtain what God Almighty before all ages has arranged to give them," as Gregory says.

§ 3. God gives us many things out of His liberality without our asking; but some things He wills to give us only on condition of our asking; which arrangement works to our advantage, teaching us to have recourse to God with confidence, and to recognize Him for the author of our good.

ARTICLE V.—*Should we in prayer ask anything definite of God?*

R. Socrates, Valerius Maximus relates, "thought that nothing further should be asked of the immortal gods than that they should give good things: because, he said, they knew what was to the advantage of each of us, whereas we often seek and pray for that which it would be better not have obtained." This advice is in some measure correct, as regards those prosperities that may come to an evil end, and that a man may use well or ill, such as riches, which, as the same author says, "have been the ruin of many; honours, that have brought many men to an overthrow; sovereignties, which are frequently seen to come to a lamentable conclusion; splendid marriages, that sometimes have been the entire overturning of houses." There are however some good things which a man cannot use badly, and which can never come to an evil end. These are the things of which our happiness is made up, and by which we merit happiness; and these things the saints pray for absolutely, according to that: "Show us thy face, and we shall be saved;"[1] and again: "Lead me in the path of thy commandments."[2]

ARTICLE VI.—*Ought a man in prayer to ask of God temporal blessings?*

R. As Augustine says, "It is lawful to pray for

[1] Psalm lxxix. 4. [2] Psalm cxviii. 35.

what it is lawful to desire." But it is lawful to desire temporal blessings, not putting them in the first place, as though setting up our rest in them, but regarding them as aids to happiness, inasmuch as they support our corporal life and serve as instruments for acts of virtue. And therefore we may lawfully pray for temporal blessings. And this is what Augustine says: "He not unbecomingly wishes for a competence in life, who wishes for that and no more. Such a competence is not desired for its own sake, but for the health of the body and the decent personal condition of the man, that he may not be out of place in the society in which he has to live. When such a competence is attained, we should pray to keep it: when we have it not, we should pray to get it."

§ 3. When our mind attends to temporal things in order to set up its rest in them, there it lies low abased; but when it attends to such things in view of gaining that which is its final happiness, it is not abased by them but rather raised on high.

ARTICLE VIII.—*Ought we to pray for our enemies?*
R. To pray for another is an office of charity. Hence we are bound to pray for our enemies in the same way that we are bound to love our enemies, that is, loving the nature, not the fault that is in them. To love our enemies in common with the rest of mankind, is matter of precept; but to love them in a special manner beyond the common is not matter of precept, except to the extent of readiness of heart: that is, a man must be prepared even

in a special manner to love his enemy and aid him in the hour of need, or if he should ask pardon. But apart from these particular calls, to love our enemies and aid them in a special manner beyond the common, is a counsel of perfection. And in like manner it is absolutely required that, in the general prayers which we say for our neighbour, we should not exclude our enemies. But to pray specially for them is a point of perfection, not of absolute requirement, except in some special cases.

§ 1. The imprecations in Holy Scripture may be understood in four ways. First, on the principle that prophets are wont "to foretell the future under the figure of an imprecation," as Augustine says. Secondly, inasmuch as temporal evils are sometimes sent by God upon sinners for their correction. Thirdly, taking the petition to be, not against persons, but against the reign of sin, that by the correction of certain persons sins may be stamped out. Fourthly, the prophets are conforming their will to the divine justice in the matter of the damnation of such as persist in sin.

§ 2. As Augustine says: "The vengeance of the martyrs[1] is the overthrow of the reign of sin, by the reigning of which they have had so much to endure." Or again: "Their cry for vengeance is not a voice, but a reason, as the blood of Abel cried from the earth." As for their rejoicing at vengeance,[2] that they do, not for vengeance' sake, but for the divine justice.

[1] Apoc. vi. 10.   [2] Psalm lvii. 11.

ARTICLE XII.—*Should a prayer be vocal?*
R. There are two sorts of prayer, public and private. Public prayer is that which is offered to God by the ministers of the Church in the person of the whole faithful people: and therefore such prayer should come to the knowledge of the people for whom it is offered; which it could not do, if it were not vocal; and therefore it is a reasonable institution for the ministers of the Church to recite public prayers in a loud voice, that they may come to the knowledge of all. Private prayer is that which is offered by a private individual praying for himself or others: such prayer need not necessarily be vocal. Still the voice is used in private prayer, and that for three reasons. First, to excite interior devotion, whereby the mind of him who prays may be raised to God: because by exterior signs, whether of word or action, a man's mind is moved to apprehend and consequently to desire. And therefore in private prayer we should so far make use of words and other such signs as is helpful to move the mind interiorly. But if the mind is distracted thereby, or in any way hindered in its operation, such signs are to be dropped; and this is especially likely to be the case with those whose minds are sufficiently ready for devotion without such signs. The second reason for adding vocal prayer is for the discharge of a debt, to the end that man should serve God to the full extent of the being which he has of God, that is, not with mind only, but also with body; and this belongs to prayer, especially as prayer has the office of satisfying for

sin. Thirdly, vocal prayer is added as a certain overflow of strong volition and emotion redounding from the soul to the body.

ARTICLE XIII.—*Is it a necessary condition of prayer that it should be attentive?*

R. This question has place particularly in vocal prayer. Regarding it we must note that a thing is said to be necessary in two ways. In one way that is necessary, by which *the end is better attained;* and in that way attention is absolutely necessary to prayer. In another way a thing is necessary, without which something *cannot take effect.* Now there are three effects of prayer. One is common to all acts informed with charity, namely merit. To this effect it is not necessarily required that attention should accompany prayer throughout, but the force of the first intention, with which one approaches prayer, renders the whole prayer meritorious, as happens in other meritorious acts. The second effect of prayer is its own proper effect, which is to obtain by asking; and to this effect also the first intention suffices, being what God principally regards. But if the first intention be wanting, the prayer is neither meritorious nor apt to obtain by its asking: for God does not hear that prayer, which the person himself who prays does not intend, as Gregory says. The third effect of prayer is that which it produces there and then, namely, a certain spiritual refection of mind; and to this effect attention during prayer is necessarily required.

Hence it is said: "If I pray in a tongue, my understanding is without fruit."[1]

You must know however that there is a threefold attention that may be paid to vocal prayer. One is attending to the words, not to make any slip in them. The second is attending to the sense of the words. The third is attending to the end and purpose of the prayer, that is, to God and to the object for which the prayer is offered. This third sort of attention is most of all necessary, and even uninstructed persons may have it: and sometimes this intention that carries the mind to God abounds so much that the mind forgets all other things.

§ 3. Mind-wandering during prayer, if it is done on purpose, is sinful and hinders the fruit of prayer; and against this Augustine says in his Rule: "When you pray to God in psalms and hymns, let that be in your heart which is uttered on your lips." But unintentional mind-wandering does not destroy the fruit of prayer. Hence Basil says: "If, weakened by sin, you cannot pray attentively, hold yourself together as well as you can, and God forgives, because it is not from negligence but from frailty that you cannot stand in His presence as a creature ought."

ARTICLE XIV.—*Ought prayer to be lengthy?*
R. We may speak of prayer either in itself or in its cause. The cause of prayer is the longing of charity, from which longing prayer ought to proceed; and this in us ought to be continual either actually

[1] 1 Cor. xiv. 14.

or virtually: for the impulse of this longing remains in all the acts that we do on a motive of charity. But we ought to do all things to the glory of God, as is said.[1] And in this respect prayer ought to be continual. But prayer considered in itself cannot be continual, because we must be busy with other works. Now the quantity of everything ought to be in proportion to the end in view, as the quantity of a potion to health. Hence it is proper that prayer should last so long as is useful for stirring up the fervour of inward desire. When it exceeds this measure, so that it cannot go on without weariness, prayer should not be further prolonged. Hence Augustine says: "The brethren in Egypt are said to have prayers frequent, but short and ejaculatory, lest that vigilant and erect attention which is most necessary to him who prays, should drop and be blunted by performances long drawn out. Thereby they clearly show that this attention is not to be strained, if it cannot of itself last; and on the other hand, if it will last, it is not to be broken off." And this is a point to observe as well in private prayer for the attention of him who prays, as in public prayer in view of the devotion of the people.

ARTICLE XV.

§ 2. The merit of prayer at times goes to obtain something else than the object that is prayed for: for merit goes towards attaining happiness principally; but the petition of prayer takes in also other

[1] 1 Cor. x. 31.

things. If therefore that other thing which the petitioner asks for himself is not conducive to his happiness, he does not merit that: nay, sometimes by asking and desiring such a thing he loses merit, as if one were to ask of God the accomplishment of something sinful; and this is not to pray *piously*. Sometimes again the thing asked is not *necessary to salvation*, nor yet plainly contrary to salvation; and then, though he who prays may merit life everlasting by his prayer, yet he does not merit to obtain the particular thing that he asks. Hence Augustine says: "A man faithfully supplicating God for the necessaries of this life, is both heard in mercy, and in mercy is not heard. For the physician knows better than the patient what is good for the sick." And therefore also Paul was not heard, because it was not expedient, when he begged to have the sting of the flesh removed. But if what is asked is conducive to the man's happiness, and makes for his salvation, he merits it, not only by prayer, but also by doing other good works; and therefore beyond doubt he receives what he asks, but at such time as he ought to receive it. "For some things are not refused, but deferred that they may be given at an appropriate time," as Augustine says, which effect however may be hindered, if the petitioners *persevere* not in prayer. And therefore Basil says: "For this reason thou sometimes askest and receivest not, because thou hast asked amiss, or without faith, or without earnestness, or what was not expedient for thee, or because thou hast given up the asking." But because one man cannot condignly merit life everlasting for another man, therefore neither can one condignly merit for another what makes for life everlasting; and on this account he is not always heard who prays *for another*. And therefore there are assigned four conditions, under a concurrence of which the petitioner always obtains what he asks: namely, that he should ask *for himself, things necessary to salvation, piously, and perseveringly*.

ARTICLE XVI.—*Do the prayers of sinners obtain anything of God?*

R. There are two things to consider in a sinner, the nature that God loves, and the fault that He hates. If therefore a sinner as such asks anything of God, that is to say, if his asking is moved by his desire of sin, in this he is not heard by God in mercy, but he is sometimes heard unto punishment, God permitting such a sinner to plunge still further into sin. For God "refuses some things in His mercy, which He grants in His anger," as Augustine says. But the prayer of a sinner proceeding from a good natural desire is heard by God, not out of justice, because the sinner deserves it not, but out of pure mercy, under the above-mentioned four conditions, that he asks for himself things necessary to salvation, piously and perseveringly.

§ 1. As Augustine says, that saying, "God heareth not sinners,"[1] is the word of a blind man not yet anointed, that is, not yet perfectly brought to the light, and therefore it is not a valid testi-

[1] St. John ix. 31.

mony; though it may be truly spoken, if it is understood of the sinner as a sinner, in which way also it is said, "His prayer shall be an abomination."[1]

§ 2. Though the sinner cannot pray *piously* in the sense that his prayer is informed by a habit of virtue,[2] still his prayer may be pious to this extent, that he asks for something appertaining to piety, as he who has not the habit of justice may will something that is just. And though his prayer is not meritorious, it may be impetratory, because merit rests on justice, but impetration on favour.

QUESTION LXXXIV.

OF THE EXTERIOR ACTS OF DIVINE WORSHIP.

ARTICLE I.

§ 1. Reverence is due to God for His excellence, which is communicated to creatures, not so far as to set them on a level with God, but in some measure of participation: and therefore the veneration with which we venerate God—a part of divine worship, or *latria*—is different from the veneration called *dulia*, with which we honour certain excellent creatures. Among the marks of reverence that we

---

[1] Prov. xxviii. 9.
[2] That is, of supernatural virtue. Cf. I-II. q. 65. art. 2.: q. 71. art. 4. (Trl.)

pay to excellent creatures the greatest is *worship*;[1] but there is one thing that is paid to God alone, namely, sacrifice. Hence Augustine says: "Men are called reverend and venerable, and by a great addition, worshipful. But who ever thought of offering sacrifice except to one whom he either knew to be God, or thought to be, or fabricated as such?"

ARTICLE II.—*Does worship suppose any bodily act?*

R. Because we are compounded of a twofold nature, intellectual and sensible, we owe to God a twofold worship—a spiritual worship consisting in the inward devotion of the mind; and a corporal worship consisting in the outward humbling of the body. The outward worship is for the sake of the inward, that by the signs of humility which we exhibit in the body our heart may be moved to subject itself to God, because it is connatural to us to proceed by way of things sensible to things intelligible.

§ 1. To the text, "True adorers shall adore the Father in spirit and in truth,"[2] it is to be said that even corporal adoration is in spirit, inasmuch as it proceeds from spiritual devotion and is directed to it.

---

[1] *Adoratio.* In Tacitus, *Histories*, i. 36, a candidate for empire is said *adorare vulgus*, "to do obeisance to the people." St. Augustine's words, that follow, are so far verified in their English dress, that the Worshipful the Mayor takes precedence in his own town of the Reverend Incumbent of the parish, and even of the Venerable Archdeacon. (Trl.)

[2] St. John iv. 23.

§ 2. Worship consists principally in inward reverence to God, but secondarily in certain corporal signs of humility: thus we bend the knee to mark our weakness in comparison with God; and we fall on our faces to profess that of ourselves we are nothing.

§ 3. Though we cannot attain to God by sense, yet by sensible signs our mind is roused to tend to God.

ARTICLE III.

§ 2. A definite place is chosen for adoration, not for the sake of the God who is adored, as though He had local bounds, but for the sake of the adorers themselves, and that on three accounts: first, on account of its being a consecrated place, from which consecration those who pray there conceive special devotion, so as to be the better heard, as appears by the prayer of Solomon;[1] secondly, on account of the sacred mysteries and other signs of holiness contained there; thirdly, on account of the concourse of many adorers, which makes the prayer more apt to be heard, as it is said: "Where there are two or three gathered together in my name, there am I in the midst of them."[2]

[1] 3 Kings viii.   [2] St Matt. xviii. 20.

QUESTION LXXXV.

OF SACRIFICE.

ARTICLE I.—*Is it of the law of nature to offer sacrifice to God?*

R. Natural reason dictates to man subjection to some higher power on account of the deficiencies which he experiences in himself, wherein he needs to be aided and guided by some one above himself; and whatever that higher power may be, that it is which amongst all men is called God. Natural reason dictates to man to show, in his own way, submission and honour to the power that is above man. Now it is a way befitting man to employ sensible signs to express his concepts, because his knowledge is derived from sensible objects. And therefore it comes of natural reason that a man should make use of sundry sensible things, offering them to God in token of due subjection and honour, after the likeness of those who offer sundry things to their lords in recognition of their seignorial rights.[1] But this belongs to the nature of sacrifice; and therefore the offering of sacrifice is a part of the natural law.

§ 1. Some things are of natural law in some general sort, the specifications thereof being of

[1] So in the feudal system, under which St. Thomas wrote.

positive law. Thus the natural law has it that evil-doers be punished; but their punishment by this or that penalty is of divine or human ordinance. In like manner also the offering of sacrifice is in some general sort of natural law: and therefore in this all men are agreed; but the specification of sacrifices is of human ordinance, or divine: and therefore in this men differ.[1]

§ 3. To signify his concepts is natural to man; but the specification of signs is according to human convention.

ARTICLE II.—*Ought sacrifice to be offered to God alone?*

R. The sacrifice that is offered outwardly, signifies the inward spiritual sacrifice whereby the soul offers itself to God. Now the soul offers itself to God in sacrifice as to the principle of its creation and the end of its beatitude. But God alone is the creator of our souls; and in Him alone does the happiness of our soul consist. And therefore as it is to God alone that we ought to offer the spiritual sacrifice, so it is to Him alone that we ought to offer exterior sacrifices. This too we see to be an observance in every commonwealth, that they honour the sovereign with some singular mark of reverence, which it would be treason to pay to any other.

§ 3. As Augustine says: "The priest does not say: I offer sacrifice to thee, Peter or Paul. But

[1] Cf. I-II. q. 94. art. 3. note. (Trl.)

we render thanks to God for their victories, and exhort one another to imitation of them."

ARTICLE III.—*Is the offering of sacrifice a special act of virtue?*

R. When the act of one virtue is directed to the end and purpose of another virtue, it participates in some manner in the species of the latter: just as when one steals to commit fornication, that theft assumes something of the deformity of fornication, so that if it were not otherwise a sin, it would be a sin by the mere fact of being referred to fornication. So then sacrifice is a special act, praiseworthy from being done in reverence of God: wherefore it belongs to a definite virtue, namely, to religion. But it may happen that the acts of other virtues are directed to the reverence of God; as when a person gives alms out of his own property for God's sake, or afflicts his body out of reverence for God; and in this way even the acts of other virtues may be called *sacrifices*. There are however certain acts which are not praiseworthy on any other ground except that of their being done for reverence to God; and these acts are properly called *sacrifices*, and belong to the virtue of religion.

§ 3. *Sacrifices* properly so called are when something is done about things offered to God, as the old practice of slaying animals and burning their bodies; and again the breaking and eating and blessing of bread. And this the name itself expresses: for it is called *sacrifice* from man's doing something sacred (*facit aliquid sacrum*).

But an *offering* is directly so called when something is offered to God, even though nothing be done about it: as pence or loaves are said to be *offered* on the altar, nothing being done about them. Hence every sacrifice is an offering, but not *vice versa*. First-fruits are offerings, because they were offered to God,[1] but not sacrifices, because nothing sacred was done about them. But tithes, properly speaking, are neither sacrifices nor offerings, because they are not paid immediately to God, but to the ministers of divine worship.

ARTICLE IV.—*Are all persons bound to offer sacrifices?*

R. There are two sorts of sacrifices, of which the first and principal is the inward sacrifice, to which all are bound: for all are bound to offer to God a devout mind. But there is another and outward sacrifice, divided into two kinds. One kind of sacrifice there is, which is praiseworthy only from the offering to God of some outward thing in protestation of subjection to God; and to this kind of sacrifice they who are under the New Law, or the Old, are bound in a different manner from those who are not under the Law. For those who are under the Law, are bound to offer fixed sacrifices according to the commandments of the Law: but those who were not under the Law, were bound to perform some outward acts to the honour of God in some decent and seemly fashion, suited to the society in which they lived,

---

[1] Deut. xxvi. 1—10.

but without determination of these or those acts. There is another class of outward sacrifices, in which the outward acts of other virtues besides religion are taken up for reverence of God: of which acts some fall under precept, and all are bound to them; others are works of supererogation, to which not all are bound.

§ 3. Priests offer sacrifices, which are specially directed to divine worship, not for themselves only, but also for others. But there are certain other sacrifices which any one can offer for himself to God.[1]

QUESTION LXXXVI.

OF OFFERINGS.

ARTICLE I.

The name of *offering* is common to all presentations made for the worship of God; so that if anything is presented for that worship, to be consumed in any sacred action, that is to be done upon it, it is both an *offering* and a *sacrifice;* but if it is so presented as to remain entire, set apart for purposes of divine worship, or to be spent for the use of the ministers of religion, it will be an *offering* and not a *sacrifice.*

[1] Namely, as explained above, the inward sacrifice of a devout mind, which is a point of religion, and the outward sacrifice of external acts of other virtues besides religion, done on a motive of religion, or done for the greater glory of God. (Trl.)

ARTICLE II.—*Are offerings due only to priests?*

R. A priest is appointed to be a sort of middle-man and mediator between God and the people, as we read of Moses;[1] and therefore it belongs to him to deliver the divine decrees to the people; and again that which comes from the people, in the way of prayers and sacrifices and offerings, ought to be paid to God through the priest. And therefore the offerings that are made by the people to God belong to the priests; not simply to convert them to their own use, but also to dispense them faithfully, partly by expending them on what belongs to divine worship, partly on what belongs to their own maintenance, because "they that serve the altar partake with the altar;"[2] partly also for the use of the poor, who are to be supported, so far as possible, out of the property of the Church, because our Lord also had a purse for the use of the poor, as Jerome says.

[1] Deut. v. 5, 27.   [2] 1 Cor. ix. 13.

QUESTION LXXXVIII.

OF A VOW WHEREBY SOMETHING IS PROMISED TO GOD.

ARTICLE I.—*Does a vow consist in a mere purpose of the will?*

R. There are three necessary requisites to a vow: deliberation, purpose of the will, and promise; and in this the essence of the vow is complete. Sometimes however two other elements are added to confirm the vow, namely, the utterance of the mouth and the witness of other persons.

ARTICLE II.—*Must a vow always be of the better good?*

R. A vow is a promise made to God. Now a promise is of something which one voluntarily does for another; for if one were to say that he would do anything against another, it would not be a promise but a threat. And therefore since every sin is against God, and no work is acceptable to God if it be not virtuous, consequently a vow must be made of no unlawful nor of any indifferent matter, but only of some act of virtue.

That which is absolutely necessary to be or not to be, in no way falls under vow. Thus it would be a folly to vow to die, or not to fly into the air. But as for that which is not absolutely necessary, but is necessary as a means to the end, being the means without which there can be no salvation—such a matter falls indeed under vow, inasmuch as it is done voluntarily, but not inasmuch as it is of necessity. But that which falls neither under absolute necessity, nor under the necessity of means to end, is altogether voluntary: it therefore is the most proper matter of a vow. This is called a *greater good*, in comparison with the good that is of ordinary necessity to salvation. Therefore, properly speaking, a vow is said to be *of the better good*.

§ 3. The maceration of the body by watchings and fastings, is not acceptable to God except so far as it is a work of virtue; and that it is in so far as it is done with due discretion, so that concupiscence may be restrained at the same time that nature is not overwhelmed. And on such terms these austerities may fall under vow. Therefore also the Apostle after saying, "Present your bodies a living sacrifice, holy, pleasing unto God," added, "your reasonable service."[1] But because a man is easily deceived in his judgment on what concerns himself, the more fitting course with such vows is to submit them to the judgment of a superior, whether they are to be kept or set aside; yet so that if the person should feel great and manifest hardship from the observance of such a vow, and had no access to a superior, he ought not to keep such a vow. As for vows of vain and useless things, they are rather to be derided than kept.

[1] Romans xii. 1.

ARTICLE IV.—*Is it expedient to make any vow?*

R. It is a different thing promising to man and promising to God. We promise to man something for his advantage; but we promise to God, not for His advantage, but for our own, because "what is rendered to Him is added to the renderer," as Augustine says. And therefore it is expedient to vow, inasmuch as by vowing we clamp our will to the doing of that which it is expedient to do.

§ 1. As inability to sin does not diminish liberty, so neither is liberty diminished by the necessity of a will fixed on good, as is evident in God and in the blessed; and such is the necessity of a vow, bearing a certain likeness to the confirmed estate of the blessed. Hence Augustine says: "Happy the necessity, that compels us to the better course."

§ 2. When the danger arises from the doing of the thing itself, then the doing thereof is not expedient, as when one crosses a river by a tumbledown bridge; but if the danger threatens from a man giving over the doing, the doing does not on that account cease to be expedient. Thus it is expedient to mount on horseback, notwithstanding the danger that threatens you of a fall from your horse. Otherwise you would have to cease from all things, because accidentally by some turn of affairs anything may prove dangerous. Hence it is said: "He that observeth the wind shall not sow; and he that considereth the clouds shall never reap."[1] But the danger that threatens one making a vow is not from the vow itself, but from the fault of the man,

[1] Eccles. xi. 4.

who changes his will in transgressing the vow. Hence Augustine says: "Repent not of having vowed: nay, rather rejoice, that it is no longer allowable for you to do that, which only could have been allowed you to your own loss."[1]

ARTICLE VI.—*Is it more praiseworthy and meritorious to do a thing by vow than without a vow?*
R. The same work done with a vow is better and more meritorious than without a vow, for three reasons. First, because to vow is an act of religion, which is the chief of the moral virtues. But the work of the nobler virtue is the better and more meritorious. Hence the act of an inferior virtue is better and more meritorious for being *commanded* by a superior virtue, of which latter it becomes an act by being *commanded* by it; as the act of faith or hope is better for being *commanded* by charity.[2] And therefore the acts of the other moral virtues, as of abstinence and of chastity, are better and more meritorious for being done by vow, because thus they come to belong to divine worship as sacrifices offered to God. Hence Augustine says: "Even virginity itself is not honoured because it is

[1] The distinction here lies between dangers that come of relaxing our efforts, and dangers that are irrespective of our efforts. An enterprise is rash when, being unnecessary, it is fraught with grave dangers of the latter sort, the issue of which, once we are in the danger, is independent of anything that we may do. By this principle a strong man and a wise one regulates even his amusements. Is it a question only of a steep Alpine ascent, or are there frequent avalanches? Is the water deep? is that all? or is it infested with sharks? (Trl.)

[2] See II-II. q. 26. art. 7. for this sense of *commanded*. (Trl.)

virginity, but because it is dedicated to God, in which capacity it is fostered and preserved by the uninterrupted practice of piety." Secondly, because he who both vows a thing and does it accordingly, subjects himself to God more thoroughly than another, who simply does the thing; for he subjects himself to God, not only as to the act, but also as to the power, because henceforth he has it not in his power to act otherwise: as he who should give a man the tree with the fruit, would give more than another who gave the fruit only. Thirdly, because by a vow the will is clamped fast to good; but to do a thing with a will, firm set on good, belongs to the perfection of virtue, as obstinacy in sin is an aggravation of the sin.

§ 2. The necessity of constraint, as being contrary to the will, causes sadness. But the necessity of vow, as strengthening the will, causes not sadness but joy, in well-disposed persons.

§ 3. He who does a thing without a vow, has his will fixed upon that particular work which he does, at the moment when he does it; but his will does not remain altogether fixed for the future, like the will of the person under vow, who has bound his will to a certain line of action, even before doing this particular act, and perhaps has bound himself to repeat the act many times over.

ARTICLE VIII.—*Are those debarred from vowing who are subject to another's control?*

R. A vow is a promise made to God. Now none can bind himself by promise irrevocably to that which is under the control of another, but only to that which is altogether under his own control. But whoever is subject to another, is not his own master to do as he likes in the matter in which he is subject, but is dependent on another's will. And therefore, in the things in which one is subject to another, he cannot bind himself irrevocably by vow without the consent of his superior.[1]

§ 2. From the time that a human being comes to the years of puberty, if his condition is not that of a slave, he is his own master in what relates to his own person, as to the contracting marriage, or binding himself by vow to religious life; but he is not his own master as to the ordering of the household: hence with respect to that he cannot vow anything that can stand without the consent of his father.

ARTICLE X.—*Does a vow admit of dispensation?*
R. Dispensation from a vow is to be looked upon in the same manner as dispensation from the observance of a law. A law is made in view of what is in the majority of cases good. But because what is good in the majority of cases may happen in a particular case not to be good, it has been found necessary to have some one to determine that the law should not be observed in that particular case. And this is the proper meaning of a dispensation from a law: for *dispensation* seems to imply a sort of commensurate distribution, or application

[1] That is, he can vow, but his superior can revoke the vow. (Trl.)

of some common attribute to the subjects that come under it: in which way one is said to *dispense* food to a family.[1] In like manner a person vowing makes in a certain way a law for himself, binding himself to something that is ordinarily and for most cases good. But it may happen that in a particular case the thing proves either simply evil, or useless, or a hindrance to greater good; which is against the idea of what falls under a vow. And therefore it is necessary to have it ruled in such a case that the vow is not to be observed. If it is ruled absolutely that a vow is not to be observed, that is called a *dispensation* from the vow. If in place of what was to be observed something else is imposed, that is called a *commutation* of the vow. Hence it is less to commute a vow than to dispense from a vow; but both the one and the other lies within the power of the Church.

§ 2. As by natural law and divine precept a man is bound to fulfil his vow, so is he also under the same obligations to obey the law or commandment of his superiors. Still, when a dispensation is granted from a human law, it is not that a human law is disobeyed, such disobedience being against the law of nature and the commandment of God; but what happens is this, that what was a law ceases to be a law in this particular case. So also it comes about by the authority of the superior dispensing, that what was contained under a vow is no longer so contained, it being ruled in this particular case that the matter is not proper matter for a vow.

[1] Nowadays they dispense medicine. (Trl.)

And therefore, when a Prelate of the Church dispenses from a vow, he does not dispense from any precept of natural or divine law; but he rules a point, which was become matter of obligation through the resolve of a human will, wherein the person who so made up his mind was not able at the time to see all round the circumstances of the case.[1]

ARTICLE XII.—*Is the authority of a Prelate requisite for the commutation or dispensation of a vow?*

R. A vow is a promise made to God of something acceptable to God. Now in any promise, what is acceptable to the recipient of the promise depends on what he chooses to have. But a Prelate in the Church holds the place of God. And therefore in the commutation or dispensation of vows there is required the authority of a Prelate, to determine in the person of God what is acceptable to God.

§ 2. Some have said that Prelates can dispense from vows just as they like, for this reason, that there is included as a condition in every vow the will of the Prelate who has authority over the person making it, as in the vows of those who are in the subject condition of slaves or sons there is understood the clause, *if my father*, or *master, approves*, or *does not object;* and in this view a subject need have no remorse of conscience in abandoning any vow, when told to do so by his superior. But the above

[1] Cf. I-II. q. 94. art. 5.; q. 100. art. 8.; II-II. q. 89. art. 9. § 1. (Trl.)

position rests on a false foundation; for since the power of a spiritual superior, who is not a master but a dispenser, or steward, is given " unto edification and not for destruction,"[1] so the superior can no more forbid what is of itself pleasing to God, namely works of virtue, than he can command what is of itself displeasing to God, to wit, sins. And therefore it is lawful to vow those works absolutely. But it is the Prelate's office to discern what course is the more virtuous and the more acceptable to God. And therefore where the case is plain, the Prelate's dispensation would not excuse from blame; for instance, if a Prelate were to dispense a person from a vow of entering religion, without there being any apparent obstacle in the way of its fulfilment. But if there were an apparent cause that made the matter at least doubtful, the subject might abide by the judgment of his superior dispensing or commuting, but not by his own judgment, because he himself does not hold the place of God, except it be in the case in which the thing vowed were manifestly unlawful, and he had no convenient access to his superior.

[1] 2 Cor. x. 8.

QUESTION LXXXIX.

OF OATHS.

ARTICLE I.—*Is swearing a calling on God to witness?*

R. As the Apostle says: "An oath is for confirmation."[1] In matters of science, confirmation is done by reasoning from premises of natural knowledge, that are infallibly true. But the particular facts of the contingent doings of men cannot be confirmed by necessary reasoning; and therefore what is alleged concerning them is usually confirmed by witnesses. Still human testimony is not sufficient for such confirmation, and that on two accounts. First, for lack of truthfulness in man, seeing that very many fall into lying. Secondly, for lack of knowledge, because men cannot discern things to come, nor the secrets of hearts, nor yet the doings of the absent. Still however men talk on all these points; and it is expedient for human society that some certainty should be had about them. And therefore it has been found necessary to recur to the witness of God; because God cannot lie, nor is anything hidden from Him.

Now to call God to witness is to swear,—sometimes about things present or past, which is an

[1] Hebrews vi. 16.

oath of asseveration; sometimes in confirmation of a future performance, and that is called a *promissory oath.*

ARTICLE II.—*Is it lawful to swear?*

R. A thing may very easily be good in itself, and yet turn to his evil who does not use it properly. Thus to receive the Eucharist is good, and yet he who receives unworthily "eateth and drinketh judgment to himself."[1] Thus then an oath is a lawful and virtuous thing in itself, as is evident from its origin and its end. From its origin: because the taking of an oath was brought in by the belief of mankind that God has infallible truth, possesses a universal knowledge, and exercises a universal providence over all things. From its end, because oaths are taken to justify men and put an end to disputes. But an oath works to the evil of a man through his using it badly, without necessity and due caution. Small indeed seems to be his reverence for God, who brings God in as witness to a light matter, which he would not presume to do with any man of honourable position. There is also the danger of perjury, because a man easily errs in word. Hence it is said: "Let not thy mouth be accustomed to swearing; for in it there are many falls."[2]

ARTICLE III.—*Are these three duly enumerated accompaniments of an oath,—justice, judgment, and truth?*[3]

[1] 1 Cor. xi. 29.   [2] Ecclus. xxiii. 9.   [3] Jerem. iv. 2.

R. There are two requisites for the good use of an oath: First, that one should not swear lightly, but with a necessary cause, and discreetly: in this respect *judgment* is necessary, or discretion on the part of him who swears. Secondly, touching the matter sworn to, it is requisite that it be neither a falsehood nor anything unlawful; and in this respect *truth* is necessary, whereby one swears to what is true; and *justice*, whereby one swears to what is lawful. *Judgment* is wanting in an incautious oath; *truth* in a lying oath; and *justice* in an iniquitous or unlawful oath.

ARTICLE V.—*Is swearing something desirable and frequently to be practised, as a thing useful and good?*

R. That which is sought only as a support and stay to infirmity and deficiency, is not counted of the number of things in themselves desirable, but of the number of things necessary, as in the case of medicine. But an oath is sought as a support and stay to the deficiency of the faith that one man can put in another. And therefore an oath is not to be held of the number of things that are in themselves desirable, but of the number of things that are necessary for this life, and which are unduly used by whosoever uses them beyond the bounds of necessity.

ARTICLE VII.

§ 1. The case of a simple affirmation is different from that of an oath, in which the witness of **God** is invoked. For the truth of a simple affirmation it is enough that the person says what he intends to do, because that is true at the time in his case, or in the purpose of the doer. But an oath ought not to come in except upon a matter on which the person's mind is immovably made up. And therefore if an oath is used, then for reverence of the witness of God that is invoked, the man is bound to make true what he has sworn to, to the best of his power, unless the issue is for the worse.

§ 2. An oath may issue for the worse in two ways. In one way *from the beginning*, either because the oath is of itself evil, as when one swears to commit adultery; or because it is an obstacle to greater good, as when one swears not to enter the religious or the ecclesiastical state,[1] or not to accept a prelacy in a case where it is expedient to accept it. An oath of this kind is unlawful from the beginning. That however it may be in different ways. In the case of a person swearing to commit a sin, he sinned in swearing, and he sins in keeping the oath. But if a person swears not to do that which is the better good, good however which he is not bound to do, he sins, to be sure, in swearing, inasmuch as he places an obstacle to the Holy Ghost, the inspirer of good purposes, but he does not sin in keeping the oath, though he does much better not to keep it. In another way an oath has issue for the worse on account of *something fresh that comes up unforeseen*. Thus Herod's oath to give

---

[1] Absolutely, such an oath is an obstacle to greater good. In a particular case it is not, especially when taken to a public authority, who can release you where he sees cause. (Trl.)

the dancing girl whatever she asked, might have been lawful from the beginning, the due condition being understood, that she should ask what was a proper thing to give, but the fulfilment of the oath was unlawful.

§ 3. In an oath taken on compulsion there is a twofold obligation: one to the man to whom the promise is made; and such obligation is destroyed by the compulsion, because he who has used violence deserves that the promise made to him be not kept.[1] There is another obligation binding the person to God, to fulfil what he has promised by His name. Such obligation is not destroyed in the court of conscience; he who has sworn should rather suffer temporal loss than violate his oath. Still he may take legal measures to recover what he has paid, or he may denounce the matter to his ecclesiastical superior, any oath to the contrary notwithstanding: because such an oath would have issue for the worse, being against public justice. The Roman Pontiffs have absolved men from oaths like these, not as ruling such oaths to be of no binding force, but relaxing the force of them for just reasons.

[1] This supposes the violence to be unjust. The promise in such a case is a promise, but the maker of it has it in his discretion to rescind it: in technical language, it is *valid but not firm*. How far one may be justified in making such a promise, is a further question. It will be seen that when the promise has been confirmed by oath, it cannot be rescinded except by Church authority. See also II-II. q. 98. art. 3. § 1. This should prevent a nation from tearing up treaties, on the plea that the war which imposed them was unjust, at leas: when the present rulers of the nation have sworn to those treaties. Cf. II-II. q. 93. art. 2. § 4. But international law is a terrible tangle, for want of an international judge. (Trl.)

§ 4. When the intention of the party taking the oath is not the same as the intention of the party to whom it is taken—if this comes of any guile in him that swears, the oath should be kept according to the sound understanding of him to whom it is taken.[1] But if the person taking it uses no guile, he is bound according to his intention in taking it.

ARTICLE VIII.—*Is the obligation of an oath greater than that of a vow?*

R. Both obligations, that of an oath and that of a vow, are caused by something referring to God, but not in the same way. The obligation of a vow is caused by the fidelity which we owe to God, to discharge our promise to Him; while the obligation of an oath is caused by the reverence that we owe Him, which binds us to make true whatever we promise by His name. Now every violation of fidelity involves irreverence, but it is not every irreverence that contains a violation of fidelity. A subject's violation of the fidelity that he owes his lord, is reckoned the greatest irreverence. And therefore a vow in its own nature is more binding than an oath.

ARTICLE IX.—*Has any one the power to dispense from oaths?*

R. The need of a dispensation, whether from a law or from a vow, arises from the fact that what is useful and right in itself, viewed generally, may

[1] *E.g.*, Cranmer's oath at his consecration, *Ethics and Natural Law*, p. 234. (Trl.)

be wrong and hurtful in a particular set of circumstances: and what is wrong and hurtful cannot be matter either of law or vow. The same is out of keeping with the conditions requisite to an oath: for if it is wrong, it is out of keeping with *justice;* if it is hurtful, it is out of keeping with *judgment.* And therefore parity of reason proves that a dispensation may be granted also from an oath.

§ 1. A dispensation from an oath does extend to the man's doing anything against his oath: that is impossible, since the observance of oaths is matter of divine precept, which admits of no dispensation.[1] But the effect of a dispensation from an oath is, that what formerly fell under oath, falls under oath no longer, not being due matter of oath, as we said above of a vow.[2] The matter of an oath of asseveration, which is of the present or past, is already gone into the region of necessity and become immutable; and therefore a dispensation could not refer to the matter, but would refer to the act itself of swearing; hence such a dispensation would be directly against the divine precept. But the matter of a promissory oath is something future, capable of variation, so that in a certain conjuncture it may be unlawful or hurtful, and consequently not due matter of oath; and therefore a dispensation may be granted from a promissory oath, because such a dispensation regards the matter of the oath, and is not contrary to the divine precept of the observance of oaths.[3]

[1] I-II. q. 100. art. 8. (Trl.)   [2] Q. 88. art. 10. § 2.
[3] This paragraph should be studied by those historians who have put it on record, that the Pope has at times granted dispensations to commit perjury. (Trl.)

§ 2. There are two ways in which a man may promise something under oath to another. One way is when he promises something to that other person's benefit, as that he will serve him, or give him money. He to whom the promise was made, can absolve from such a promise; for the maker of the promise is understood to have discharged his promise to the other, when he acts in the matter according to that other's will. The other way is when one promises to another something that makes for the honour of God, or for the advantage of a third party; as when one promises another under oath to enter religion, or to do some work of piety; and then he to whom the promise is made cannot absolve the promiser; because the promise was made not to him mainly, but to God; unless it happens that a condition has been inserted, giving him that power.

§ 3. Occasionally a thing is promised on oath, of which it is doubtful whether it is lawful or unlawful, beneficial or hurtful, either absolutely or in a special case; and from such an oath any Bishop can dispense.[1] Sometimes again a thing is promised on oath, which is manifestly lawful and useful; and in such an oath there seems to be no room for dispensation or commutation, unless something better occurs to be done for the common advantage, which seems to appertain above all to the power of the Pope, who has care of the Universal Church. Or even there may be an absolute relaxation of the oath, which again appertains to the Pope in all

---

[1] In his own diocese. (Trl.)

things alike that are part of the administration of Church matters, over which he has plenitude of power. In the same way any man in authority may make void an oath that has been taken by his subjects in the matter that is subject to his authority. Thus a father may make void the oath of one but yet a girl in age, and a husband his wife's oath, as is said in Numbers xxx.

QUESTION XCI.

OF THE TAKING OF THE DIVINE NAME TO INVOKE IT IN PRAYER OR PRAISE.

ARTICLE I.—*Is God to be praised by word of mouth?*
R. We address words to a man to express to him the thought of our heart, which he cannot know otherwise than by our words. And therefore we praise a man by word of mouth, to let him or others know that we have a good opinion of him, that thereby we may provoke him who is praised to do still better, and lead others who hear him praised to think well of him, and revere him and imitate him. But we address words to God, not to manifest our thoughts to Him who is the searcher of hearts, but to lead ourselves and others who hear us to revere Him. And therefore the praise of the lips is necessary, not for the sake of God, but for the sake of him who gives the praise, whose heart is raised to God thereby. The praise of the

lips is also useful for moving the affections of other men towards God; hence it is said: "His praise shall be always in my mouth: let the meek hear and rejoice. O magnify the Lord with me."[1]

ARTICLE II.—*Ought singing to be employed in the divine praises?*

R. Vocal praise is necessary to move man's heart and raise it to God. And therefore all that can help to this purpose is properly employed in the divine praises. And therefore it was a wholesome institution to bring in singing into the divine praises, that the minds of the weak might be more stirred to devotion. Hence Augustine says: "I am led to approve of the custom of singing in church, that by the delight of the ears the weaker mind may rise to an affection of piety;" and he says of himself: "I wept at thy hymns and canticles, much moved by the voices of thy sweet-resounding church."

§ 1. "Spiritual canticles"[2] may mean, not only those that are inwardly sung in the spirit, but also those that are sung outwardly with the mouth, inasmuch as by such canticles devotion is called forth.

§ 2. Jerome when he says, "God is to be sung to, not with the voice, but with the heart," is not absolutely condemning singing, but is rebuking those who sing in the church in a theatrical strain,

[1] Psalm xxxiii. 2, 3, 4. For further reasons see *Ethics and Natural Law*, pp 194, 195. (Trl)
[2] Coloss. iii. 16.

not for the exciting of devotion, but for ostentation or to give pleasure.

§ 5. By singing of set purpose for pleasure, the mind is withdrawn from the consideration of the things that are sung. But if any one sings for devotion, he considers more attentively what is said, lingering longer upon the same phrase. And among the hearers, though some understand not what is sung, still they understand why it is sung, namely, to the praise of God; and this is enough to excite devotion.

QUESTION XCII.

OF VICES OPPOSED TO RELIGION, AND FIRST OF SUPERSTITION.

ARTICLE I.—*Is superstition a vice opposed to religion?*

R. Religion is a moral virtue. Now every moral virtue lies in some golden mean. And therefore two manner of vices are opposed to moral virtue, one by excess, and one by defect. Now the golden mean of virtue may be exceeded, not only in the circumstance of quantity, but also in other circumstances. Hence in some virtues, as munificence and magnanimity, the vice exceeds the mean of the virtue, not because it tends to a greater height than the virtue does—very possibly it tends to less—but it oversteps the mean of virtue, inasmuch as it does something to the wrong *person*, or at the wrong *time*, or something of that sort. Thus then superstition is a vice opposed to religion in point of excess, not that it renders more to divine worship than true religion does, but because it pays divine worship either to the wrong object, or in some way in which it ought not to be paid.

QUESTION XCIII.

OF THE SPECIES OF SUPERSTITION; AND FIRST OF SUPERSTITION BY UNDUE WORSHIP OF THE TRUE GOD.

ARTICLE I.—*Can there be anything pernicious in the worship of the true God?*

R. As Augustine says: "A lie is most pernicious in what appertains to the Christian religion." A lie is when one gives outward signification of something contrary to truth. Signification may be given by deed as well as by word: it is in this signification given by deed, that the outward worship of religion consists. And therefore if by outward worship any false signification is given, the worship will be pernicious. This may happen in either of two ways: in one way on the part of the *thing signified*, if the signification of the worship be in disagreement with it. Thus in the time of the New Law, the mysteries of Christ being now accomplished, it is pernicious to use the ceremonies of the Old Law, by which the mysteries of Christ were signified as things to come: as it would be pernicious also if one were to avow in word that Christ was still to suffer. In another way, falsehood may arise in exterior worship on the part of the *worshipper*, and this especially in public worship, which is rendered by ministers of religion on the part of the whole Church. For as he would be a forger, who should make any proposition on the part of his principal, which he had not been commissioned to make, so the vice of falsehood or forgery is incurred by whoever on the part of the Church renders worship to God, contrary to the rite which the Church has ordained by divine authority, and which is customary in the Church.[1] Hence Ambrose says: "He is unworthy, who celebrates the mystery otherwise than as Christ has delivered." And the gloss: "It is superstition, when the name of religion is applied to human tradition."

ARTICLE II.—*Can there be anything superfluous in the worship of the true God?*

R. There are two ways in which a thing may be called *superfluous*. In one way in point of *absolute quantity*; and in this way there can be nothing superfluous in divine worship, because man can do nothing that is not less than what he owes to God. In another way, a thing may be superfluous in point of *quantity of proportion*, because it is not proportionate to the end. Now the end of divine

---

[1] Did the compilers of the Book of Common Prayer think of these words, when they were hacking and hewing down the ancient rite of the Church of England? (Trl.)

worship is that a man should give glory to God, and subject himself to God in mind and body. And therefore whatever a man does that bears on the glory of God, and on the subjection of man's mind to God, and of his body also by a moderate restraint of the appetites, according to God's and the Church's ordinance, and the custom of the community with whom he lives,—that is not superfluous in divine worship. But if there be anything that of itself belongs not to God's glory, nor to the carrying of man's thoughts to God, nor to the restraint of the inordinate lusts of the flesh,—or again, if it be against the institution of God and of the Church, or against the common custom, which is to be held for a law,—all this is to be accounted superfluous and superstitious, because it rests on externals alone, and reaches not to the inward worship of God.

QUESTION XCIV.

OF IDOLATRY.

ARTICLE I.—*Is idolatry rightly set down as a species of superstition?*

R. It belongs to superstition to exceed the due mode and measure of divine worship. This is done most of all when divine worship is paid to an object to which it ought not to be paid. Now it ought to be paid to the supreme, uncreated God alone; and therefore whenever divine worship is paid to any creature whatsoever, it is a superstitious practice. Divine worship thus paid to sensible creatures[1] was shown by sensible signs, as sacrifices, games, &c.; so also it was paid to creatures represented by some sensible form or figure, which is termed an *idol*. But there were different ways in which divine worship was paid to idols. Some persons by a nefarious art put together certain images, which wrought certain effects due to the power of demons: hence they thought that there was some divinity in the images themselves, and consequently that divine honour was due to them. Others did not pay divine honours to the mere images themselves, but

[1] Read *creaturæ sensibili*. (Trl.)

to the creatures whose images they were.[1] Among these latter worshippers there were three opinions. Some thought that certain men had been gods, whom they worshipped through their images, as Jupiter, Mercury, and other such. Some thought that the whole world was one god, not for its corporal substance, but for its soul, which they believed to be God, saying that God was nothing else than a soul, by movement and reason governing the world. Hence they thought that divine worship should be paid to the world and to all the parts thereof, to the heavens, to the air, to water, and to all such parts. Others, the Platonists, laid it down that there was one supreme God, the cause of all; after whom they placed certain spiritual substances, called gods, created by the supreme God with some participation of Divinity; after these they placed the souls of the heavenly bodies, and under them the *genii*, who they said were certain living creatures in the air; and under them they placed the souls of men, which they believed to be raised by the merit of virtue to the society of the gods or of the *genii*; and to all these beings they paid divine honours. These last two opinions they said belonged to *natural theology*, which philosophers studied in nature and taught in the schools. That other opinion, of the worship of men, they said belonged to *legendary theology*, which was represented in theatres according to the fancies of poets. The

---

[1] "We set up likenesses of the gods and honour them, because we deem that the living gods will be much beholden to us for venerating their lifeless images." Plato, *Laws*, 931. (Trl.)

other opinion, about images, they said belonged to *political theology*, which is matter of celebration by pontiffs in temples. Now all these things were part of the superstition of idolatry.

§ 1. As religion is not faith, but a protestation of faith by external signs; so superstition is a protestation of infidelity by external worship.

§ 3. From the common heathen custom of worshipping all manner of creatures under certain images, the name of *idolatry* has been applied to any worship whatever of a creature, even if it be without images.

ARTICLE II.—*Is idolatry a sin?*

R. Some have thought that it was lawful and in itself good to offer sacrifice and other acts of divine worship, not only to the supreme God, but also to other beings above mentioned, on the ground that divine reverence was to be paid to every superior nature, as being nearer to God. But this is an irrational thing to say. For though we ought to reverence all superior beings, yet the same reverence is not due to all; but something special is due to the supreme God, who in a singular manner excels them all: and that is the worship of *latria*. Others have thought that the paying of the exterior worship of *latria* to idols was not to be adopted as a practice in itself good or the best thing, but as being in accordance with the custom of the vulgar, as Augustine introduces Seneca saying: "In adoring we will still remember that this worship is rather a point of convention than of reality." Some heretics also have fallen into this error, saying that there is no danger in one externally worshipping idols, if he is seized in time of persecution, provided he keeps the faith in his heart. The falsity of this position is clear and manifest: for seeing that exterior worship is a sign of the worship that is interior, it is quite as pernicious a falsehood for one to pay exterior worship to any object against the inner sentiment of his mind, as for one to assert in words the contrary of that which with true belief he holds in his heart. Hence Augustine says against Seneca that "his worship of idols was all the more condemnable, for that, acting as he was mendaciously in the matter, he yet so acted as to cause people to think that he was acting veraciously."

§ 1. Neither in the Tabernacle, or Temple of the Old Law, nor again now in the Church, are images set up for divine worship to be paid to them; but they are there for a symbolical purpose, that by these images faith in the exalted prerogatives of the angels and the saints may be imprinted and confirmed in the minds of men. But it is otherwise with the image of Christ, to which on account of His Divinity divine worship is due, as will be explained in Part III. Question xxv. Article iii.[1]

ARTICLE III.[2]—*Is the image of Christ to be adored with the adoration of "latria"?*

R. There are two affections of the soul towards

[1] It appears best to subjoin the Article to which St. Thomas refers. (Trl.)
[2] Part III. q. xxv.

an image: one towards the image itself, considered as an object; the other towards the image, considered as the image of another being. And between these two affections there is this difference: that the first affection—that towards the image considered as an object—is different from the affection towards the object itself which the image represents: whereas the second affection—that towards the image considered as an image—is one and the same with the affection towards the object which the image represents. Thus then we must say that to the image of Christ, considered as an object—a sculptured or painted piece of wood—no reverence is paid; because reverence is due only to a rational nature. It remains therefore that reverence is paid to it, only inasmuch as it is an image; and thus it follows that the same reverence is paid to the image of Christ as to Christ Himself. Since then Christ is adored with the adoration of *latria*, it follows that His image is to be adored with the adoration of *latria*.

§ 1. The precept: "Thou shalt not make to thyself any graven thing, nor the likeness of any thing,"[1] does not forbid the making of any sculptured figure or likeness, but the making of them for adoration. Hence it is added: "Thou shalt not adore them nor serve them." And because the affection to the image and to the thing is one affection, the prohibition of the adoration of the image stands on the same footing as the prohibition of the adoration of the thing, of which it is

[1] Exodus xx. 4.

the image. Hence the text is to be understood as prohibiting the adoration of the images which the Gentiles made for the veneration of their gods, that is, of demons. And therefore it is prefaced with the command: "Thou shalt not have strange gods before me." But of the true God Himself, seeing that He is incorporeal, no material image could be set up, because, as the Damascene says: "It is the height of folly and impiety to make a figure of the Divinity." Since however in the New Covenant God has become man, He may be adored in His material image.

§ 2. The Apostle forbids us[1] to have any fellowship with the unfruitful works of the Gentiles; but fellowship with their fruitful works the Apostle does not forbid. Now the adoration of images is to be counted among unfruitful works from two points of view: first, inasmuch as some of the Gentiles adored the images themselves as objects, believing that there was a divinity resident in them, on account of the answers which the devils in them gave, and other such wonderful effects; secondly, by reason of the objects which the images represented; for they erected these images to certain creatures, which they venerated in them with the veneration of *latria*. But we adore with the adoration of *latria* the image of Christ, who is true God; adoring it, not for the sake of the image itself, but for the sake of the object of which it is an image.

[1] Ephes. v. 11.

QUESTION XCV.

OF THE SUPERSTITION OF DIVINATION.

ARTICLE I.—*Is divination a sin?*

R. By the name of *divination* is understood some sort of prediction of things to come. Now things to come may be predicted in two ways: one way in their causes; in another way in themselves. Causes of things to come fall into three classes. Some there are that produce their effects necessarily and invariably: such effects may be known for certain, and predicted by foreknowledge of their causes, as astronomers predict eclipses. Some causes produce their effects, not necessarily and invariably, but generally, failing however at times; and through such causes future effects may be foreknown, not indeed with certainty, but conjecturally, as astronomers can predict rain or drought, and physicians recovery or death. There are other causes that, considered in themselves, are indeterminate, and may work either way, as is seen especially in the rational powers; and such effects, as also any effects that happen unusually and by chance from natural causes, cannot be foreknown from the consideration of their causes, because their causes have no determinate inclination to such effects. And therefore effects of this kind cannot be foreknown, unless they be viewed in themselves. Now human eyes can view these effects in themselves only while they are present, as when a man sees Socrates running or walking: but to consider such effects in themselves before they take place, is proper to God, who alone in His eternity sees future things as present. Hence it is said: "Show the things that are to come hereafter, and we shall know that ye are gods."[1] If any one therefore presumes to foretell or foreknow future things of this character, otherwise than by God's revealing them to him, he manifestly usurps to himself the prerogative of God; and from this some are called *diviners*. Hence Isidore says: "Diviners are so called as being full of God: for they pretend to be full of the Divinity, and with fraudulent cunning they conjecture what is to befall men in the future." It is not therefore called *divination*, if one foretells things that happen of necessity, or happen generally, which things can be foreknown by human reason; or if one knows by revelation of God other events that are to happen, though not of necessity, in the future: for then he is not himself *divining*, that is, doing what is divine, rather he is receiving what is divine. But then only is a man said to *divine*, when he arrogates to himself in an undue manner the foretelling of future events; and this is certainly a sin: hence divination is always sinful.

[1] Isaias xli. 23.

ARTICLE IV.—*Is divination by invocation of evil spirits lawful?*

R. All divination by invocation of evil spirits is unlawful for two reasons. The first is taken from consideration of the principle, or prime means of this divination, which is a pact expressly entered into with the Evil One, by invocation of the same: and this is altogether unlawful; and it would be still more grievous if sacrifice or reverence were paid to the fiend thus invoked. The second reason is taken from consideration of the future event. For the devil, who aims at the perdition of mankind, though he sometimes tells the truth, intends by these his answers to accustom men to give him credence, and thus he seeks to lure them on to something prejudicial to their salvation. Hence Athanasius says: "Though the devil told the truth, Christ restrained his speech, lest he might utter his iniquity along with the truth: to accustom us not to care for such utterances, though they seem to be true; for it is monstrous that, having the Divine Scripture at hand, we should take instruction of the devil."

ARTICLE VIII.—*Is divination by lot unlawful?*

R. If the point to be determined by lot is, what is to be assigned and to whom, be it a matter of property or of dignity, or of punishment, or of employment; that is called a *dividing lot*. If the inquiry is, what is to be done, it is called a *consulting lot*. If the inquiry is, what is to happen in the future, that is called a *divining lot*. Now the issue of proceedings that are committed to lot, must be looked for either from chance or from spiritual cause directing the lot. If from chance—which can have place only in a *dividing lot*—there seems to be no fault there, except perhaps the fault of silliness. Thus parties unable to agree to a division may draw lots for it, leaving the apportionment to chance. But if the decision by lot is looked for from a spiritual cause, that cause sometimes is the agency of evil spirits. Thus we read: "The king of Babylon stood in the highway, at the head of two ways, seeking divination, shuffling arrows: he inquired of the idols and consulted entrails."[1] Such use of lots is unlawful. Sometimes again the issue is looked for from God, according to the text: "Lots are cast into the lap, but they are disposed of by the Lord."[2] Such use of lots is not evil in itself, but sin may attach to it incidentally; and first of all, if recourse is had to lots without any need; for that looks like tempting God. Secondly, if even in need lots are used without show of reverence for God. Hence Bede says: "But if any persons under stress of necessity think that they should consult God by lot after the example of the Apostles,[3] let them observe that the Apostles did not do this except after gathering an assembly of the brethren, and pouring forth prayers to God." Thirdly, if the divine oracles are turned to use for earthly business. Hence Augustine says: "As for those who gather decisions by lot from opening the pages of the Gospels, though one is glad to see them doing that rather than consulting evil spirits, still I must

[1] Ezech. xxi. 21.   [2] Prov. xvi. 33.   [3] Acts i. 23—26.

say I like not the custom of trying to turn the divine oracles to use of secular business and the vanity of this life."[1]

But in case of necessity it is lawful, with due reverence, to implore the judgment of God by recourse to lots. Hence Augustine says: "If there arises among the ministers of God a discussion, which of them are to stay at their posts in time of persecution, that there be not a flight of all, and which of them are to fly, that the Church be not left deserted by the death of all; if this discussion cannot be otherwise terminated, my opinion is that the selection should be made by lot, who are to stay and who are to fly." And again: "If you had something in abundance, to give to one who had none, and there was no giving of it to two; and two persons came in your way, neither of whom surpassed the other either in need or in any connection with you; you could do nothing fairer than to select by lot him to whom you should give what could not be given to both."

§ 3. The ordeal of the hot iron, or of the boiling water, is intended for the detection of secret sin by means of something done by man: still there is further expected a miraculous effect to be wrought by God. Hence this kind of judicial inquiry is

---

[1] The place where the Gospels open when they are laid on the shoulders of a Bishop at his consecration, is often regarded with interest, though not intended by the Church as any divination of the future. Another opening of the Gospel page, this time at the end of an episcopal career—a consultation that could not have displeased St. Augustine—is related in Father Bridgett's *Life of Blessed John Fisher*, p. 394. (Trl.)

rendered unlawful, both because it is directed to the judging of secret things that are reserved to the divine judgment; and also because such a judicial procedure is not sanctioned by divine authority. Hence in a decree of Pope Stephen V.[1] it is said: "The holy canons do not approve of confession being extorted from any one by the ordeal of the hot iron or boiling water; and what is not sanctioned by the testimony of the holy Fathers, no modern superstitious invention must presume to do. It is offences made public by spontaneous confession or the evidence of witnesses, that are granted to our government to judge, having the fear of God before our eyes; but things hidden and unknown are to be left to Him who alone knows the hearts of the children of men."

[1] Pope in 816. (Trl.)

QUESTION XCVI.

OF SUPERSTITIOUS OBSERVANCES.

ARTICLE II.—*Are those observances unlawful, that are directed to producing changes in animal bodies, health, and the like effects?*

R. In what is done for the producing of any particular effects, we must consider whether the agents employed seem naturally capable of producing such effects; for in that case the operation will not be unlawful, for it is lawful to employ natural causes to their own proper effects. Hence if the agents used do not seem naturally capable of causing such effects, it follows that they are not employed as causes to the causation of these effects, but only as signs; and thus they are part of a concerted system of signalling to evil spirits.

§ 1. If physical agents are simply employed to produce certain effects, for which they are thought to have a natural efficiency, that will not be superstitious or unlawful. But it will be superstitious and unlawful, if letters are brought in, or names, or any other vain observances, which manifestly have no natural efficiency in the case.

§ 3. It belongs to the dominion of the Divine Majesty, to which the devils are subject, that God should use them for whatever purpose He wills. But man has no authority given him over the devils, lawfully to use them for whatever purpose he will, but he has a war declared against the devils. Hence it is nowise lawful for man to employ the aid of devils by any compacts tacit or express.

ARTICLE III.—*Is it unlawful to observe omens of good or bad luck?*

R. Men make these observations, not as observing causes, but as observing signs of future events, good or evil. Now they are not observed as signs given by God, seeing that they are not introduced by divine authority, but rather by human folly, abetted by diabolical malice, as the devils endeavour to entangle the minds of men in such follies. Manifestly therefore all such observations are superstitious and unlawful, and seem to be relics of idolatry.

§ 2. The fact that, in the beginning, men have found some truth in these observances, is a result of chance; but once men begin to entangle their minds in such observances, many things turn out accordingly by the deception of evil spirits,—" to the end that, entangled in these observances, men may become more curious, and put their necks further and further into the manifold snares of pernicious error," as Augustine says.

ARTICLE IV.

§ 3. As for the wearing of relics upon the person, if they are worn from a motive of confidence in God and the saints, whose relics they are, it will not be unlawful; but if there were any vain observance about the matter, as taking care that the locket should be triangular, or anything of that sort, which has nothing to do with reverence to God and to the saints, it would be a superstitious and unlawful observance.

QUESTION XCVII.

OF TEMPTING GOD.

ARTICLE I.—*Does tempting God consist in certain proceedings, in which an effect is looked for that is possible to divine power alone?*

R. A man tempts God sometimes in words, sometimes in deeds. In words we speak with God in prayer. Hence a man expressly tempts God in his petition, when he asks anything of God with the intention of making trial of God's knowledge, power, or will. A man expressly tempts God in deeds, when he means by what he does to make experiment of the divine power, or loving-kindness, or knowledge. He tempts God, as we may say, *constructively*, who though he does not intend to make experiment of God, nevertheless asks for something, or does something, which is useful for nothing else but to put God's power, or goodness, or knowledge, to the test. Thus if one gallops a horse to escape the enemy, that is not making trial of the horse; but if one gallops a horse without any useful purpose, that is reckoned to be nothing else than making trial of the horse's speed. When then for some necessary or useful purpose, a man trusts himself to divine help in his petitions or deeds, that is not tempting God, for it is said: "As we know not what to do, we can only turn our eyes to thee."[1] But when this is done without any useful and necessary purpose, it is constructive tempting of God. Hence on the text, "Thou shalt not tempt the Lord thy God,"[2] the gloss says: "He tempts God, who, having a safe line of action open to him, unreasonably puts himself in danger by way of making trial of the possibility of a divine deliverance."

§ 2. The saints, when they work miracles by their prayers, are moved by some consideration of necessity or utility to seek for effects of divine power.

§ 3. It is in view of great necessity and utility that the preachers of the Kingdom of God leave aside temporal succours, that they more readily give themselves to preaching the Word of God; but if they were to abandon human aids without any utility or necessity, they would be tempting God.

[1] 2 Paral. xx. 12.   [2] Deut. vi. 16.

QUESTION XCVIII.

OF PERJURY.

ARTICLE II.—*Is all perjury a sin?*

R. To swear is to call God to witness. Now it is an irreverence to God to call Him to witness to a falsehood, as though God either did not know the truth, or were willing to be a witness to what is false. And therefore perjury is manifestly a sin against religion, the virtue which has for its office to show reverence to God.

§ 1. He who swears to do an unlawful act, in swearing incurs the guilt of perjury for lack of *justice*.[1] If however he does not fulfil his oath, he does not thereby incur the guilt of perjury: because it was not a matter that could fall under oath.

§ 2. He who swears not to enter religion,[2] or not to give alms, or anything of that nature, in swearing incurs the guilt of perjury for lack of *judgment*. And therefore when he goes and does the better thing, it is not perjury, but quite the contrary: for the contrary of what he now does could not be matter of an oath.

[1] See II-II. q. 89. art. 3. (Trl.)
[2] See II-II. q. 89. art. 7. § 2. with note. (Trl.)

§ 4. An oath being a personal action, a newly admitted citizen is not bound on oath to observe what the city has sworn to observe. He is bound however in fidelity to share the burdens and obligations of the city, as he has become a partaker in its advantages. A canon who swears to observe the statutes made in any college, is not bound on oath to observe the statutes to be made hereafter, unless it was his intention to bind himself to all statutes past and to come. He is bound however to observe them by the mere force of the statutes themselves, which are compulsory.

ARTICLE III.—*Is all perjury a mortal sin?*
R. According to the doctrine of the Philosopher, "that which makes other things of this or that quality, is itself of the same quality in a higher degree." But we see that sins of themselves venial, or even actions good of their kind, are mortal sins, if they are done on a motive of contempt of God. Much more therefore is everything a mortal sin, that of its own nature appertains to contempt of God. But perjury of its own nature implies a contempt of God: for this is the element of guilt in it, that it is a piece of irreverence to God. Hence perjury of its own nature is a mortal sin.

§ 1. As was said above, q. 89. art. 7. § 3. compulsion does not take away from a promissory oath its binding power in respect of that which may lawfully be done. And therefore if a party does not keep an oath taken on compulsion, he none the less commits perjury and sins mortally. He may, however, be absolved from the obligation of his oath by the authority of the Sovereign Pontiff, especially if he were constrained by threats, formidable enough to cause fear in a resolute man.

QUESTION XCIX.

OF SACRILEGE.

ARTICLE I.—*Is sacrilege the violation of a sacred thing?*

R. A thing is called *sacred* from its being ordained to divine worship. From the fact of a thing being set aside for the worship of God, it is rendered something divine; and thus there is due to it a certain reverence, which is referred to God. And therefore every piece of irreverence to sacred things is something of an injury to God, and bears the character of sacrilege.

ARTICLE II.—*Is sacrilege a special sin?*

R. Wherever there is found a special ground of deformity, there must needs be there a special sin; because the species of everything is fixed principally according to the formal character, not according to the matter or the subject. But in sacrilege there is found a special ground of deformity, by which a sacred thing is violated by irreverence; and therefore it is a special sin, and is opposed to religion.

For as Damascene says: "The purple is honoured and glorified for being made the royal robe; and if any makes a rent in it, he is condemned to death," —as acting against the King.

§ 2. One special character of sin may be found in many different kinds of sins, according as these different sins are directed to the end of one sin. The like is seen in different virtues, all *commanded*[1] by one virtue. And thus whatever be the kind of sin by which one acts against the reverence due to sacred things, he *formally* commits sacrilege, though *materially* there be there different kinds of sin.

§ 3. Sacrilege is sometimes found separate from other sins, for that the act in question has no other deformity than being in violation of a sacred thing: as if a judge should arrest and carry off from a sacred place one whom he might lawfully arrest in other places.

ARTICLE III.—*Are the species of sacrilege distinguished according to the distinction of sacred things?*

R. The sin of sacrilege consists in irreverent behaviour towards a sacred thing. Now reverence is due to a sacred thing on account of its sanctity. And therefore according to difference in the character of sanctity attaching to the sacred things to which irreverence is done, we must distinguish different species of sacrilege. For the greater the sanctity that attaches to the sacred thing that is sinned against, the more grievous is the sacrilege. Now sanctity is attributed both to *sacred persons*, that is,

---

[1] *Commanded*, II-II. q. 26. art. 7. note. (Trl.)

persons dedicated to divine worship, and to *sacred places*, and to certain other *sacred things*. The sanctity of a place is referred to the sanctity of the man who pays worship to God in the sacred place. For it is said: "God did not choose the people for the place's sake, but the place for the people's sake."[1] And therefore the sacrilege that sins against a sacred person, is a graver sin than the sacrilege that sins against a sacred place. There are however in both these species of sacrilege different grades, according to differences of sacred persons and places. In like manner also the third species of sacrilege, that is committed on sacred things, admits of different grades according to the differences of sacred things. Among them the highest place is held by the sacraments, whereby man is sanctified, chief of which is the Sacrament of the Eucharist, which contains Christ Himself. And therefore sacrilege against this Sacrament is the most grievous of all sacrileges. The second place after the sacraments is held by the vessels consecrated for the receiving of the sacraments, and by sacred images, and by the relics of the saints, in which in a manner the very persons of the saints are venerated or dishonoured; then by what belongs to the ornamentation of the church and of its ministers; lastly, by what is set aside for the sustenance of the ministers of religion, in the shape either of movable goods or of immovable. Whoever sins against any of the afore-mentioned objects,. incurs the crime of sacrilege.

[1] 2 Mach. v. 19.

§ 3. Every sin that a sacred person commits is materially and incidentally a sacrilege. Hence Bernard says: "Trifles are trifles among seculars: in a priest's mouth they are blasphemies."[1] But formally and properly that sin alone in a sacred person is a sacrilege, which is committed directly against the sanctity of the said person, as if a virgin dedicated to God should be guilty of fornication.

QUESTION C.

OF SIMONY.

ARTICLE I.—*Is simony a will of deliberate choice to buy or sell something spiritual, or annexed to what is spiritual?*

R. An act is evil of its kind from falling upon undue matter. Now there are three reasons that render a spiritual thing undue matter of buying and selling. First, because a spiritual thing cannot have its equivalent in any earthly price, as is said of wisdom: "She is more precious than all riches."[2] Therefore also Peter, condemning the wickedness of Simon at its very root, said: "Keep thy money to thyself to perish with thee, because thou hast thought that the gift of God may be purchased with

---

[1] These are the exact words of St. Bernard, *De Consid.* l. 2. c. 13. St. Thomas quotes from memory, not quite accurately. The sentiment must be checked by what is said below, q. 168. arts. 2 and 4. (Trl.)

[2] Prov. iii. 15.

money."[1] Secondly, because that cannot be due matter of sale, of which the seller is not the owner; but a prelate in the Church is not owner of spiritual goods, but steward or dispenser, according to the text: "Let a man so account of us as of the ministers of Christ and dispensers of the mysteries of God."[2] Thirdly, because selling is inconsistent with the origin of spiritual things, which proceed from the gratuitous will of God: hence the Lord says, "Freely have you received, freely give."[3]

ARTICLE II.—*Is it always unlawful to give money for the sacraments?*

R. The sacraments of the New Law are especially spiritual, seeing that they are the cause of spiritual grace, which has not a money price; and it is inconsistent with the essential notion of this grace that it should not be given gratuitously. But the sacraments are dispensed by the ministers of the Church, who ought to be supported by the people, according to the Apostle.[4] Thus then we must say that to take money for the spiritual grace of the sacraments is the crime of simony, which no custom can excuse, because custom avails not to the prejudice of natural or divine law. Now by money is understood everything that has a money price. But to take something for the sustenance of those who administer the sacraments of Christ, when it is done according to the ordinance of the

[1] Acts viii. 20.   [2] 1 Cor. iv. 1.   [3] St. Matt. x. 8.
[4] 1 Cor. ix. 13, 14.

Church and approved customs, is not simony, nor any sin; for it is not taken as the price of hire, but as the wages of necessity. Hence on 1 Tim. v. 17, Augustine's gloss says: "Let them receive the sustenance of necessity from the people, the reward of their dispensation from the Lord."

§ 6. Matrimony is not only a sacrament of the Church, but also an office of nature. Hence it is lawful to give money for matrimony, inasmuch as it is an office of nature; unlawful, inasmuch as it is a sacrament of the Church.

ARTICLE III.

§ 2. It would be an unlawful ordinance to enact in any church, that there should be no procession at any one's funeral unless he paid a certain sum of money: because such a statute would bar the way to any gratuitous rendering of that pious office. But it would be a more lawful ordinance to enact that such an honour should be paid to all who gave a certain alms: because that would not bar the way to paying it to others. And besides, the first ordinance has the appearance of an exaction, but the second the appearance of a return of gratitude.

§ 4. It is not lawful to exact anything or take anything as a price for entrance into a monastery. But if the monastery is poor, and not able to maintain so many persons, it is lawful, while granting entrance to the monastery gratuitously, to take something for the keep of the person received, if the funds of the monastery are not sufficient for that purpose.

ARTICLE IV.—*Is it lawful to take money for what is annexed to spiritualities?*

R. A thing may be annexed to spiritualities in either of two ways: in one way as depending on spiritualities, as the holding of ecclesiastical benefices is said to be annexed to spiritualities, because it is not within the competence of any but the holder of clerical office: hence such things can nowise be at all without spiritualities. And therefore it is nowise lawful to sell them, because in the sale of them spiritualities also are understood to be subject to sale. Other things again are annexed to spiritualities as being directed to spiritual ends: as the right of patronage, which is directed to the presentation of clerics to ecclesiastical benefices; and the sacred vessels, which are meant for use in the sacraments: hence such things do not presuppose spiritualities, but rather precede them in order of time. And therefore in some respect they may be sold, but not inasmuch as they are annexed to spiritualities.

§ 2. The sacred vessels are annexed to spiritualities as to their end, and therefore their consecration cannot be sold; but the material of them may be sold for the need of the Church and of the poor.

QUESTION CI.

OF NATURAL AFFECTION.

ARTICLE I.—*Are there certain definite persons who come within the range of natural affection?*

R. A man comes to stand in the debt of others in various ways, according to their various excellences and various benefits received from them. In both these respects God holds the chief place: for He is at once most excellent, and is to us the first principle of being and of government. In the second place our parents and our country, of whom and in which we were born and reared, are the principles of our being and government. And therefore, after God, man is most in debt to his parents and to his country. Hence as it belongs to religion to worship God, so in a secondary degree it belongs to natural affection to worship parents and country. In the *cultus* of parents is included the *cultus* of all kinsmen who are sprung of the same parents. Again, in the *cultus* of country is included the *cultus* of all fellow-citizens and friends of our country. And these are mainly the bounds of natural affection.

ARTICLE II.—*Does natural affection find sustenance for parents?*

R. There are two ways in which a thing is due to parents and fellow-countrymen: in one way a thing is due *ordinarily*, in another way *incidentally*. *Ordinarily* there is due to them that which becomes a father, inasmuch as he is a father: now a father being the superior, and as it were the origin and principle of his son, there is due to him from the son reverence and service. A thing is due to a father *incidentally*, when it becomes him to receive it in respect of some accident that has befallen him: for instance, if he is sick, it is becoming that he should be visited and endeavour made to cure him; if he is poor, it is becoming that he should receive sustenance—and so of the rest, all which attentions come under the head of due service.

§ 1. Under the *honouring* of parents is understood all the support that ought to be rendered to parents, as our Lord interprets the commandment;[1] and this because support is rendered to a father as a tribute due to a superior.

§ 2. To the text, "Neither ought the children to lay up for the parents,"[2] it is to be said that because a father stands for a source and originating principle, and a child for that which has being of that originating principle, therefore it is *ordinarily* proper for a father to support his child; and therefore he ought to support him not for a season only, but for the whole course of his life, and this is the meaning of "laying up." But as for the son bestow-

[1] St. Matt. xv. 3—6.   [2] 2 Cor. xii. 14.

ing anything on his father, that happens *incidentally*, on account of some need of the hour, in which he is bound to give him support; but he is not bound to lay up for a distant day, because in the natural course of things parents are not the successors of their children, but children of their parents.

ARTICLE III.—*Is natural affection a special virtue distinct from others?*

R. A virtue is special by regarding some object in some special light. But since it belongs to the notion of justice to give another his due, there is a special virtue wherever there is found a special way in which anything is due to any person. Now there is something specially due to a person for being a connatural originating principle, productive of existence and governing the same. This is the principle that natural affection regards in paying duty and worship to parents and country and their adjuncts. And therefore natural affection is a special virtue.

§ 1. As religion is a protestation of faith, hope, and charity, by which virtues a man is primarily referred to God, so natural affection is a protestation of the charity which one has to his parents and his country.

ARTICLE IV.—*Is religion an occasion for laying aside the offices of natural affection to parents?*

R. Religion and natural affection are two virtues. Now no virtue is contrary to or inconsistent with any other virtue, because according to the Philosopher, "good is not contrary to good." Hence religion and natural affection cannot possibly get in one another's way, so that the act of the one should be excluded by the act of the other. But the act of every virtue is limited by due circumstances, transgressing which it will cease to be an act of virtue, and become vicious. Hence it is the part of natural affection to render duty and worship to parents according to the manner due. But it is not the manner due, that a man should lay himself out more for worshipping his father than for worshipping God; but as Ambrose says, "The piety of divine worship is preferred to the tie of kindred."

If therefore the worship of parents were to withdraw us from the worship of God, it would no longer be the part of natural affection to go on with the worship of parents against God. Hence Jerome says: "Go your way, pass over father and mother; fly with dry eyes to the standard of the Cross; it is the highest kind of natural affection in this matter to have been cruel." And therefore in such a case the offices of natural affection for parents are to be dropped for the sake of worshipping God in religion. But if it be that by paying due services to parents we are not withdrawn from the worship of God, then such services will belong to natural affection; and in that case there will be no need to abandon natural affection for the sake of religion.

§ 1. Gregory on that word of our Lord[1] says: "We ought to ignore our parents, hating them and flying from them when they are an obstacle to

[1] St. Luke xiv. 26.

us in the way of the Lord." For if our parents incite us to sin, and withdraw us from worshipping God, we ought in that respect to abandon and hate them. And in this way the Levites are said[1] not to have known their kinsmen, because according to the command of the Lord[2] they spared not the idolaters.

§ 4. A different tone must be taken in speaking of one who is still in the world, and of one who is already professed in religion. For he who is still in the world, if he has parents who cannot be supported without him, ought not to leave them and enter religion, because in so doing he would be transgressing the commandment of honouring parents. Some indeed say that even in this case he may lawfully abandon them and commit the care of them to God. But looking at the matter rightly, we see that it would be tempting God, for a man who has human means at his command, to go and expose his parents to danger in the hope of divine assistance. But if his parents could contrive to live without him, it would be lawful for him to leave his parents and enter religion: because children are not bound to support their parents except in case of necessity. But he who is already professed in religon, counts as one dead to the world: hence he ought not, on any plea of supporting his parents, to quit the cloister in which he is buried with Christ, and entangle himself again in worldly business. He is bound however, saving his obedience to his superior and his state as a religious, to make pious efforts to get relief for his parents.

[1] Deut. xxxiii. 9.   [2] Exodus xxxii. 27.

QUESTION CIV.

OF OBEDIENCE.

Article II.—*Is obedience a special virtue?*

R. A special virtue is set and appointed for all good works that have a special character of praiseworthiness: for it is the proper function of virtue to render a work good. Now to obey a superior is due according to the divine order laid down in creation, and consequently is a good thing, since goodness consists in measure, decency, and order, as Augustine says. This act has a special character of praiseworthiness from having a special object. For among the many other things that inferiors are bound to render to their superiors, this is one thing special, that they are bound to obey their commands. Hence obedience is a special virtue, and its special object is a command, tacit or express; for the will of a superior, in whatsoever way it becomes known, is a sort of tacit command, and the obedience seems all the readier when, understanding the superior's will, it forestalls any express command.

§ 1. Two special ideas, regarded by two special virtues, may easily meet in one and the same material object. Thus a soldier defending a royal fortress performs at once a work of fortitude, in not shrinking from the danger of death in a good cause; and a work of justice, in yielding due service to his Sovereign. So then the idea which obedience fixes upon, that of a *command*, goes along with acts of all virtues, but not with all acts of virtue, because not all acts of virtue are enjoined under a command. In like manner also some things fall under a command which belong to no other virtue but obedience, as is clear in things that are not evil except for their being forbidden. Thus then if obedience is taken in its proper sense, as regarding and going upon the precise idea of a *command*, it will be a special virtue, and disobedience a special sin: for, taking it in this way, it is requisite for obedience that one should perform an act of justice, or of any other virtue, with the intention of accomplishing a command; and for disobedience it is requisite that one should actually set at nought a command.

§ 3. Obedience, like any other virtue, ought to have a ready will for its own proper object, and not for anything inconsistent with that object. But the proper object of obedience is a command, proceeding from the will of another. Hence obedience renders a man's will prompt and ready to fulfil the will of another commanding him. But if what is commanded him is something willed on its own account, apart from any idea of a command, as happens in prosperity, he is already tending to it of his own will, and seems to accomplish it, not for the command, but for the gratification of his own will. But when what is commanded is in no way willed of itself, but, looked at in itself, is repugnant to the person's own will, as happens in hard times, then it is quite clear that the thing is done only on account of the command. And therefore Gregory says that "the obedience that has something of its own in prosperity, is either no obedience at all, or is of inferior degree; but in adversity or difficulty the obedience is greater."[1] This however is to be understood, *judging by external appearances.* But in the judgment of God, who searches hearts, it may happen that, even in prosperity, obedience, having something of the man's own about it, may not be on this account less praiseworthy, if the man's own will does none the less devoutly tend to the accomplishment of the precept.

ARTICLE III.—*Is obedience the greatest of virtues?*

R. As sin consists in man's cleaving to changeable goods, to the contempt of God; so the merit of a virtuous act consists in man's cleaving to God, as to his last end, to the contempt of created goods. But the end has the preference over the means to the end. If then created goods are contemned in order that the soul may cleave to God, it is greater praise of a virtue to say that it cleaves to God than to say that it contemns earthly goods. And therefore those virtues which of themselves make the soul cleave to God, namely, the theological virtues, have the preference over the moral virtues, by which some earthly object is contemned in order

[1] See St. Francis of Sales, *On the Love of God,* ix. 2. (Trl.)

that the soul may cleave to God. But among moral virtues a virtue has the preference, the greater the object that it contemns in order to cleave to God. Now there are three kinds of human goods which a man may contemn for God's sake. The lowest of the three are external goods; intermediate are goods of the body; and highest of all are goods of the soul. Of these last chiefest in one way is the will, inasmuch as by the will it is that a man uses all other goods. And therefore, ordinarily speaking, the virtue of obedience, which contemns the man's own will for God's sake, is more praiseworthy than the other moral virtues, which contemn for God's sake sundry other goods. Hence also all other works of virtue are meritorious with God as being done in obedience to the divine will. For if one even were to endure martyrdom, or had distributed all his goods to the poor, unless he referred it to the fulfilment of the divine will, which reference belongs directly to obedience, there could be no merit in such acts, no more than if they were done without charity; and indeed charity cannot be without obedience, for it is said: "He that keepeth his word, in him in very deed the charity of God is perfected;"[1] and that because friendship makes identity in willing and willing not.

§ 3. Good is of two sorts: one sort which a man is necessarily bound to do, as to love God; and such good nowise ought to be omitted for obedience. There is another sort of good which

[1] 1 St. John ii. 5.

a man is not necessarily bound to do; and such good a man ought at times to omit for the obedience to which he is necessarily bound, because one ought not to incur any fault in doing good; and yet, as Gregory says: "He who forbids his subjects any one good deed, must needs allow them many others, lest the spirit of him who obeys die out entirely, if he is kept fasting and quite turned away from all good deeds." And thus by obedience and other good exercises the loss of one good exercise may be made up.

ARTICLE IV.

§ 2. As God works no effect against nature, because "that is the nature of everything, which God works in the thing," as the gloss says, quoting Augustine; and yet He works sundry effects against the usual course of nature: so God can command nothing against virtue, because virtue and the rectitude of the human will consist principally in conformity to the will of God and compliance with His command, though that command be against the usual manner of virtue.[1] Thus then the command given to Abraham to slay his innocent son was not against justice, because God is the author of life and death.

---

[1] On this delicate question, see *Ethics and Natural Law*, p 131, n. 6; p. 149, n. 3; and the references to Suarez given p. 152. Suarez holds that God, as Master, can alter the *matter* of the law, but He cannot as Lawgiver alter or dispense from the law itself. And this accords well with St. Thomas, II-II. q. 88. art. 10. § 2.; q. 89. art. 9. § 1. Cf. also I-II. q. 100. art. 8. (Trl.)

ARTICLE V.—*Are subjects bound to obey their superiors in all things?*

R. It may happen on two grounds that a subject is not bound to obey his superior in all things. One ground is the commandment of a higher authority to the contrary. Another ground is in the case of a command being given in a matter in which the receiver of the command is not subject to the authority from which the command proceeds. For Seneca says: "It is a mistake to suppose that slavery descends upon the whole man; the better part of the man remains free: bodies are liable to ownership and are made over as property, but the mind is its own master."[1] And therefore in what concerns the inward motion of the will man is not bound to obey man, but only God. Still man is bound to obey man in what has to be done externally by the body. Yet even here man is not bound to obey man, but only God, in what belongs to the nature and physical being of the body, because in the physical order all men are equal,[2] as touching the nourishment of the body and the begetting of offspring. Hence neither slaves are bound to obey their masters, nor children their parents, about contracting marriage, or preserving virginity, or anything of that kind. But in the laying out of his day and the transaction of business

---

[1] Christianity allowed the slave-owner's property, not in the man himself whom he called his slave, but in all the man's labour. He was a slave-labour-owner. (Trl.)

[2] Such is the true meaning of *omnes homines natura sunt pares*, a maxim borrowed by St. Thomas from the Roman jurists. (Trl.)

the subject is bound to obey his superior according to the character of his superiority, a soldier his commanding officer in matters of war, a slave his master in doing slave's work, a son his father in conduct of life and household management, and so of the rest.

§ 2. Man is subject to God absolutely in all respects both within and without, and therefore he is bound to obey Him in all things. But inferiors are subject to their superiors, not in all things, but in certain matters of limited range; and in those matters superiors are intermediaries between God and their subjects: in other matters the latter are subject immediately to God, by whom they are instructed through the natural or the written law.

§ 3. Religious profess obedience according to regular observance, in which they are subject to their superiors; and therefore they are bound to obey in those points only which can form a part of regular observance; and this is obedience sufficient for salvation. But if they choose to obey in other matters also, that will be carrying perfection to a height; provided the things enjoined be not against God, nor against the perfection of the rule, because such obedience would be unlawful. Thus then we may distinguish three degrees of obedience: one sufficient for salvation, which obeys in what it is obliged to; another, perfect obedience, which obeys in all things lawful; a third, indiscreet, which obeys even in things unlawful.

ARTICLE VI.—*Are Christians bound to obey civil authority?*

R. The faith of Christ is the principle and cause of justice, according to the text: "The justice of God by the faith of Jesus Christ;"[1] and therefore by the faith of Jesus Christ the order of justice is not taken away, but is rather confirmed. But the order of justice requires that inferiors obey their superiors: otherwise the state and condition of human society could not be preserved. And therefore the faith of Christ does not excuse the faithful from the duty of obedience to secular princes.[2]

§ 1. The slavery by which man is subject to man reaches to the body, not to the soul, which remains free. But in the present state of this life we are set free by the grace of Christ from the defects of the soul, but not from the defects of the body, as is clear by the Apostle, who says of himself: "With the mind I serve the law of God, but with the flesh the law of sin."[3] And therefore they who become the children of God by grace are free from the spiritual slavery of sin, but not from the slavery of the body, by which they are bound over to temporal masters.

[1] Romans iii. 22.
[2] Cf. I-II. q. 96. art. 5. § 2. (Trl.)
[3] Romans vii. 25.

QUESTION CVI.

OF GRATITUDE.

ARTICLE II.—*Is the innocent more bound to render thanks to God than the penitent?*

R. Where the favour is greater, there greater gratitude is requisite. But a favour is a favour because it is bestowed gratuitously. Hence there are two ways in which a favour may be greater: in one way from the amount of the thing given; and in this way the innocent is bound to greater return of thanks, because, absolutely speaking, other things being equal, there is given him a greater gift from God, and a more continuous gift. In another way a favour may be said to be greater because it is bestowed more gratuitously; and in this way the penitent is more bound to return thanks than the innocent, because, being as he was worthy of punishment, there is given him grace and favour. And thus, though the gift that is given to the innocent is, absolutely considered, the greater, still the gift that is given to the penitent is greater in reference to him, as a small gift given to a poor man is greater than a great gift to a rich one.

§ 4. "To whom less is forgiven, he loveth less."[1]

[1] St. Luke vii. 47.

ARTICLE IV.—*Ought a benefit received to be requited on the spot?*

R. As in the conferring of a benefit there are two things to consider, the affection and the gift, so the same two things are to be considered in returning a benefit. As for the affection, the return should be made immediately: hence Seneca says, "Do you wish to return a benefit? accept it graciously." But as for the gift, a time should be waited for in which the return may be opportune for the benefactor; but if at an inconvenient time one wishes at once to render service for service, that has not the air of a virtuous, but of an unwilling return. For as Seneca says: "If he seeks to pay too quickly, he owes unwillingly; and he who owes unwillingly, is ungrateful."

§ 4. "He who is in a hurry to return a kindness, has not the mind of a grateful man, but of a debtor."[1]

ARTICLE VI.—*Ought the return of kindness to exceed the kindness received?*

R. The return of kindness has regard to the benefit, as the benefit was in the will of the benefactor. Now in the benefactor this is reckoned specially commendable, that he has gratuitously conferred a benefit to which he was not obliged. And therefore the recipient of the benefit is bound by a debt of moral decency to some similar gratuitous payment. But the payment does not seem to be gratuitous, unless it exceeds the quantity of the

[1] Seneca.

benefit received: because so long as the requital is less or equal, it has not the look of a thing gratuitously done, but of a return of something received. And therefore the return of kindness always strives to the best of the person's ability to give back something greater than has been received.

§ 2. The debt of gratitude is derived from charity; and charity, the more it is paid, the more it is due, according to the text: "Owe no man anything but to love one another."[1] And therefore no harm if the obligation of gratitude is interminable.

QUESTION CVII.

OF INGRATITUDE.

ARTICLE II.—*Is ingratitude a special sin?*

R. Ingratitude means want of gratitude. Now every want or privation has its species according to the opposite habit: for blindness and deafness differ according to the difference of sight and hearing. Hence as gratitude is one special virtue, so ingratitude is one special sin. But it has different degrees, according to the order of things requisite for gratitude. There the first thing requisite is that the man should recognize the benefit he has received; the second is praise and rendering of thanks; the third is that he should give something in return according to place and time and his

[1] Romans xiii. 8.

ability. But because what is last to be generated is the first to decay, therefore the first degree of ingratitude is not to return the kindness; the second is to dissemble the kindness, as being unwilling to show that you have received any; the third and most grievous is failing to recognize it as such, either by forgetting it or in any other way. And because in an affirmation there is understood the denial of the opposite statement,[1] therefore it belongs to the first degree of ingratitude that a man should render evil for good; to the second, that he should disparage the benefit he has received; to the third, that he should account the benefit an ill turn done him.

ARTICLE IV.—*Are kindnesses to be withdrawn from the ungrateful?*

R. About the ungrateful person two things are to be considered: first, what it is that he deserves to have done to him; and putting the question that way, it is certain that he deserves withdrawal of kindness. In another way it is to be considered, what it befits the benefactor to do. In the first place, he ought not to be too ready to judge that there is ingratitude, for "frequently," as Seneca says, "he who has made no return is grateful," the reason being perhaps that he has not had the means or due opportunity of making any return. Secondly, he ought to aim at making the ungrateful person grateful; which if he cannot do with the first act of

[1] *i.e.*, if you affirm, as below, that a man renders evil for good, you deny the opposite, that he returns good for good. (Trl.)

kindness, he will perhaps do with the second. But if after repeated kindnesses the other increases his ingratitude and becomes worse, the benefactor ought to desist from bestowing kindnesses.

§ 2. He who bestows a kindness on an ungrateful person, does not give him an occasion of sin, but rather of gratitude and love. If the recipient thence takes occasion of ingratitude, that is not to be imputed to the giver.

§ 3. He who bestows a kindness, ought not to pose as a punisher of ingratitude, but rather as a benevolent physician, seeking to cure ingratitude by reiterated acts of kindness.

QUESTION CVIII.

OF VENGEANCE.[1]

ARTICLE I.—*Is vengeance lawful?*

R. Vengeance is taken by some penal evil inflicted on the offender. In judging of vengeance then we are to consider the mind and purpose of him who takes it. For if his intention makes principally for the evil of him on whom he takes vengeance, and rests there, it will be altogether unlawful; because to take delight in the evil of another belongs to hatred, which is repugnant to the charity with which we are bound to love all men. Nor is it an excuse for any one to say that he intends the evil of him who has unjustly inflicted

[1] *Ethics and Natural Law*, pp. 169—176. (Trl.)

evil on him, as it is no excuse for a man that he hates another who hates him; for a man ought not to sin against another, simply because that other has first sinned against him; for this is being overcome by evil, which the Apostle tells us not to be, saying, "Be not overcome by evil, but overcome evil by good."[1] But if the intention of him who takes vengeance makes principally for some good that is reached by the punishment of the offender, say his amendment, or the restraint of that party and the quiet of others, and the maintenance of justice, and the honour of God, then vengeance may be lawful, other due circumstances being observed.

§ 1. To the text, "Vengeance is mine, I will repay,"[2] it is to be said that he who according to his rank and order exercises vengeance upon evildoers, does not usurp to himself what is God's, but uses the power divinely bestowed on him; for it is said of the earthly prince: "He is God's minister, an avenger to execute wrath upon him that doth evil."[3] But if any one exercises vengeance contrary to the order of divine institution, he usurps to himself what is God's, and therefore sins.[4]

§ 2. The good bear with the wicked to this extent, that, so far as it is proper to do so, they patiently endure at their hands the injuries done to themselves; but they do not bear with them to the extent of enduring the injuries done to God and

---

[1] Romans xii 21. [2] Deut. xxxii. 35; Romans xii. 19.
[3] Romans xiii. 4.
[4] Lawful vengeance is in fact the vengeance of the law (Trl.)

their neighbours. For [pseudo-] Chrysostom says: "It is praiseworthy to be patient under one's own wrongs, but the height of impiety to dissemble injuries done to God."

§ 3. The Gospel law is a law of love; and therefore into them who do good works on a motive of love, who alone properly belong to the Gospel, fear is not to be inspired by punishments, but only into such as are not moved by love to good, who though they are of the Church in number, are not so in merit.

§ 4. The wrong that is done to an individual, sometimes redounds to God and to the Church, and then the person ought to avenge his own wrong: as is clear of Elias, who made fire to descend upon them who had come to arrest him;[1] and in like manner Eliseus cursed the boys that mocked him;[2] and Pope Silverius excommunicated those that sent him into exile. But inasmuch as the wrong done you concerns your own individual person, you ought to put up with it patiently, if so it be expedient: for these precepts of patience[3] are to be understood as obligatory "in readiness of heart," as Augustine says.[4]

§ 5. When a whole people sins, vengeance is to be taken upon them either to the extent of the whole people, as the Egyptians were drowned in the Red Sea, and as the Sodomites all perished together, or to the extent of a great portion of the people, as in the punishment of those who adored

---

[1] 4 Kings i 10.   [2] 4 Kings ii. 24.
[3] St. Matt. v. 39, 40.   [4] Cf. II-II. q. 72. art. 3. (Trl.)

the golden calf.[1] But sometimes, if there is hope of the amendment of the many, the severity of vengeance should be exercised only upon a few ringleaders, whose punishment may serve to terrify the rest, as the Lord[2] ordered the princes of the people to be hung for the sin of the multitude. But if it is not the whole community that has sinned, but only a part, then if the wicked can be got at apart from the good, vengeance should be exercised on them alone, provided it can be done without scandal to others; otherwise the community must be spared, and abatement of severity made. And the same holds good for the prince whom the people follow. For his sin must be borne with, if it cannot be punished without scandal of the people, unless it happens to be such a sin on his part as would do more harm to the people in spirituals or temporals than the scandal to be apprehended from his punishment.

ARTICLE II.—*Is vengeance a special virtue?*

R. As the Philosopher says, fitness for virtue is in us by nature, but the fulness of virtue comes by practice, or by some other cause.[3] Hence it appears that the virtues perfect us, duly to carry out those natural inclinations which are part of the ordinance of nature. And therefore to every definite natural inclination there is attached some special virtue. Now there is one special inclination of nature to

---

[1] Exodus xxxii. 28.   [2] Numbers xxv. 4.
[3] *i.e*, by *infusion*, in the case of the supernatural virtues. Cf. II-II. q. 47. art. 14. § 3. (Trl.)

remove causes of hurt: hence to animals there is given an irascible faculty distinct from the concupiscible faculty. Now a man repels causes of hurt by defending himself against wrongs, to prevent their being done him; or in case of wrongs already done, revenging them, not with any intention of hurting, but with the intention of removing causes of hurt.

ARTICLE III.—*Ought vengeance to be taken by means of the punishments customary amongst men?*
R. Vengeance is so far lawful and virtuous, as it makes for the restraint of evil. Now they who have no love of virtue, are restrained from offending by fear of losing something that they love more than what they gain by offending. And therefore vengeance is to be taken for offences by the withdrawal of all that the offender most loves—life, limb, liberty, property, country, and glory.

§ 2. All who sin mortally are worthy of eternal death in the retribution of the world to come, which is according to the truth of divine judgment. But the punishments of the present life are rather medicinal; and therefore the punishment of death is inflicted on those sins alone which tend to do serious mischief to others.

§ 3. When along with the fault the punishment also becomes known, be it death or any other of those things that man has a dread of, his will is thereby weaned from sin; because the punishment terrifies him more than the example of the fault allures him.[1]

[1] See *Ethics and Natural Law*, p. 348. (Trl.)

ARTICLE IV.—*Is vengeance to be exercised on those who have sinned involuntarily?*[1]

R. Punishment may be considered in two ways, in one way precisely as *punishment*, and in this way punishment is not due except to sin, because by punishment the equilibrium of justice is restored, inasmuch as he who by sinning has had too much of his own will, suffers something now against his will. In another way punishment may be considered as a *medicine*, inasmuch as medicine is not only remedial of past sin, but is also preservative against future sin, or promotive of some good; and in this way one is sometimes punished without fault, but not without cause. It is to be observed however that medical treatment never withdraws a greater good to promote a less; it never blinds the eye to cure the heel; but it does sometimes inflict hurt in lesser matters to afford remedy in greater things. And because spiritual goods are the greatest goods, and temporal goods the least, therefore a man is sometimes punished in temporal goods without his fault; this is the case in many of the punishments of the present life, divinely inflicted to prove a man or to humble him; but never is a man punished in spiritual goods without his own fault, neither in the present life nor in the life to come: because there in the world to come punishments are not medicines, but follow upon spiritual condemnation.

§ 1. One man is never punished with a spiritual punishment for the sin of another, because spiritual

[1] Cf. I-II. q. 87. arts. 7. 8. (Trl.)

punishment reaches to the soul, in which every man is free and independent. But sometimes one is punished with temporal punishment for the sin of another, for three reasons. First, because one man is temporally the chattel of another; and so he is punished to punish that other: thus children are in the body the chattels of their father, and slaves in a certain sense the chattels of their owners. In another way, inasmuch as the sin of one spreads to another, either by *imitation*, as children imitate their parents' sins, and slaves their masters', to sin more boldly; or by way of *merit*, as the sins of subjects merit a sinner to be set over them, according to the text, "Who maketh a man that is a hypocrite to reign for the sins of the people;"[1] or by way of some *consent* or *dissembling*, as sometimes the good are temporally punished with the wicked because they have not rebuked their sins, as Augustine says. Thirdly, to commend the unity of human society, in consequence of which unity one man ought to be solicitous for another that he sin not; and to excite a detestation of sin, when it is found that the punishment of one redounds to all, as though all made one body, as Augustine says of the sin of Achan.[2] But as for the saying of the Lord, "Visiting the iniquity of the fathers upon the children unto the third and fourth generation,"[3] that seems rather to point to mercy than to severity, in that He does not wreak His vengeance at once, but waits for the time to come, that posterity at least may mend their ways; but as the malice of posterity

[1] Job xxxiv. 30.   [2] Josue vii.   [3] Exodus xx. 5.

increases, it becomes in a manner necessary for vengeance to fall.

§ 2. The secret judgments of God, whereby He temporally punishes some persons without fault of theirs, are not within the competence of human judgment to imitate; because man cannot comprehend the reasons of these judgments so as to know what is expedient for each individual soul. And therefore never by human judgment ought a man to be punished with the *pain of the lash*, so as to be put to death, or maimed, or beaten with stripes, without his own fault.[1] But with the *pain of loss* one is punished even in human judgment without fault, but not without cause.

[1] Cf. II-II. q 64. art. 2. § 3.; *Ethics and Natural Law*, pp. 349, 350, n. 8. (Trl.)

QUESTION CIX.

OF TRUTHFULNESS.

ARTICLE I.

§ 3. He who speaks the truth, utters certain signs conformable to things, the signs being either words or outward deeds or any outward things whatever. But such things are the matter of the moral virtues only: for to them belongs the use of the outward members under the control of the will. Hence truthfulness is a moral virtue. And it is in the golden mean between excess and defect in two ways,—on the part of the *object* and on the part of the *act*. On the part of the object, because truth essentially involves a certain equality: now equality is something intermediate between too much and too little: hence by the fact of a person's saying what is true of himself, he holds an intermediate place between him who says too great things of himself and him who says too small things. On the part of the act it holds the golden mean, inasmuch as it speaks the truth when it ought and as it ought. Now excess is attributable to him who blurts out his own doings and feelings unseasonably; and defect to him who conceals them when he ought to declare them.

ARTICLE II.—*Is truthfulness a special virtue?*

R. The idea of human virtue is that it should render man's work good. Hence wherever a special character of goodness is found in the act of man, man needs to be disposed thereto by a special virtue. But since goodness consists in order, a special character of goodness must accompany every definable order. But there is a certain special order whereby our outward behaviour whether in word or deed is ordained as a sign to something signified; and to this effect man is perfected by the virtue of truthfulness. Clearly then truthfulness is a special virtue.

ARTICLE III.—*Is truthfulness a part of justice?*

R. The qualification for a virtue to be annexed to justice as a secondary to a primary virtue, is that it should partly coincide with justice and partly fall short of the perfect character thereof. Now the virtue of truthfulness coincides with justice in two particulars. One particular is this, that it is exercised *in relation to another* person: for the declaration is made *to another*, the man declaring to that other the truth about himself. The other particular is touching the *equality* that justice establishes in things; and the virtue of truthfulness does likewise: for it equalizes and adapts signs to existent matters of fact about the speaker. But it falls short of the proper character of justice in respect of the nature of the thing *due:* for this virtue does not deal with what is legally due, as justice does, but rather with what is morally due, inasmuch as on grounds of moral seemliness one man owes to another a declaration of the truth. Hence truthfulness is a part of justice, being annexed to it as a secondary virtue to its primary.

§ 1. Because man is a social animal, one man naturally *owes* another that without which human society could not go on. But men could not live with one another, if they did not believe one another as declaring the truth to one another. And therefore the virtue of truthfulness in some way hinges upon the notion of a thing *due*.

QUESTION CX.

OF VICES OPPOSED TO TRUTHFULNESS, AND FIRST OF LYING.

ARTICLE I.—*Is lying always opposed to truthfulness?*

R. A moral act has its species assigned to it according to its *object* and its *end in view;* for the *end* is the object of the will, and the will is the prime mover in moral acts. Again the power set in motion by the will has its own *object*, which is the proximate object of the voluntary act; and in the act of the will this object stands to the end in view as the material element to the formal.[1] Now the virtue of truth, and consequently the opposite vices, both consist in a declaration made by means of certain signs, which declaration or assertion is an act of reason applying the sign to the thing.

[1] As explained above, I-II. q. 18. art. 6.

signified: for every representation is a certain putting of things together, which is the proper act of reason. Hence though dumb animals give certain declarations or indications, yet they do not intend to indicate or declare anything; but they do some action by natural instinct, and on that instinct declaration ensues. In so far however as such declaration or assertion is a moral act, it must be voluntary, and dependent upon the intention of the will. The proper object of any declaration or assertion is truth or falsehood. And the intention of an inordinate will may be carried to two purposes: one is the utterance of a false assertion; the other is the proper effect of a false assertion, the deceiving of somebody. If then these three elements all combine, that the assertion made is false, that there is the will to make a false assertion, and lastly the intention to deceive: then there is falsehood *materially*, because what is said is false; and falsehood *formally*, on account of the will to utter what was false; and falsehood *effectively*, on account of the will to create a false impression. Nevertheless the essential character of lying is derived from formal falsehood, or from the fact of one having the will to assert what is false: a lie is *speech against one's mind*. And therefore if any one asserts what is false, believing it to be true, it is a falsehood materially but not formally, because the falseness is beside the intention of the speaker. Hence it does not bear the perfect character of a lie: for what is beside the intention of the speaker is accidental, and therefore cannot constitute a specific difference. But if one utters a formal falsehood, with the intention of saying what is false, then though what is said be true, still such an act, so far as it is voluntary and moral, has falsehood of its own portion, and truth only accidentally: hence it attains to the species of lying. But as for one's intending to create falsehood in the opinion and belief of another by deceiving him, that is not part of the specific nature of a lie, but goes to give the lie perfection: as in the physical world a thing attains to the species, if it has the form, even though the effect of the form be wanting.[1] Thus it is clear that lying is directly and formally opposed to the virtue of truthfulness.

§ 1. Everything is rather judged by what is in it formally and ordinarily than by what is in it materially and incidentally. And therefore it is more opposed to the moral virtue of truthfulness for one to tell the truth, intending to tell a falsehood, than for one to tell a falsehood, intending to tell the truth.

§ 2. Speech holds the foremost place among signs. And therefore when it is said that a lie is a false intimation given by speech, under the name of *speech* is understood every sign. Hence he would not be guiltless of lying, who by nods and becks should endeavour to give any false intimation.

§ 3. The desire to deceive goes to make the lie perfect, but does not enter into its specific essence, as neither does any effect belong to the specific essence of its cause.

See *Ethics and Natural Law*, p. 225, n. 2 (Trl.)

ARTICLE III.—*Is every lie a sin?*

R. What is evil of its kind can nowise be good and lawful: because for a thing to be good, all must be right that goes to make it up; for goodness supposes soundness all round, but any single defect makes an evil case. But a lie is evil of its kind; for it is an act falling on undue matter: for words being naturally signs of thoughts, it is a thing unnatural and undue for any one to signify in word what he has not in his mind.[1]

§ 4. A lie has the character of sinfulness, not only from the damage done to a neighbour, but also from its own inordinateness. Now it is not lawful to employ any unlawful inordinateness for the hindering of hurts and losses to others; as it is not lawful to steal in order to give alms. And therefore it is not lawful to tell a lie to deliver another from any danger whatever. It is lawful however to hide the truth prudently under some dissimulation, as Augustine says.[2]

§ 5. He who promises anything, if he has the intention of doing what he promises, does not lie; because he does not speak contrary to what he bears in his mind. But if afterwards he does not do what he has promised, then he seems to act unfaithfully by changing his mind. He may however be excused on two accounts. One is, if the thing promised is manifestly unlawful; in which case he sinned in promising, and does well in changing his mind. The other is, if the conditions

[1] *Ethics and Natural Law*, pp. 228—230, nn. 4, 5, 6. (Trl.)
[2] A word to the wise: see *Ethics and Natural Law*, pp. 232—237.

of persons and things are changed. For as Seneca says, for a man to be bound to do as he has promised, it is requisite that all things remain unchanged: otherwise neither was he a liar in promising, because he promised what he had in his mind, due conditions being understood; nor is he unfaithful in not fulfilling what he promised, because the conditions do not remain the same.

§ 6. An act may be considered in one way in itself, in another way on the part of the agent. A jocose lie then has a character of deceit from the very kind of the act, though in the intention of the speaker it be not spoken to deceive, and from the manner of speaking actually do not deceive.[1]

ARTICLE IV.—*Is every lie a mortal sin?*

R. Mortal sin is properly that which is inconsistent with the charity whereby a soul is united to God. Now a lie may be contrary to charity in three ways: *in itself, in the end intended,* and *accidentally. In itself* it is contrary to charity as regards the falsity of the intimation given.. If this is about divine things, it is contrary to the charity of God, whose truth is obscured or misrepresented by such a lie. Hence a lie of this nature is not only opposed to the virtue of charity, but also to the virtue of faith and religion: and accordingly this is a lie most grievous and mortal. But if the false intimation be about something that it appertains to man's good to know of, for instance something bearing on the progress of knowledge and the formation of character, thereby bringing the prejudice of false

[1] See however *Ethics and Natural Law*, p. 226. (Trl.)

opinion to a neighbour, it is contrary to charity in the department of love of our neighbour: hence it is a mortal sin. But if the false opinion generated by a lie turns on a point about which it does not matter whether one view or another be taken of it, —as if one should be deceived on some particular incidents that were no concern of his—then by such a lie no damage is done to our neighbour: hence it is not *in itself* a mortal sin. On the ground of *the end intended*, a lie is opposed to charity by being uttered either to the injury of God, which is always a mortal sin, as being opposed to religion; or to the hurt of our neighbour in his person, wealth, or good name; and this also is a mortal sin, since it is a mortal sin to hurt our neighbour, and the mere intention of mortal sin makes a mortal sin. But if the end intended be not contrary to charity, neither will the lie be a mortal sin in this respect; as appears in a *jocose lie*, that is intended to create some slight amusement, and in an *officious lie*, in which is intended even the advantage of our neighbour. *Accidentally* the lie may be contrary to charity by reason of the scandal it gives, or other damage ensuing from it; and so again it will be a mortal sin, for that the party is not deterred by fear of scandal from a barefaced, open lie.[1]

[1] Once more it is to be remembered that the mortal sin against charity, so often insisted on by St. Thomas, supposes serious harm; where the harm is not serious, the sin is not mortal, on account of *parvity of matter*. Modern Catholic theologians agree, with what St. Thomas implicitly teaches here, that a lie pure and simple, as a sin against truth, is never a mortal sin, but becomes mortal by being complicated with some other sin, as against justice, charity, or religion. (Trl.)

§ 5. Some say that in perfect men every lie is a mortal sin. But that is an irrational thing to say; for no circumstance aggravates infinitely unless by transferring the sin to another species. But the circumstance of *person*, who it is that offends—does not transfer the sin to another species, unless it be by reason of some adjunct, as of a vow that the person has made, which reason cannot be said to hold in the case of an officious or jocose lie. And therefore an officious or jocose lie is not a [grave] sin in perfect men, except it happen to become so by reason of the scandal given.

QUESTION CXI.

OF SIMULATION AND HYPOCRISY.

ARTICLE I.—*Is all simulation sinful?*

R. It belongs to the virtue of truthfulness that one should show himself exteriorly by outward signs to be such as he really is. Now outward signs are not only words but also deeds. And therefore, as it is opposed to truth for any one to signify by outward words anything different from what he has in his heart, so also is it opposed to truth for any one by any signs consisting in actions or outward things to signify that which is not in him; and such a proceeding is properly called simulation. Hence simulation is properly a lie enacted in certain signs, consisting of outward actions; and it makes no difference whether one lies in word or in action. Hence as all lying is sinful, so also is all simulation.

§ 4. As one lies in word when he signifies that which is not, but not when he is silent over what is,—which is sometimes lawful; so it is *simulation* when by outward signs, consisting of actions or things, any one signifies that which is not, but not when one omits to signify that which is: hence without any simulation a person may conceal his own sin.[1]

ARTICLE II.—*Is hypocrisy the same as simulation?*

R. Augustine says: "As actors [*hypocritae*, ὑποκριταί] pretend to other characters than their own, and act the part of that which they are not; so in the churches and in all human life, whoever wishes to seem what he is not, is a hypocrite, or actor: for he pretends to be just without rendering himself such." So then hypocrisy is simulation, not however any and every simulation, but only that by which a person pretends to a character not his own, as when a sinner pretends to the character of a just man.

§ 2. The habit or garment of holiness, religious or clerical, signifies a state wherein one is bound to works of perfection. And therefore, when one takes the holy habit intending to betake himself to a state of perfection, if afterwards he fails by weakness, he is not a pretender or hypocrite, because he is not

[1] Understand, when he is not interrogated by any one who has the right to hear it of him. (Trl.)

bound to declare his sin by laying the holy habit aside. But if he were to take the holy habit in order to figure as a just man, he would be a hypocrite and pretender.

ARTICLE. IV.—*Is hypocrisy always a mortal sin?*

R. There are two things in hypocrisy, the want of holiness and the simulation of possessing it. If therefore by *hypocrite* we are to understand one whose intention is carried to both these points, so that he cares not to have holiness but only to appear holy—as the word is usually taken in Holy Scripture—in that understanding it is clearly a mortal sin: for no one is totally deprived of holiness otherwise than by mortal sin. But if by *hypocrite* is meant one who intends to counterfeit the holiness which mortal sin makes him fall short of, then though he is in mortal sin, and is thereby deprived of holiness, still the mere pretence on his part is not always a mortal sin, but is sometimes only venial. To tell when it is venial and when mortal, we must observe the end in view. If that end be inconsistent with the love of God and of one's neighbour, it will be a mortal sin, as when one pretends to holiness in order to disseminate false doctrine,[1] or to gain some ecclesiastical dignity of which he is unworthy, or any other temporal goods, placing his last end in them. But if the end intended be not inconsistent with charity, it will be a venial sin, as when one finds pleasure and satisfaction in the mere assumption of a character

[1] Like Father Clement in the *Fair Maid of Perth*. (Trl.)

that does not belong to him: of such a one it is said that "there is more vanity than malice in him."

QUESTION CXII.

OF BOASTING.

ARTICLE I.—*Is boasting opposed to the virtue of truthfulness?*

R. Boasting (*jactantia*) seems properly to mean a man's extolling himself and raising himself aloft in words; for what a man wants to throw (*jactare*) far, he raises aloft. A man is then properly said to *extol* himself, when he says something of himself *above himself;* and that may happen in either of two ways. For sometimes a man speaks of himself, not above what he is in himself, but above what men think of him, which the Apostle shrank from doing: " But I forbear, lest any man should think of me above that which he seeth in me."[1] A man extols himself in another way by speaking of himself above what he is in truth and reality. And because a thing is rather to be judged according to what it is in itself than according to what it is in the opinion of others, hence it is more properly called *boasting*, when a man raises himself above what he is in himself, than when he raises himself above what he is in the opinion of others; though it may be called boasting either way. And therefore boasting,

[1] 2 Cor. xii. 6.

properly so called, is opposed to truth by way of excess.

§ 2. If we look for the cause from which boasting proceeds generally though not always, we find that its inner motive and impellent cause is pride. For usually it is in consequence of a person being inwardly lifted up by arrogant esteem of himself above his merits, that he outwardly boasts of himself to excess: though sometimes it is not arrogance, but a sort of vanity, that moves a man to boasting, and gives him delight therein because that is his way.

QUESTION CXIII.

OF SELF-DEPRECIATION.

ARTICLE I.—*Is the self-depreciation by which a person feigns to possess lower endowments than he really has, a sin?*

R. It may happen in two ways that men in speaking attribute to themselves lower endowments than are really theirs. In one way without infringement of truth, by reticence of the higher endowments that are in them, and unfolding and bringing out as their own certain lesser endowments, which however they recognize to be in their possession. This way of attributing to oneself less than one possesses is not a piece of self-depreciation, nor is it sinful of its kind, unless by some circumstance it come to be not what it should be. The other way of attributing to oneself less endowments than one has, contains a departure from truth, as when a person avers of himself some meanness, which he does not recognize in himself, or denies of himself some greatness, which at the same time he perceives to be in himself: this is a piece of self-depreciation which is always sinful.

§ 1. Wisdom is twofold, and folly also; for there is a certain wisdom according to God, that has annexed to it folly in the eyes of the world, according to the text: "If any man among you seem to be wise in this world, let him become a fool that he may be wise."[1] There is another, a worldly wisdom, which, as is added there, "is foolishness with God." He then who is strengthened by God, confesses that he is an utter fool according to human notions, because he despises the human things that the wisdom of men seeks after.

§ 2. To what Gregory writes in his letter to Augustine, Bishop of the English, "It is the part of good souls to recognize fault of their own where there is no fault," it is to be said that it belongs to goodness of soul to tend to the perfection of justice. And therefore a good soul reckons it a fault, not only to fall short of common justice, which is really a fault, but also to fall short of the perfection of justice, which sometimes is not a fault. But such a soul does not call that a fault, which it does not recognize for a fault, which would be a lie of self-depreciation.

[1] 1 Cor. iii. 18.

§ 3. A man ought not to commit one sin to avoid another; and therefore he ought not in any way to lie to avoid pride.

QUESTION CXIV.

OF THE FRIENDLINESS THAT IS CALLED AFFABILITY.

ARTICLE I.—*Is friendliness a special virtue?*

R. Where there occurs a special character of goodness, there must be a special character of virtue. But goodness consists in order. And a man must be suitably ordered and adapted to his fellow-men in social intercourse as well in action as in word, that he may behave to each appropriately. And therefore there must be a special virtue that observes this suitable order; and it is called *friendliness*, or *affability*.

§ 1. The Philosopher mentions two varieties of friendship: one of which consists principally in the affection with which one man loves another; the other variety consists only in outward words or actions, and has not the perfect nature of friendship, but a certain likeness to it, inasmuch as one behaves becomingly to those with whom he converses.

§ 2. Every man is naturally every man's friend with a certain general love, as it is said: "Every beast loveth its like."[1] This love is represented by the signs of friendliness that one exteriorly shows in word or action even to foreigners or strangers.

[1] Ecclus. xiii. 19.

Hence there is no simulation or pretence about the matter: for one does not show them perfect signs of friendship, not bearing oneself with the same familiarity towards strangers as towards special friends.

§ 3. "The heart of the wise" is said to be "where there is mourning,"[1] not that his presence may bring grief to his neighbour, for the Apostle says: "If because of thy meat thy brother be grieved, thou walkest not now according to charity,"[2] but that he may carry consolation to them that are in grief, according to the text: "Be not wanting in comforting them that weep, and walk with them that mourn."[3] But "the heart of fools is where there is mirth,"[4] not that they may bring mirth to others, but that they may enjoy others' mirth. It belongs therefore to the wise man to be good company to those with whom he converses, not in wantonness that virtue shuns, but with propriety, according to the text: "Behold how good and how pleasant it is for brethren to dwell together in unity."[5] Sometimes however, for good to come of it, or for the avoidance of evil, the virtuous man will not shrink from making those sorrowful with whom he associates: hence the Apostle says, "Although I made you sorrowful by my epistle, I do not repent: now I am glad, not because you were made sorrowful, but because you were made sorrowful unto penance."[6]

[1] Eccles. vii. 5. [2] Romans xiv. 15.
[3] Ecclus. vii. 38. [4] Eccles. vii. 5. [5] Psalm cxxxii. 1.
[6] 2 Cor. vii. 8.

Article II.

§ 1. As said above, because man is by nature a social animal, he owes by a certain moral fitness that declaration of truth to other men without which human society could not endure. But as man could not live in society without truth, so neither can he without pleasure, because, as the Philosopher says, "None can stay all day with a gloomy person, or with a person who is not pleasant." And therefore a man is bound by a natural debt of propriety to be pleasant in his intercourse with other men, unless for some reason it be necessary at times to make others sorrowful to good purpose.[1]

QUESTION CXV.

OF FLATTERY.

Article I.

§ 1. To praise another is a thing that may be done well or ill, according as due circumstances are observed or neglected. For if one wishes to give pleasure by praising, thereby to console the person that he fail not in tribulation, or also that he may be eager to advance in good, if other due circumstances are observed, this will be part of the aforesaid virtue of friendliness. But it will be a piece of flattery, if one will praise another on points on which he ought not to have praise, either

[1] See further on this matter II-II. q. 168 arts. 2. 4 (Trl)

because they are evil things, according to the text, "The sinner is praised in the desires of his soul,"[1] or because they are uncertainties, as it is said, "Praise not a man before he speaketh;"[2] and again, "Praise not a man for his look;"[3] or again, if there be fear of his being moved by human praise to vainglory, hence it is said: "Praise not any man before death."[4]

ARTICLE II.—*Is flattery a mortal sin?*

R. That is a mortal sin, which is contrary to charity. Now flattery is sometimes contrary to charity, and sometimes not. There are three ways in which it may be contrary to charity. One is in virtue of the *matter* praised, when one praises another's sin: for this is contrary to the love of God, being an impugning of His justice, and contrary also to the love of your neighbour, whom you foster and encourage in his sin. Another way is in virtue of the *intention* of him who praises, when one flatters another in order fraudulently to hurt him either in body or in soul: this again is a mortal sin, and of it there is said, "Better are the wounds of a friend than the deceitful kisses of an enemy."[5] The third way is in virtue of the *occasion* given, when the flatterer's praise becomes to the other an occasion of sin, even beside the intention of the flatterer. And here we must consider whether the occasion be *given* or *taken*, and what is the nature of the ruin that follows, as

[1] Psalm ix. 24.   [2] Ecclus. xxviii. 8.
[3] Ecclus xi. 2.   [4] Ecclus. xi. 20.   [5] Prov. xxvii. 6.

in the case of what was said above of scandal.[1] But if the motive of the flattery is mere eagerness to give pleasure, or to avoid some evil, or to get something in a case of need, it is not against charity, and therefore not a mortal but a venial sin.

QUESTION CXVI.

OF THE SPIRIT OF CONTRADICTION.

ARTICLE II.—*Is the spirit of contradiction a more grievous sin than flattery?*

R. In point of species, a vice is more grievous the more it is opposed to the opposite virtue. But the virtue of friendly behaviour tends rather to give pleasure than to give annoyance; and therefore he who is possessed with the spirit of contradiction, going to excess in annoyance, sins more grievously than the complaisant man, or flatterer, who goes to excess in giving pleasure. In point of exterior motives, sometimes flattery is the graver sin, and sometimes the spirit of contradiction.

§ 2. In human acts that is not always the more grievous sin which is the fouler and more unseemly. For the comeliness of man is of reason; and therefore carnal sins, whereby the flesh carries the day over reason, are fouler and more unseemly, although spiritual sins are more grievous, because they proceed from greater contempt. In like manner, sins that are committed by stealth and

[1] II-II. q. 43. art. 3.

treachery look worse, because they appear to have their origin in weakness and a certain falseness of reason; and yet sins openly committed come sometimes of greater contempt. And therefore flattery, as being conjoined with treachery, seems to be the more ill-looking; but the spirit of contradiction, as proceeding from greater contempt, seems to be the graver sin.

§ 3. Shame has regard to the unsightliness of sin: hence a man is not always more ashamed of the more grievous sin, but of that which looks uglier. Hence a man is more ashamed of flattery than of the spirit of contradiction, though the spirit of contradiction is the more grievous.

QUESTION CXVII.

OF LIBERALITY.

ARTICLE III.

§ 3. It belongs to liberality particularly, not to be held back by any inordinate affection for money from any right use of the same. Now there is a twofold use of money: one upon oneself—a matter of personal expenses; another upon others—a matter of gifts. It belongs therefore to liberality, not to be held back by immoderate love of money either from suitable expenses or from suitable gifts. Hence liberality is conversant with gifts and expenses.

ARTICLE IV.

§ 2. It belongs to liberality to use money seasonably, and therefore seasonably to give it away, which is one use of money. Now every virtue is distressed at what is contrary to its act, and avoids hinderances thereto. But to seasonable giving two things are opposed: *not giving* where there is occasion for a seasonable gift, and *giving unseasonably*. Hence liberality is distressed at both the one proceeding and the other, but more at the former, because it is more opposed to its own proper act. And therefore also it does not give to all: for its own proper act would be injured if it gave to every one, for it would not have the means of giving to others to whom a gift would really be seasonable.

ARTICLE V.—*Is liberality a part of justice?*

R. Liberality is not a species of justice: because justice renders to another what is his, but liberality gives him what is the giver's own. Still it has a certain agreement with justice on two points: first, that it is *to another*, as justice also is; secondly, that it is about exterior things, like justice, though in another way. And therefore liberality is laid down by some to be a part of justice, as a virtue annexed to justice as its primary.

§ 1. Though liberality supposes not any legal debt, as justice does, still it supposes a certain moral debt, considering what is becoming in the person himself who practises the virtue, not as though he had any obligation to the other party; and therefore there is about it very little of the character of a debt.

QUESTION CXVIII.

OF COVETOUSNESS.

ARTICLE I.—*Is covetousness a sin?*

R. In all that is for an end, goodness consists in the observance of a certain measure: for means to the end must be commensurate with the end, as medicine with health. But exterior goods have the character of things useful to an end. Hence human goodness in the matter of these goods must consist in the observance of a certain measure, as is done by a man seeking to have exterior riches in so far as they are necessary to his life according to his rank and condition. And therefore sin consists in exceeding this measure, and trying to acquire or retain riches beyond the due limit; and this is the proper nature of covetousness, which is defined to be "an immoderate love of having."[1]

§ 2. Covetousness may involve immoderation regarding exterior things in two ways: in one way immediately as to the receiving or keeping of them, when one acquires or keeps beyond the due amount; and in this respect it is directly a sin against one's neighbour, because in exterior riches one man cannot have superabundance without another being

[1] Cf. II-II. q. 77. art. 4. (Trl.)

in want, since temporal goods cannot be simultaneously possessed by many.[1] The other way in which covetousness may involve immoderation, is in interior affections, in immoderate love or desire of, or delight in riches. In this way covetousness is a sin of man against himself by the disordering of his affection. It is also a sin against God by the despising of eternal good for temporal.

ARTICLE IV.—*Is covetousness always a mortal sin?*
R. Covetousness may be taken in two ways. As opposed to *justice*, covetousness is a mortal sin of its kind: for, taken in this way, it is the part of covetousness unjustly to get or keep the goods of others, which is an act of robbery or theft, and those are mortal sins. It may however be in this kind of covetousness that the offence is only a venial sin on account of *the imperfection of the act*.[2] Taken in another way, covetousness is opposed to *liberality;* and in this way it involves an inordinate attachment to riches. If therefore the love of riches grows so far as to be preferred to charity, so that for love of riches one hesitates not to act against the love of God and of his neighbour, at that rate covetousness will be a mortal sin. But if the inordination of the love is confined within such bounds that, though the man loves riches to excess, still he

[1] Except the case in which one man's superabundance is the means of opening new sources of wealth to the whole community. There were not *capitalists* in St. Thomas' day, but only *hoarders*. That was one of the many temporal miseries of the thirteenth century as compared with our own. (Trl.)

[2] See above, q. 66. art. 6. § 3. (Trl.)

does not prefer the love of them to the love of God, and would not for riches' sake do anything against God and his neighbour, under those limits covetousness is a venial sin.

ARTICLE V.—*Is covetousness the greatest of sins?*

R. Every sin, by the very fact of its being evil, consists in the destruction or removal of some good; while in so far as it is voluntary, it consists in the fixing of the heart on some good. We may rank sins then with regard to the good that is contemned or destroyed by sin; and the greater that is, the more grievous is the sin; and in this point of view sin against God is the most grievous; and after that, sin against the human person; and after that, sin against the exterior things which are assigned to the use of man; and this last category seems to include covetousness. Or in another way we may rank sins in regard of the good on which the human heart is inordinately fixed; and the less that is, the more unseemly is the sin: for it is baser to bow to an inferior good than to a higher and better one. But the good of exterior things is the lowest of human goods: for it is less than the good of the body, and that is less than the good of the soul, and that is less than the good that is for man in God. And in this way the sin of covetousness, whereby the human heart is subjected even to exterior things, has in some sense a greater deformity than the rest. Since however the destruction or removal of good is the formal element in sin, and the turning to the perishable good of creatures is the material element, the grievousness of sin is rather to be judged in respect of the good that is destroyed than in respect of the good to which the desire and heart is subjected. And therefore covetousness is not absolutely the greatest of sins.

ARTICLE VII.—*Is covetousness a capital sin?*

R. That is called a *capital vice*, from which other vices arise having it as their end. For as an end is much to be desired, the desire of it moves a man to do many things good or evil. But the end most to be desired is happiness, the supreme end of human life. And therefore the more anything partakes of the condition of happiness, the more it is to be desired. Now one of the conditions of happiness is that it should be self-sufficient: otherwise it could not do the office of a supreme end in setting desire to rest. But this self-sufficiency is exactly what riches most of all promise: because, as the Philosopher says, "We use coin as a surety for the acquisition of property;" and it is said, "All things obey money."[1] And therefore covetousness, consisting in the desire of money, is a capital sin.

[1] Eccles. x. 19.

QUESTION CXIX.

OF PRODIGALITY.

ARTICLE I.—*Is prodigality the opposite of covetousness?*

R. In affection to riches the miser superabounds, loving them to excess: while the prodigal falls short, not taking due care of them. In exterior behaviour it belongs to the prodigal to exceed in giving, but to fail in keeping or acquiring: while it belongs to the miser to come short in giving, but to superabound in getting and in keeping.

§ 1. Opposite qualities may be found in the same subject in different respects. Sometimes one fails in giving who yet does not exceed in getting. In like manner also sometimes one goes to excess in giving, and therein is prodigal, and at the same time runs to excess in getting,—either from necessity, because his superabundant giving exhausts his resources and forces him to undue acquiring, which is the part of covetousness; or again through the inordination of his affections: for as he gives not for any good motive, setting virtue to scorn, so neither does he care whence and how he acquires; and thus, though not under the same respect, he is at once a prodigal and a miser.

§ 3. On what is said of the prodigal son, that "he wasted his substance living riotously,"[1]—it is to be observed that prodigals generally fall into sins of dissipation and debauchery, because as they run into idle expenses on other accounts, so also they do not shrink from lavishing money on their pleasures; and also because, having no delight in virtuous good, they seek for themselves bodily delights.

ARTICLE II.—*Is prodigality a sin?*
R. Prodigality is opposed to covetousness as superabundance to defect. But by those extremes the good of virtue is destroyed; and a thing is vicious and sinful by destroying the good of virtue: hence it remains that prodigality is a sin.

§ 1. Covetousness is said to be "the root of all evils,"[2] not that all evils always spring from covetousness, but that there is no evil which does not sometimes spring from covetousness. Hence even prodigality at times is born of covetousness: as when one prodigally expends large sums with the intention of currying favour with persons of whom he may get money.[3]

ARTICLE III.—*Is prodigality a more grievous sin than covetousness?*
R. Prodigality considered in itself is a less sin than avarice, for three reasons. First, because

---
[1] St. Luke xv. 13.   [2] 1 Timothy vi. 10.
[3] Cf. the Earl of Leicester's entertainment of Queen Elizabeth at Kenilworth. (Trl.)

avarice differs more from the opposite virtue: for it belongs more to the liberal man to give, in which matter the prodigal superabounds, than to get or keep, in which the miser superabounds. Secondly, because the prodigal is useful to many, to whom he gives; but the miser to none, not even to himself. Thirdly, because the prodigal is easy to cure, as well by the approach of old age, which is contrary to prodigality, as by his easily sinking into poverty through his many useless expenses, and thus impoverished, he cannot run to excess in giving; and also because he is easily brought to virtue by the likeness that he bears to it. But the miser's is no easy cure.

§ 1. The prodigal sins against himself, squandering his own goods on which he ought to live: he also sins against his neighbour, squandering the goods out of which he ought to provide for others. And this appears most of all in clerics, who are dispensers of the goods of the Church, which belong to the poor, and the poor they defraud by their prodigal expenditure.

§ 3. All vices are opposed to prudence, as all virtues are directed to prudence; and therefore a vice is accounted so much the less grave for the fact of its being opposed to prudence only.

QUESTION CXX.

OF EQUITY.

ARTICLE I.—*Is equity a virtue?*

R. Human acts, about which laws are framed, are so many singular occurrences of infinite possible variety. Hence it was found impossible for any rule of law to be established that should in no case fall short of what was desirable; but legislators have their eye on what commonly occurs, and frame their law for that: yet in some cases the observance of that law is against the equality of justice and against the public good. In such cases it is evil to abide by the law as it stands, and good to overlook the words of the law, and follow the course that is dictated by regard to justice and public expediency. And this is the end of equity: hence clearly equity is a virtue.[1]

§ 1. Equity does not abandon justice absolutely, but only justice as fixed by law. Nor is it opposed to that severity, which abides by the words of the law in cases where it is proper to abide by them: to abide by them otherwise is an error. Hence it is said in the Codex: "Beyond doubt he offends against the law, who holds fast to the words of the

[1] Cf. I-II. q. 96. art. 6. (Trl.)

law, while striving against the will of the legislator."[1]

§ 2. To Augustine's words: "Once laws are established and sanctioned, it must not be allowed to the judge to judge of them, but to judge according to them," it is to be said that he judges of the law, who says that it is not a good enactment; but he who says that the terms of the law are not to be observed *in this case*, does not judge of the law, but of a particular business that has occurred.

§ 3. Interpretation has place in doubtful cases, and in them it is not allowable to depart from the terms of the law without the decision of the ruler; but in clear cases the need is, not of interpretation, but of execution.

ARTICLE II.—*Is equity a part of justice?*

R. As said above, q. 48, a virtue has three sorts of parts, *subjective, integral,* and *potential.* Equity is a *subjective* part of justice. Legal justice is directed according to equity. Hence equity is a kind of higher rule of human acts.

§ 1. Equity in some sort is contained under legal justice, and in some sort goes beyond it. For if legal justice is said to be that which obeys the law, whether as to the terms of the law or as to the intention of the legislator—a weightier consideration; in that view, equity is the weightier part of

---

[1] Aristotle, *Rhetoric,* I. 15. nn. 1—12. gives these and other stock arguments for counsel to use when the letter of the law is against his client, and a set of counter-arguments to produce when the letter makes in his favour. (Trl.)

legal justice. But if by legal justice is meant only that which obeys the law according to the terms of the law, at that rate equity is not a part of legal justice, but a part of justice in the widest sense of the term, marked off from legal justice as going beyond it.

QUESTION CXXIII.

OF FORTITUDE.

ARTICLE I.—*Is fortitude a virtue?*

R. It belongs to human virtue to make a man good, and his work according to reason. And this is done in three ways; in one way by the rectification of reason itself, which is done by the intellectual virtues; in another way by the right order of reason being established in human affairs, which is the work of justice; in a third way by the removal of the obstacles to the setting up of this order in human affairs. Now the human will finds two sorts of hinderances in following the right order of reason: one is the attraction of some pleasurable object, drawing it to follow some other course than what the right order of reason requires; and this hinderance is removed by the virtue of temperance: the other sort of hinderance is the difficulty of doing what is according to reason, and for the removal of this hinderance fortitude is required. Hence fortitude is a virtue, as making man to be according to reason.

§ 1. Virtue of soul is not perfected in infirmity of soul, but in infirmity of the flesh, of which the Apostle spoke.[1] It belongs to fortitude of mind, bravely to bear the infirmity of the flesh.

§ 2. The outward act of a virtue is sometimes performed by persons who have not the virtue, on some other motive than the motive of the virtue. And therefore the Philosopher assigns five classes of persons who have the semblance of fortitude, as exercising the act of the virtue apart from the virtue. And this is done in three ways. First, by people rushing at a difficulty as though it were no difficulty at all; and this way has three varieties. Sometimes it comes of ignorance, the man not perceiving the greatness of the danger. Sometimes it comes of good hope of overcoming the danger, as when the man has found by experience that he has often come safe out of such perils. Sometimes it comes of knowledge and professional skill, as in soldiers, who by practice of arms and exercise do not think much of the dangers of war, reckoning their skill sufficient for their security. A second way of doing the act of fortitude without the virtue is under the impulse of some passion, as of grief, which one wishes to throw off, or again of anger. A third way is by deliberate choice of action, in view, not of the due end of the virtue, but of some temporal advantage, as honour, pleasure, or gain; or in view of avoiding something disagreeable, as reproach, distress of body, or loss of goods.

[1] 2 Cor. xii. 9.

ARTICLE II.—*Is fortitude a special virtue?*

R. The name of fortitude may be taken either as absolutely signifying firmness of mind; and in this understanding it is a general virtue, or rather a condition of every virtue, because, as the Philosopher says, for virtue it is necessary to act firmly and unflinchingly; or in another way it may be taken as signifying firmness in the enduring and resisting of those difficulties only, in which it is hardest to have firmness; and thus fortitude is set down as a special virtue, having a definite matter.

ARTICLE III.—*Is fortitude about fears and ventures?*

R. It belongs to the virtue of fortitude to remove the obstacle by which the will is diverted from the following of reason. Now it is fear especially that diverts the will from a difficult line of action; for fear means retirement before an evil fraught with difficulty. And therefore fortitude deals principally with fears of things difficult, which may divert the will from the following of reason. But it is necessary, not only to restrain fear, and firmly endure the onset of these difficulties, but also with due moderation to attack them, when there is a call to exterminate them in view of security for the future; and this seems to belong to the idea of venturing a bold stroke. And therefore fortitude deals with fears and with ventures, repressing fears and moderating ventures.

Article IV.—*Is fortitude about dangers of death only?*

R. It belongs to the virtue of fortitude to preserve the will of man from being withdrawn from rational good by the fear of bodily evil. Now rational good must be maintained against any evil whatsoever, because no bodily good can weigh in the scales against rational good. And therefore that must be called fortitude, that holds the will of man firm in the good of reason against the greatest evils: because he who stands firm against the greater, consequently stands firm against the less; but not conversely. Now the most terrible of all bodily evils is death, that takes away all the goods of the body. And therefore the virtue of fortitude is about fears of dangers of death.

§ 1. Fortitude behaves well in bearing all adversity; still it is not from the bearing of any sort of adversity that a man is accounted absolutely a brave man, but only from bearing well the very greatest evils; from the others he gets the name of being relatively brave.

Article V.—*Is fortitude properly conversant with the dangers of death that occur in war?*

R. Fortitude strengthens the mind of man against the greatest dangers, which are the dangers of death. But because fortitude is a virtue, and it is of the essence of virtue always to tend to good, it follows that the pursuit of some good should be man's motive for not shrinking from dangers of death. But dangers of death from sickness, or from a storm at sea, or from an attack of brigands, or other such cause, do not seem to threaten a man in direct consequence of his pursuit of good, as do dangers of death in war, which are imminent directly in consequence of his just defence of the public good. But there are two sorts of just war, one general, as when people fight on a battlefield; the other particular, as when a judge, or even a private person, goes not back upon a just decision for any fear of the sword threatening him, or of any danger even unto death. It belongs therefore to fortitude to show a firm heart against dangers of death, not only in a general war, but also in a particular conflict, which may be called by the common name of war. And in this sense we must grant that fortitude is properly shown in meeting dangers of death in war. The brave man however behaves well in dangers of any other sort of death; because the danger of any death may be encountered for virtue's sake, as when one shrinks not from attending a sick friend for fear of a mortal infection; or shrinks not from journeying on a pious errand for fear of shipwreck or of brigands.[1]

§ 1. Martyrs endure personal combats for the sake of the sovereign good, which is God: therefore their fortitude is above all commended. Nor is it foreign to that kind of fortitude which is shown in things of war; hence it is said that they "became valiant in battle."[2]

[1] See *Ethics and Natural Law*, p. 96. (Trl.)
[2] Hebrews xi. 34.

§ 3. The peace of the commonwealth is in itself good, and is not rendered evil by the evil use that some make of it, for there are many others who use it well; and by it much greater evils are prevented, as homicides and sacrilege, than the evils that are occasioned by it, which evils principally belong to the class of sins of the flesh.

ARTICLE VI.—*Is endurance the principal act of fortitude?*

R. As the Philosopher says: "Fortitude has more to do with repressing fears than with keeping fiery daring within bounds." For it is harder to repress fear than to keep fiery daring within bounds, because the mere danger, which is the object of venturesomeness and of fear, of itself contributes to the checking of fiery daring, but to the augmentation of fear. And therefore the principal act of fortitude is endurance, or the remaining steady and unflinching in dangers, rather than attacking.

§ 1. Endurance is more difficult than taking the offensive, for three reasons. First, because one seems to endure or withstand the assault of an adversary more powerful than oneself, but he who takes the offensive comes on as having the upper hand. Now it is harder to fight with the stronger than with the weaker. Secondly, because he who endures feels the danger now on him; but he who attacks has it before him in the future. Now it is harder not to be moved by the present than by the future. Thirdly, because endurance takes a long time; but one may attack by a sudden movement.

Now it is harder to remain long immovable than with a sudden motion to move forward to an arduous task.

ARTICLE VIII.—*Does the man of fortitude find pleasure in the exercise of it?*

R. There are two sorts of delight: one *physical*, following upon bodily contact; and another *psychical*, following the soul's apprehension. This latter it is that properly follows acts of virtue; because in them the good of reason is considered. Now the principal act of fortitude is to endure things that are at once distressing according to the soul's apprehension,—as in the case where a man sacrifices his bodily life, which the virtuous man loves, not only as a natural good, but also as a necessary instrument for works of virtue,—and at the same time are painful according to the bodily sense of touch, as wounds or stripes. And therefore the brave man on the one side has matter of pleasure, that is to say, of psychical delight, in the act of virtue and in the end thereof; and on the other side he has matter of pain, as well of *psychical* pain, considering the loss of his life, as also of that which is *physical*. But the sensible pain of the body prevents the psychical delight of virtue from making itself felt; except in the case of an abundant grace from God raising the soul to the delight of divine things too potently for it to be affected by the pains of the body, as blessed Tiburtius, when walking barefoot on hot coals, said that he seemed to himself to be treading on roses. Still the virtue of fortitude prevents the reason from being swallowed up in the pains of the body; and the psychical distress is overcome by the delight of virtue, whereby a man prefers the good of virtue to the life of the body and to all that goes therewith.

ARTICLE X.

§ 2. To the words of Seneca, "Reason suffices for the doing of her own business: what more foolish than for her to beg aid of anger, —steadiness begging of unsteadiness, faith of faithlessness, health of disease?"—it is to be said that reason does not employ anger for her act as begging aid of anger; but reason uses the sensitive appetite for an instrument, as she uses also the members of the body. Nor is there any unsuitableness in the instrument being less perfect than the prime agent, as the hammer than the workman. As for Seneca, he was a follower of the Stoics; and his words, quoted above, are aimed directly against Aristotle.[1]

§ 3. Fortitude having two acts, to endure and to attack, does not employ anger for the act of endurance,—that act is done by the mere sole force of reason; but for the act of attack. For this act anger is employed rather than other passions, because it is the part of anger to assault the vexatious object; and thus anger lends direct co-operation to fortitude in making the attack.

[1] See I-II. q 24. art. 2. (Trl.)

QUESTION CXXIV.

OF MARTYRDOM.

ARTICLE II.

§ 2. The first and principal motive of martyrdom is charity, acting in the capacity of the *virtue commanding;* but fortitude is its proper motive in the capacity of the *virtue eliciting*.[1] Martyrdom then is a display of both virtues. But the merit of it comes of charity, like the merit of every other act of virtue. And therefore without charity it avails nothing.

ARTICLE III.—*Is martyrdom the act above all others of greatest perfection?*

R. We may speak of an act of virtue in two ways: in one way according to the species of the act itself, as fixed by reference to the virtue that proximately elicits it; and in that way martyrdom, consisting in the due suffering of death, cannot possibly be the most perfect of acts of virtue, because the suffering of death is not praiseworthy in itself, but only inasmuch as it is directed to some good end consisting in an act of virtue, as faith or

---

[1] An act is *elicited* by the virtue to which it immediately belongs, but *commanded* by a higher virtue which puts in motion the virtue that elicits the act. Cf. II-II. q. 26. art. 7. (Trl.)

the love of God: hence that act of virtue, being the end, is the better. In another way an act of virtue may be considered in reference to the prime motive, which is the love of charity; and it is from this relation particularly that an act derives its value as tending to perfection of life, because as the Apostle says: "Charity is the bond of perfection."[1] But of all virtuous acts martyrdom pre-eminently argues the perfection of charity; because a man proves himself to love a thing the more, the more lovable the thing that he despises for its sake, and the more hateful the thing that he chooses to suffer rather than lose it. But of all the goods of the present life man most loves life itself, and contrariwise most hates death, especially a death attended with pain and bodily torments, "by the fear of which," as Augustine says, "even brute animals are restrained from the greatest pleasures." And therefore, of human acts, martyrdom is the most perfect of its kind, as being the sign of the greatest charity, according to the text: "Greater love than this no man hath, that a man lay down his life for his friends."[2]

§ 1. There is no act of perfection falling under counsel, that in some contingency may not fall under precept, and be of necessity to salvation: as Augustine says that a man falls under the necessity of observing continence by reason of the absence or illness of his wife. And therefore it is not against the perfection of martyrdom, if in some case it is of necessity to salvation.

[1] Coloss. iii. 14. [2] St. John xv. 13.

ARTICLE IV.—*Is death essential to martyrdom?*

R. A martyr is so called as being a *witness* of the Christian faith, that faith which proposes to us to despise the things that are seen for the things that are unseen. Martyrdom therefore supposes a man to bear witness to his faith, showing in very deed that he despises all present advantages in order to arrive at future and invisible goods. But so long as his bodily life remains to a man, he has not yet shown in very deed his contempt of all the goods of the body. For men are wont to make light of kinsmen and possessions, and even to suffer bodily agonies, to save their lives. Hence it is that Satan urged against Job: "Skin for skin, and all that a man hath he will give for his life."[1] And therefore the essence of martyrdom, full and perfect, requires the suffering of death for Christ.

[1] Job iii 4.

QUESTION CXXV.

OF FEAR.

ARTICLE I.—*Is fear a sin?*
R. A thing is said to be sinful in human acts on account of its inordinateness: for the goodness of a human act consists in a certain order. Now the due order is for appetite to be subject to the guidance of reason. Reason dictates that some things are to be shunned, and some things sought; and of things to be shunned, that some are more to be shunned than others; and of things again to be sought, that some are more to be sought than others; and that the more any good is to be sought, the more the opposite evil is to be shunned. Hence reason dictates that sundry good things are to be more sought than sundry other evil things are to be shunned. When then appetite shuns that which reason declares ought to be met and encountered, lest by shunning it other things more to be sought after have to be relinquished, such fear is inordinate and sinful.

ARTICLE IV.—*Does fear excuse from sin?*
R. If any one for fear, in view of shunning evils that are less to be shunned, were to rush upon evils

that are more to be shunned, he could not be totally excused from sin, because such fear would be inordinate. Now evils of the soul are more to be feared than evils of the body, and evils of the body more than evils in exterior things. And therefore if any one rushes upon evils of the soul, that is to say, sins, by way of shunning evils of the body, as stripes or death, or evils in exterior things, as the loss of money; or even if he endures evils of the body to avoid loss of money,[1]—he is not totally excused from sin. Nevertheless his sin is in some respect diminished, because what is done for fear is less voluntary.

QUESTION CXXVI.

OF INSENSIBILITY TO FEAR.

ARTICLE I.—*Is insensibility to fear a sin?*

R. Because fear is born of love, the same judgment seems to hold of love and of fear. The question now is of the fear wherewith temporal ills are feared, which arises out of the love of temporal goods. Now it is natural to every one to love his own life, and aids to life, in due measure, which means that these things be not so loved as that a man should set up his rest in them finally, but they should be loved as things that have to be used for the last end. Hence for any one to fall short of the due measure of love of these things, is against

[1] Like King John's famous Jew. (Trl.)

the inclination of nature, and is consequently a sin.[1] Never however does any one totally fall away from this love: for what is natural cannot be totally lost: wherefore the Apostle says: "No man ever hated his own flesh."[2] Hence even they who kill themselves do so from love of their flesh, which they wish to deliver from present hardship. Hence it may happen that a man fears death and other temporal ills less than he ought, for the reason that he loves the opposite goods less than is their due. But his fearing nothing of these ills cannot arise from a total want of love of those goods, but only from his reckoning that the evils opposite to the goods that he loves cannot possibly come upon him. And this arises sometimes from pride, self-assurance, and contempt of others, as it is said [of the leviathan], that he "was made to fear no one: he beholdeth every high thing."[3] Sometimes again it happens for want of reason, as the Philosopher says that "folly makes the Celts impervious to fear."[4] Hence it appears that insensibility to fear is a flaw in the character, caused it may be by want of love, or by elation of mind, or by stolidity, which last cause however excuses from sin, if it be invincible.

§ 1. To the text, "The just, bold as a lion, shall be without dread,"[5] it is to be said that the just is commended for the fact that fear holds him not

---

[1] For this consequence, see *Ethics and Natural Law*, p. 112.
[2] Ephes. v. 29.   [3] Job xli. 24, 25.
[4] The Philosopher's exact words are: "A man would be mad or insensate, if he feared nothing, neither earthquake nor waves, as they say of the Celts." Aristotle, *Ethics*, III. 7. 7. (Trl.)
[5] Prov. xxviii. 1.

back from good, not as though he were without all fear: for it is said, "He that is without fear cannot be justified."[1]

§ 2. To the texts, "Fear ye not them that kill the body," and "Who art thou that thou shouldst be afraid of a mortal man?"[2]—it is to be said that death, or aught else that can be inflicted by a mortal man, is not to be feared in such fashion as that justice should be departed from on that account: still it is to be feared inasmuch as man may thereby be hindered from doing virtuous works, either for his own person or for the improvement of others.

§ 3. To the saying of Augustine, that "the love of God even to the contempt of self makes citizens of the heavenly city," it is to be said that temporal goods ought to be contemned inasmuch as they hinder us from the love and fear of God; and to this extent also no fear should be entertained about them: hence it is said, "He that feareth the Lord shall tremble at nothing."[3] But temporal goods are not to be despised as instruments to aid us to the exercises of the fear and love of God.

ARTICLE II.—*Is insensibility to fear opposed to fortitude?*

R. Fortitude regards fears and ventures. Now every moral virtue fixes the golden mean of reason in the matter which it regards. Hence to fortitude belongs fear, moderated according to reason, that man should fear what he ought and when he ought.

[1] Ecclus. i. 28.   [2] St. Matt. x. 28; Isaias li. 12.
[3] Ecclus. xxxiv. 16.

This golden mean of reason may be spoilt by defect, as it may be spoilt by excess. Hence as timidity is opposed to fortitude by excess of fear, the man fearing what he ought not: so insensibility in the matter of fear is opposed to fortitude by defect, a man not fearing what he ought to fear.

QUESTION CXXVII.

OF FIERY DARING.[1]

ARTICLE I.—*Is fiery daring a sin?*

R. Fiery daring is a passion. A passion is sometimes regulated according to reason, and sometimes unregulated, passing either into excess or into defect; and in this condition passion is vicious. Now the names of the passions are sometimes taken to signify excess of passion. Thus by *anger* is not meant any anger whatever, but excessive anger, according as it is vicious; and in the same way also *fiery daring*, meaning that which is carried to excess, is set down as a sin.

§ 3. Vices are designated by the names of those passions especially, the object of which is evil, as hatred, fear, anger, and fiery daring: whereas hope and love having good for their object, their names are rather used to designate virtues.

[1] Cf. I-II. q. 45 (Trl.)

QUESTION CXXVIII.

OF THE PARTS OF FORTITUDE.

ARTICLE I.—*Are the parts of fortitude suitably enumerated?*

R. To any virtue there may be three sorts of parts, *subjective, integral,* and *potential.*[1] But to fortitude as a special virtue no *subjective* parts can be assigned, because it is not divided into many virtues specifically different, seeing that it is about a very special matter. But there are assigned to it *integral* and *potential* parts: *integral,* as representing the qualities that must concur to an act of fortitude; *potential,* inasmuch as what fortitude observes in very difficult matters, that is, where there is danger of death, the same is observed by other virtues in other matters less difficult; and these virtues are attached to fortitude as secondary virtues to their primary. Now the act of fortitude is twofold, to attack and to endure. To the act of attacking a difficulty there are two requisites. The first regards preparation of soul, that one should have a prompt and ready mind for the attack; and to this Tully assigns *self-confidence.* The second regards the execution, that one should not fail in the execu-

[1] Q. 48.

tion of what he has confidently begun; and to this Tully assigns *magnificence*. If these two virtues are limited to the proper matter of fortitude, that is to dangers of death, they will be *integral* parts of it, or qualities without which fortitude cannot be. But if they are referred to other matters in which there is less difficulty, they will be virtues distinct from fortitude in their species; still they will be attached to it as secondaries to their primary.[1] In this way *magnificence* is assigned by the Philosopher to the matter of large expenses; and *magnanimity*, which seems to be the same as *self-confidence*, to the matter of great honours. To the other act of fortitude, which is endurance, there are again two requisites. The first is that the mind be not crushed and broken by sadness, and fall from its greatness in face of the difficulty of imminent evils; and to this purpose Tully assigns *patience*. The other is that a man be not wearied out by protracted suffering of difficulties, and brought to the point of desisting from his enterprise, as the text has it: "Be not wearied, fainting in your minds;"[2] and to this he assigns *perseverance*. These two virtues also, if they are confined to the proper matter of fortitude, will be *integral* parts thereof: but if they are referred to any difficult matters whatsoever, they will be virtues distinct from fortitude, and yet attached to it as secondaries to their primary.

§ 1. Magnificence in the matter of liberality adds a certain magnitude, which reaches to the idea of

[1] And therefore they will be *potential* parts of fortitude. (Trl.)
[2] Hebrews xii. 3.

arduousness; and that is the object of the irascible faculty, which faculty it is the principal office of fortitude to perfect; and under this aspect magnificence belongs to fortitude.

§ 2. The hope whereby one confides in God ranks as a theological virtue. But by the self-confidence here set down to be a part of fortitude, a man has hope in himself, yet under God.

§ 3. To attack any great matters may be accounted dangerous, because to fail in such matters is very hurtful. Hence, though self-confidence and magnificence are assigned to the doing or attacking of great businesses other than those that are the proper matter of fortitude, still they have a certain affinity with fortitude on the score of danger imminent.

QUESTION CXXIX.

OF MAGNANIMITY.[1]

ARTICLE I.—*Does magnanimity obtain in the matter of honours?*

R. Magnanimity from its name implies a reaching out of the soul to great things. A man is called *magnanimous* principally from this, that he has a mind bent upon some great act. Now an act may be great either relatively or absolutely. It is indeed a great act, relatively speaking, to make an excellent use of a trifle. But speaking absolutely, that is a great act which uses a grand thing excellently. Now of the exterior things that come into man's use, absolutely the greatest is honour, both because it is nearest to virtue, as being a testimony thereto, and also because it is paid to God and to the most excellent of creatures; and again because men postpone all other considerations to the gaining of honour and the avoidance of disgrace. But a man is called *magnanimous* from what is absolutely and without qualification *great*, as he is called *brave* from what is without qualification *difficult*. And therefore magnanimity obtains in the matter of honours.

[1] See *Ethics and Natural Law*, pp. 98—101. (Trl.)

§ 3. Those who despise honours in such a way as to do nothing unbecoming to gain them, and do not value them too highly, deserve praise. But if a man were so to despise honours as not to care to acquit himself of performances worthy of honour, that would be blamable. And in this way magnanimity is in the matter of honours: that is to say, it endeavours to make its performances worthy of honour, yet not so as to have great esteem of human honour.

ARTICLE II.
§ 3. The magnanimous man aims at high honours as being worthy of them, or even as things less than what he is worthy of, seeing that virtue cannot be enough honoured by man, since honour is due to it from God. And therefore the magnanimous man is not puffed up by great honours, because he does not account them to be above himself, but rather despises them, and much more does he despise petty honours. And in like manner his spirit is not broken by marks of dishonour, but he despises them, reckoning them to be indignities done him.

ARTICLE III.—*Is magnanimity a virtue?*
R. It is of the essence of human virtue to secure in human life attention to rational good, which is the proper good of man. Now of all the exterior things that enter into human life, honours hold the highest place. And therefore magnanimity, that

fixes the golden mean of reason in the matter of great honours, is a virtue.

§ 3. On the saying of Aristotle, "Slow seems to be the gait of the magnanimous man, and his voice deep, and his utterance grave and leisurely," it is to be remarked that rapidity of gait comes from a man having many things in view, and being in a hurry to accomplish them: whereas the magnanimous man has only great objects in view, and there are few such, and what there are require great attention; and therefore he is slow of gait. In like manner also shrillness and rapidity of utterance belongs to those who are ready to contend on any question that occurs, which is not the habit of magnanimous men: they meddle only with big things.

§ 4. In man there is found something great, which he possesses by the gift of God; and some shortcoming which attaches to him from the weakness of his nature. Now magnanimity makes a man deem himself worthy of great honours in consideration of the gifts that he possesses of God; while humility makes him think little of himself in consideration of his own shortcomings. In like manner also magnanimity despises others inasmuch as they come short of the gifts of God: for it does not set such store by others as to do anything unbecoming for their sakes. But humility honours others and accounts them superior beings, in so far as it discerns in them any of the gifts of God. Hence it is said of the just man: "In his sight the malignant is brought to nothing,"[1] which points to

[1] Psalm xiv. 4.

the contempt which the magnanimous man feels: "but he glorifieth them that fear the Lord," which points to the honour that the humble man pays. And thus evidently magnanimity and humility are not contrary, because they proceed on different considerations.

§ 5. On the sayings of Aristotle that the magnanimous man "does not remember people from whom he has received benefits;" that he is "inactive and a lingerer;" that he "understates his own qualities to the world at large;" that he "cannot live with others;" that he "rather holds unfruitful than fruitful possessions;"—it is to be remarked that these properties, in the way that they belong to the magnanimous man, are not blameworthy, but exceedingly to be praised. First of all, as to his being said not to bear in mind the persons of whom he has received benefits, that is to be understood of his not liking to receive benefits from others without conferring on them greater benefits in return, which belongs to the perfection of gratitude, in the act of which he wishes highly to excel, as in the acts of other virtues. In like manner also it is said, in the second place, that he is inactive and a lingerer, not that he fails in doing the work that is proper to him, but that he does not mix himself up in all manner of works indiscriminately, but only in great works, such as become him. It is said, in the third place, that he practises understatement of his own powers, not in a way opposed to truth by saying abject things of himself that are not true, or denying great things of himself that are true, but by not showing all his greatness, especially to the multitude of meaner persons. In the fourth place it is said that he cannot live with others, that is to say, not on terms of familiarity, except with friends; because he altogether avoids flattery and pretence, which are parts of meanness of spirit. He does however live and converse with others, both great and small, with due discrimination. Again, in the fifth place, it is said that he wills rather to have unfruitful possessions, not of any sort, but good, that is virtuous: for in all things he prefers virtue to utility, as something greater: for useful things are sought after for the supplying of some deficiency, such as stands not with magnanimity.

ARTICLE IV.
§ 1. Magnanimity fixes not on any manner of honour, but on great honour. But great honour is due to a great work of virtue. Hence the magnanimous man aims at great works in every line of virtue, making it his aim to do things worthy of great honour.

§ 3. There is a certain beauty of its kind proper to every virtue: but there is a certain added grace from the mere magnitude of the virtuous work, due to magnanimity, which makes all the virtues greater.

ARTICLE VI.
§ 1. As the Philosopher says: "It belongs to the magnanimous man to want nothing, or hardly

anything." This however must be understood in human measure: for it is beyond the condition of man to have no wants at all. For every man needs first of all the divine assistance, and secondly also human assistance, for man is naturally a social animal, not being self-sufficient for the purposes of life.

ARTICLE VIII.—*Do the goods of fortune contribute to magnanimity?*

R. Magnanimity regards two objects, honour as its matter, and some great deed in view as its end. Goods of fortune co-operate to both these objects. For honour is paid to the virtuous, not by the wise only, but also by the multitude. Now the multitude make most account of exterior goods of fortune: consequently greater honour is paid by them to those who have the exterior goods of fortune. In like manner again goods of fortune serve as instruments to acts of virtue, because by riches and positions of authority and friends there is given us opportunity for action. Clearly then goods of fortune contribute to magnanimity.

§ 1. Virtue is said to be self-sufficient, because it can exist even without these exterior goods: nevertheless it needs these exterior goods to have more of a free hand in its working.

§ 2. The magnanimous man despises exterior goods, as not accounting them great goods for which he ought to do anything unbecoming, yet not without accounting them useful for doing the work of virtue.

§ 3. Whoever does not account a thing great, is neither very glad if he gets it, nor very much grieved if he loses it; and therefore because the magnanimous man does not account as great the exterior goods of fortune, he is not much elated at their presence, nor greatly dejected at their loss.

QUESTION CXXX.

OF PRESUMPTION.[1]

ARTICLE I.—*Is presumption a sin?*

R. Since the operations of nature are ordained by divine reason, which human reason ought to imitate, it follows that whatever human reason does contrary to the order commonly found in the operations of nature is vicious and sinful. Now this is commonly found in all the operations of nature, that every action is measured by the strength of the agent; nor does any natural agent endeavour to do what exceeds its ability. And therefore it is vicious and sinful, as being against the natural order, for any one to take upon himself to do what transcends his powers, which is the part of presumption.

§ 1. A thing may very well be beyond the active power of some natural agent, and yet not beyond the passive power of the same; for there is passive

[1] There is presumption against *magnanimity*, and presumption against *hope*. See II-II. q. 21. art. 1. (Trl.)

power in *air* whereby it may be transmuted into something that has the action and movement of *fire*, which exceeds the active power of air.[1] Thus it would be vicious and presumptuous for any one in a state of imperfect virtue to attempt to attain at once to the practices of perfect virtue. But if one aims at making progress to perfect virtue, that is not presumptuous nor vicious. And in that way the Apostle[2] was stretching forth himself to the things that were before, to wit, by continual progress.

§ 3. As the Philosopher says: "What we can do by others, we can in a manner do of ourselves." And therefore because we can think and do good by the help of God, it does not wholly exceed our ability to do good. And therefore there is no presumption in setting about a work of virtue, as there would be if one set about it otherwise than in confidence of help from God.

ARTICLE II.—*Is presumption opposed to magnanimity by way of excess?*

R. Magnanimity stands in the mean, not in respect of the amount that it aims at, for it aims at the highest amount; but as observing the proportion of its own powers: for it aims no higher than befits it. The presumptuous man, in the amount that he aims at, does not exceed the magnanimous man, but often falls far short of

---

[1] For *air* read *water;* and for *fire, vapour;* and the illustration suits the nineteenth century. (Trl.)

[2] Philipp. iii. 13.

him; but he is in excess as going beyond the proportion of his own powers, a limit which the magnanimous man does not overstep. And thus presumption is opposed to magnanimity by way of excess.

QUESTION CXXXI.

OF AMBITION.

ARTICLE I.—*Is ambition a sin?*

R. Honour implies reverence paid to another in testimony of his excellence. Now regarding excellence in man there are two things to observe: first, that whatever it is that a man excels in, he has it not of himself, but as a divine gift within him; and therefore not for that is honour due to him in the first place, but to God. Secondly, it is to be considered that whatever excellence a man has, is given to him by God, to use for the service of his fellow-men: hence the testimony that other men render to his excellence ought so far forth to be matter of complacency to him, as it shows the way open to him to make himself of service to others.[1]

In three ways the seeking after honour may come to be inordinate. In one way, by a person

---

[1] A better lesson this than Atheistic Socialism can teach, of the functions of a gifted man in society. God is the giver, not society. Under God, we are all one another's servants. (Trl.)

seeking testimony to excellence that he has not got, which is seeking honour beyond the measure of himself. In another way, by a man desiring honour for himself without referring it to God. In a third way, by his appetite fixing on the mere honour, without referring the honour to the benefit and advantage of others. But ambition means an inordinate craving after honour: hence plainly ambition is always a sin.

§ 1. The craving after a good thing ought to be regulated according to reason: if it overpasses reason's rule, it must be vicious. And in this way the desire of honour, not according to the order of reason, is vicious. But they are blamed who care nothing for honour as reason dictates that they should—in other words, who do not avoid transactions contrary to honour.

§ 2. Honour is not the reward of virtue in regard of the virtuous man himself, as though he ought to seek after that as his reward: the reward he rather seeks is happiness, which is the end of virtue. But honour is understood to be the reward of virtue on the part of other men, who have nothing greater to bestow on the virtuous than honour.

§ 3. As the craving after honour, duly regulated, is to some men an incitement to good and a check upon evil, so, unduly indulged, it may be to man an occasion of many evil deeds. At the same time, they who do good or avoid evil merely for honour's sake, are not vicious, as appears by the Philosopher, where he says that they are not truly brave who do brave deeds for honour.[1]

ARTICLE II.

§ 1. Magnanimity regards two things, one as its *end in view*, some great work that the magnanimous man undertakes according to his ability; and in this respect *presumption* is opposed to magnanimity by excess: for presumption undertakes some great work above its ability. There is another thing that magnanimity regards as the *matter* that it uses duly, namely, honour; and in this respect *ambition* is opposed by excess to magnanimity. Nor is there any difficulty in there being several excesses in different respects to one golden mean.

[1] Aristotle, *Ethics*, III. 8, distinguishes from fortitude what he calls *civic virtue*, the bravery of those who fight because they fear the reproach of their fellow-townsmen if they fly—after all, a more honourable motive than "the worthy Kempe of Kinfauns bending a large cross-bow," held out to encourage Simon Glover to stay where he was on the walls of Perth. (Trl.)

QUESTION CXXXII.

OF VAINGLORY.

ARTICLE I.—*Is the seeking after glory a sin?*

R. Properly by the name *glory* is denoted the coming of somebody's good qualities to the knowledge and approbation of many. In the larger sense of the word however glory consists in being known, not necessarily to many, but to a few, to one, even to oneself alone, where one regards one's own good qualities as worthy of praise. Now it is no sin to recognize and approve of your own good qualities, for it is said: "We have received the spirit that is of God, that we may know the things that are given us from God."[1] In like manner it is not a sin to wish your own good works to meet with approval, for it is said: "Let your light shine before men."[2] And therefore the seeking after glory does not of itself imply anything vicious; but the seeking after empty or vainglory means vice. Now glory may be called *vain* in three ways. In one way, on the part of the endowment for which one seeks to receive glory, if it be something not worthy of glory, but frail and perishable;

[1] 1 Cor. ii. 12.   [2] St. Matt. v. 16.

in another way, on the part of the man of whom one seeks glory, if he be a man whose judgment is not to be depended upon; in a third way, on the part of the person seeking the glory, if he directs not the seeking of it to the due end, that is, to the honour of God or his neighbour's salvation.

§ 1. God seeks His glory, not for His own sake, but for ours; and in like manner man also may commendably seek his own glory for the advantage of others.

§ 2. Some men are incited to works of virtue by the desire of human glory, as are others by the desire of other earthly goods. Still he is not truly virtuous, who does the works of virtue for the sake of human glory.

§ 3. It is a point of the perfection of man that he should know himself; but that he should be known by others is no point of his perfection, and therefore not a thing to be of itself desired. It may however be desired for the utility of it, either as a means to God being glorified by men, or as a means to men making progress in consequence of the good that they observe in another, or to the end that the man himself, moved by the good qualities that he recognizes in himself by the testimony of another's praise, may endeavour to persevere in them and to advance to better things. And under these conditions it is praiseworthy to "take care of a good name,"[1] and to "provide good things in the sight of God and of men;"[2] not however to take idle delight in the praise of men.

[1] Ecclus. xli. 15.   [2] Romans xii. 17.

ARTICLE II.—*Is vainglory opposed to magnanimity?*

R. Because magnanimity is about honour, it is also about glory,[1] that one should make moderate use both of the one and of the other; and therefore the inordinate seeking after glory is directly opposed to magnanimity.

§ 1. It is precisely this that is opposed to magnanimity, that one should have such a care of trifles as to glory in them. Hence it is said of the magnanimous man, that "honour is a small thing to him."[2] In like manner also other things that are sought after for the honour they bring, as high station and wealth, are accounted small by the magnanimous man. Again, it is opposed to magnanimity that one should glory in what is not: hence it is said of the magnanimous man that "he cares more for truth than for opinion." Again, it is opposed to magnanimity that one should glory in the testimony of human praise, counting that anything great: hence it is said of the magnanimous man that "he has no care to be praised." Thus weaknesses that are opposed to other virtues may be opposed to magnanimity in this, that they take small things for great.

[1] *Honour* is paid to a man to his face, where he is present either in person or by his representative. *Glory* is the good opinion and talk that is held of a man, his celebrity in fact, even where he is not present. Cf. II-II. q. 73. (Trl.)

[2] The reference is to Aristotle, *Ethics*, IV. 3. 18.: "He is not even so disposed to honour as to count it a very great thing; . . . and he to whom even honour is a little thing, holds all other things cheap." (Trl.)

ARTICLE III.—*Is vainglory a mortal sin?*

R. In a case where the love of human glory, though vain, still is not inconsistent with charity, neither in respect of the matter gloried in nor in respect of the intention of him who seeks the glory, then the sin is not mortal but venial.

§ 2. It is not every one vainly desirous of glory that seeks after the pre-eminence which belongs to God alone; for the glory due to God alone is different from that due to a virtuous or wealthy man.

§ 3. Vainglory is said to be a dangerous sin, not so much for its own grievousness, as because it predisposes people to grievous sins, making them presumptuous and too confident in themselves, and thus on the way gradually to be deprived of interior goods.

ARTICLE IV.—*Is vainglory a capital vice?*

R. Gregory makes pride the queen of all vices; and vainglory, that immediately arises from pride, he makes a capital sin. And reasonably so: for pride means an inordinate seeking to stand high. Now from everything that a man seeks he attains a certain perfection and high standing; and therefore the ends of all vices are directed to the end of pride; and therefore pride seems to exercise a *general* causality over the other vices, and not to hold a place among the *special* heads of vice, which are the capital vices. And because many vices arise from the inordinate seeking after glory, therefore vainglory is a capital vice.

§ 3. It is not requisite for a capital vice to be always a mortal sin: because even from venial sin mortal sin may arise, the former predisposing to the latter.

ARTICLE V.—*Are the daughters of vainglory properly stated to be disobedience, boasting, hypocrisy, contention, obstinacy, discord, and presumption of novelties?*

R. Those vices that have a connatural bearing on the end of any capital vice, are said to be its *daughters*. Now the end of vainglory is the showing forth of one's own excellence. To this a man may bend his efforts in two ways: in one way directly, whether by words, and that is *boasting*, or by deeds; and that, if the deeds are real, having something about them to admire, is *presumption of novelties*, which men are wont the rather to admire; but if the deeds are fictitious, it is *hypocrisy*. The other way of trying to show forth one's excellence is indirectly, by showing that you are not inferior to any one else, which may be done in four several departments. First, in point of intellect, and that is *obstinacy*, whereby a man clings too much to his own opinion, refusing to accept a better. Secondly, in point of will, and that is *discord*, when one will not give up his own will, to live at peace with others. Thirdly, in speech, and that is *contention*, when one wrangles in words clamorously with another. Fourthly, in deed, and that is *disobedience*, when one refuses to fulfil a superior's command.

QUESTION CXXXIII.

OF PUSILLANIMITY.

ARTICLE I.—*Is pusillanimity a sin?*
R. Everything that is contrary to natural inclination is a sin, because it is contrary to the law of nature.[1] Now there is a natural inclination in every agent to put forth action commensurate with its power. But as by presumption one exceeds the proportion of his power, aiming at greater things than he can accomplish, so the pusillanimous man on the other hand falls short of the proportion of his power, and refuses to bend his efforts to what is quite within the measure of his ability. Hence as presumption is a sin, so is pusillanimity. Hence the servant who has buried in the earth the money that he has received of his lord, and done no work with it, through a certain pusillanimous fear, is punished by his lord.[2]

§ 3. Even pusillanimity may arise in some way from pride, in this that a man rests too much on his own judgment in pronouncing himself incompetent for things for which he is competent. Hence it is said: "The sluggard is wiser in his own

[1] *Ethics and Natural Law*, pp. 111, 112. (Trl.)
[2] St. Matt. xxv.; St. Luke xix.

conceit than seven men who speak sentences."[1] It is quite possible for man unduly to abase himself on some points, and lift himself aloft on others. Hence Gregory says of Moses: "He would be guilty of pride perhaps, if he took up the leadership of a countless people without trembling; and again guilty of pride, if he refused to obey his Creator's command."

QUESTION CXXXIV.

OF MUNIFICENCE.[2]

ARTICLE II.

§ 3. Magnificence, or munificence, aims at doing a great work. But no end or aim of human works is so great as the honour of God, and therefore the great work of magnificence is shown especially in view of the honour of God. Hence the Philosopher says: "Those expenses are most honourable which relate to sacrifices to the Deity;" and about these the munificent man is most zealous. And therefore *magnificence* is joined with *holiness*,[3] because its principal work is directed to religion or holiness.

ARTICLE III.—*Are large expenses the matter of munificence?*

R. Great works cannot be done without great expenses. Hence it belongs to munificence to go

---
[1] Prov. xxvii. 16.
[2] St. Thomas says *magnificence*, but our word is *munificence*. (Trl.)
[3] Exodus xv. 11; Psalm xcv. 6.

to great expense for the suitable doing of a great work. Now expense means parting with money, from which a man may be restrained by excessive love of money. And therefore as matter of munificence we may assign both the *expenses* themselves which the munificent man incurs for the doing of a great work, and the *love of money* which he curbs that these great expenses may not be stopped.

§ 2. The use of money appertains to liberality and to munificence in different ways. All due use of money in the way of gifts appertains to liberality. But to the munificent man it appertains to use money for some great work, that cannot be without expenditure and cost.

§ 3. The principal act of virtue is the interior choice, which the virtue can make without exterior fortune; and in that way even the poor man may be munificent. But to exterior acts of virtue the goods of fortune are requisite as instruments; and so far forth a poor man cannot exercise the exterior act of munificence in things that are great, absolutely speaking; but perhaps he may exercise it in things that are great in relation to some work, which though small in itself may yet be done magnificently in its way: for *great* and *small* are relative terms, as the Philosopher remarks.[1]

ARTICLE IV.—*Is munificence a part of fortitude?*

R. Munificence as a special virtue cannot be

[1] The *munificent* or *magnificent man* is the *princely* man. *Magnificence* means doing things on a *handsome* scale. It is opposed to *shabbiness*, or *petty economy*, which St. Thomas calls *parvificentia*. (Trl.)

set down to be a *subjective* part of fortitude, because it does not agree with it in matter; but it is set down to be a part of it inasmuch as it is annexed to it as a secondary virtue to its primary. For such annexation two things are required: one, that the secondary virtue agree with the primary; the other, that in some respect it be transcended by it. Now munificence agrees with fortitude in this, that as fortitude tends to something arduous and difficult, so also does munificence: hence it seems, like fortitude, to be in the irascible faculty. But munificence falls short of fortitude in this, that the arduous goal to which fortitude tends has its difficulty in the danger which is threatened to the person; whereas the arduous goal of munificence has its difficulty in the expenditure of pecuniary means, a much less matter than danger to the person. Thus munificence is set down to be a part of fortitude.[1]

[1] A *potential* part, q. 128. (Trl.)

QUESTION CXXXV.

OF PETTY ECONOMY.

ARTICLE I.—*Is petty economy a vice?*

R. The munificent man primarily intends the greatness of his work, and secondarily the greatness of his expense, which he does not shrink from, to make the work great. But the pettily economical man primarily intends the smallness of his expense, and consequently the paltriness of his work, an effect which he does not stick at, so that he can make the expense small. Thus then it is clear that the pettily economical man falls short of the proportion which there ought in reason to exist between expense and work. But a falling short of what is according to reason, brings about what answers to the idea of a vice. Hence it appears that petty economy is a vice.

§ 2. As the Philosopher says, "Fear makes people prone to consultation," and therefore the pettily economical man diligently applies himself to accounts, because he has an inordinate fear of wasting his goods even in the least things. Hence this habit is not praiseworthy, but vicious and blamable, because the man does not direct his affection according to the reckoning of reason, but rather applies his powers of reckoning to serve the inordinateness of his affection.[1]

QUESTION CXXXVI.

OF PATIENCE.

ARTICLE I.—*Is patience a virtue?*

R. The moral virtues preserve the good of reason against the assaults of passion. Now among other passions sadness operates powerfully in hindering the good of reason, according to the texts: "The sorrow of the world worketh death;"[2] and "Sadness hath killed many, and there is no profit on it."[3] Hence it is necessary to have some virtue by which the good of reason may be preserved against sadness. This is the work of patience. Hence Augustine says: "It is by patience that we bear evils with equanimity, lest by loss of equanimity we abandon the goods whereby we arrive at better goods." Hence clearly patience is a virtue.

---

[1] A bit of character-painting, perhaps from life, not unworthy of Theophrastus or Clarendon. Aristotle (*Ethics*, IV. ii. 21.) has thus much of the μικροπρεπής: "The man of petty economies will be under the mark in everything. He will spoil the beauty of a costly work by sordidness in detail. Whatever he does, he does with hesitation, and much consideration how to cut down expense, and still will go lamenting and thinking that all he does is on too grand a scale." The rest of the portrait is of St. Thomas's own finding. (Trl.)

[2] 2 Cor. vii. 12.   [3] Ecclus. xxx. 25.

ARTICLE II.—*Is patience the chief of virtues?*

R. Virtue is what makes its possessor good and his work good. Hence a virtue must be more eminent and preferable, the more powerfully and directly it sets a man in the way of good. Now the virtues which are themselves constituent of good put a man in the way of good more directly than those which are preventive of seduction from good. And as among those that are constituent of good one is preferred to another inasmuch as it sets a man in possession of greater good—thus faith, hope, and charity are preferred to prudence and justice,—so among those that are preventive of withdrawal from good, one is preferred to another in proportion to the strength of the perturbing agency which it counteracts. But the perils of death, with which fortitude is conversant, or the delights of touch with which temperance deals, are more potent perturbing agents to withdraw men from good than the whole line of adversities that make the subject-matter of patience. And therefore patience is not chief of virtues, but falls short, not only of the theological virtues, and of prudence and justice, which directly set a man up in good, but also of fortitude and temperance, which remove greater obstacles from the right path than are removed by patience.

ARTICLE IV.

§ 1. It belongs to fortitude to face, not any adversity whatever, but that which is most difficult to face, namely, danger of death. But the endurance of any evils whatsoever may belong to patience.

§ 2. Fortitude is particularly about fears: fears lead to flight, and that is just what fortitude avoids. But patience is rather about annoyances, griefs, and sadnesses: for a man is called patient, not because he does not fly, but because he behaves himself commendably in suffering present hurts without inordinate sadness. And therefore fortitude is properly in the irascible faculty, but patience in the concupiscible. Nor does this hinder patience from being a part of fortitude: because the annexation of virtue to virtue is not arranged according to the subject faculty wherein the virtue resides, but according to its matter and form. Patience is particularly about the griefs and annoyances that are caused us by others.

QUESTION CXXXVII.

OF PERSEVERANCE.

ARTICLE I.—*Is perseverance a virtue?*
R. Virtue is in matter difficult and good; and therefore where there occurs a special style of difficulty or goodness, there is a special virtue. Now a work of virtue may have difficulty from the mere length of time it takes; and therefore long persistence in good, even to the complete accomplishment of the same, belongs to a special virtue. And therefore as temperance and fortitude are special virtues, so also is perseverance, to which it belongs in these or other virtues to endure long continuance according as is necessary.

§ 2. The name of perseverance is sometimes taken for the habit whereby one chooses to persevere, sometimes for the act whereby one does actually persevere. Now sometimes one having the habit of perseverance chooses indeed to persevere, and begins to put his choice into execution by holding on for some time, but does not complete the act, because he does not hold on to the end. There are two ends, one that of a particular work, the other that of human life. Of itself it belongs to perseverance that one should persevere even to the end of a virtuous work, as a soldier to the end of the conflict, and the munificent man to the completion of his work. But there are some virtues, the acts of which ought to last all life long, as faith, hope, and charity, which regard the last end of human life. And in respect of these virtues, being as they are primary, the act of perseverance is not completed even till the end of life.

ARTICLE II.—*Is perseverance a part of fortitude?*

R. To fortitude there must be attached, as a secondary virtue to its primary, every virtue the praise of which consists in enduring firmly anything that is difficult. But to endure the difficulty that arises from the length of a good work, gives praise to perseverance; nor is this so difficult as it is to face perils of death. And therefore perseverance is attached to fortitude as a secondary virtue to its primary.

QUESTION CXLI.

OF TEMPERANCE.

ARTICLE I.

§ 1. Nature inclines to that which is proper to each. Hence man naturally seeks after the delight proper to himself. But because man as such is rational, it follows that those delights are proper to man that are according to reason; and from these temperance does not withdraw him, but rather from those which are against reason. Hence clearly temperance is not contrary to the inclination of human nature, but in accordance with it. But it is contrary to the inclination of bestial nature not subject to reason.

ARTICLE II.—*Is temperance a special virtue?*

R. In the usage of human speech some common nouns are restricted to that which is principal in the class denoted by them: as the name of *the City* is understood eminently of Rome. Thus then the name of temperance may be taken in two ways: in one way in its general signification, and in that way temperance is not a special but a general virtue, since the name signifies a certain *attempering,* or moderation, which is the work of reason upon human actions and passions; and that moderation is common to every virtue. But if temperance is considered in the eminent use of the word, as something refraining the appetite from the things that most of all entice and allure man, in that way it is a special virtue with a special matter.

§ 3. Though beauty attaches to every virtue, yet it is singularly the attribute of temperance, for two reasons: first, from analysis of the general idea of temperance, which involves a certain regular and appropriate proportion, in which the essence of beauty consists; secondly, because the things from which temperance restrains us are the lowest things in man, and befit him in respect of the nature that he has in common with beasts; and therefore man is most exposed to degradation and disfigurement herein: consequently beauty is the singular attribute of temperance, as that virtue particularly removes what disfigures man.

ARTICLE IV.—*Is temperance confined to the matter of the desires and delights of touch?*

R. Temperance is about desires and delights as fortitude is about fears and daring ventures. But the fears and daring ventures with which fortitude is conversant, have respect to the greatest evils, those by which nature itself is extinguished, which are dangers of death. Hence in like manner temperance must be about the desires of the greatest delights. And because delight follows upon natural activity, certain delights must be all the more intense, the more natural are the activities upon which they follow. But to animals the most natural activities are those by which the nature of the individual is maintained by means of meat and drink, and the nature of the species by the union of the sexes; and therefore the delights of meat and drink and of sexual pleasure are the proper matter of temperance. But these delights attend the sense of touch. Hence it remains that temperance is in the matter of the delights of touch.

§ 2. Not all the delights of touch belong to the maintenance of nature; and therefore no need for temperance to be in the matter of all the delights of touch.[1]

ARTICLE VI.

§ 2. There are two ways of taking the phrase, *necessary to human life*. In one way we may call that *necessary*, without which the thing cannot be at all, as food is necessary to an animal; in another way we call that *necessary*, without which the thing cannot be in a suitable condition. Now temperance regards not the former necessity only, but also the latter. Hence the Philosopher says that "the temperate man goes after pleasant things in view of health or of a good habit of body." But other things, that are not necessary to these ends, may

[1] The reduction of the two appetites of Food and Sex to Touch, is a whim of Aristotelian physiology. If any one chooses to pass that over, he may still keep in perfect accordance with St. Thomas by saying that "Temperance is a virtue, which regulates by the judgment of reason those desires and delights, which attend upon the operations whereby human nature is preserved in the individual and propagated in the species." *Ethics and Natural Law*, p. 90. (Trl.)

T   VOL. II.

be of two sorts. Some there are that are positive hinderances to health or a good habit of body; and these the temperate man in no way uses: for that would be a sin against temperance. Others there are that are not hinderances to these ends; and these he uses moderately according to place, time, and company. And therefore the Philosopher adds that even the temperate man "goes after other pleasant things," that is, things not necessary to health or a good habit of body, " when they are not in the way of those ends."[1]

ARTICLE VII.—*Is temperance a cardinal virtue?*
R. The moderation which is requisite in every virtue is particularly praiseworthy in regard of the delights of touch, with which temperance has to deal: as well because such delights are more natural to us, and therefore more difficult to abstain from, and to moderate the desires of them; as also because their objects are more necessary to the present life. And therefore temperance is a primary or cardinal virtue.

[1] This passage is well illustrated by Devas, *Groundwork of Economics*, § 147. (Trl.)

QUESTION CXLII.

OF VICES OPPOSED TO TEMPERANCE.

ARTICLE I.—*Is insensibility a vice?*

R. Everything that is contrary to the natural order is vicious. But nature has attached delight to the activities that are necessary for the life of man. And therefore the natural order requires that man should use such delights so far as is necessary to human well-being, in point either of the maintenance of the individual or of the species. If any man therefore were so far to shun delight as to omit what was necessary for the maintenance of nature, he would sin as going against the natural order; and such a sin belongs to the vice of insensibility. It is to be observed however that sometimes it is praiseworthy, or even necessary, for a particular purpose, to abstain from the delights that are attendant upon such activities. Thus for the health of their bodies some abstain; and again for the execution of some charge, as athletes and soldiers have to abstain from many delights to fulfil their task. And in like manner penitents, to recover their soul's health, follow a sort of dietary scheme of abstinence from things delightful; and men who wish to give themselves to contemplation and divine things must withdraw themselves more than other men from fleshly desires. Nor do any of these courses belong to the vice of insensibility, because they are according to right reason.

§ 2. Because man cannot use reason without using the sensitive powers that require a bodily organ, man is obliged to give sustenance to his body in order to have the use of his reason. And bodily sustenance is taken by actions that give pleasure. Hence the good of reason cannot be in man, if he abstain from all pleasures. According however as man in performing the act that his reason approves requires more or less of bodily strength, in that proportion he has more or less need to make use of things pleasant to the body. And therefore men who have taken up the office of contemplation, and of transmitting to others by à sort of spiritual generation spiritual good, do well in abstaining from many sources of pleasure, from which others do well in not abstaining, whose office it is to give themselves to corporal works and to raising up posterity in the flesh.

ARTICLE II.—*Is intemperance a childish sin?*

R. A thing is said to be childish, either because it befits children, and in that way the Philosopher does not mean to say that the sin of intemperance is childish; or else it is called childish in point of a certain likeness to a child. For the sin of intemperance is the sin of appetite running to excess; and that is likened to a child in three respects. First, in respect of that which both the one and the other seek after: for appetite, like a child, seeks after what is unseemly. And the reason is, because beauty in human things consists in being ordered according to reason: now a child pays no attention to the order of reason, and appetite in like manner has no regard for reason. Secondly, they agree in the event and outcome. For a child, left to its own will, waxes strong in its own will: hence it is said, "A horse not broken becometh stubborn, and a child left to himself will become headstrong."[1] So also appetite, if gratified, takes new strength. Hence Augustine says: "Lust yielded to becomes a habit, and a habit not resisted becomes a necessity." Thirdly, in point of the remedy that is applied to each. For a child is amended by constraint: hence it is said, "Withhold not correction from a child: thou shalt beat him with the rod and deliver his soul from hell."[2] And in like manner appetite, by being resisted, is reduced to due measure of propriety.

§ 2. Desire may be said to be *natural* in two ways: in one way, in its *kind;* and in that way temperance and intemperance are about natural desires; for they are about desires of food and sex, which are ordained to the maintenance of nature. In another way, desire may be said to be *natural* in respect of the *species* of that which nature requires for its maintenance; and in this way there is not much opening for sin in the matter of natural desires: for nature requires no more than the relief of its own necessity; and in the desire of that there

[1] Ecclus. xxx. 8. [2] Prov. xxiii. 13, 14.

is no opening for sin except in the way of excess in quantity. And this is the only way that sin is committed in the matter of natural desire, as the Philosopher says. But other matter of much sin is found in certain incentives to desire which human artificiality has invented, as dishes, the work of *artistes*, and elaborate toilets.[1]

§ 3. What belongs to nature in boys is to be developed and fostered: but what belongs to the deficiency of reason in them is not to be fostered, but corrected.

ARTICLE III.—*Is cowardice a greater vice than intemperance?*

R. One vice may be compared with another either in respect of its matter or object, or in respect of the man himself who sins; and in both respects intemperance is a more grievous vice than cowardice. First, in respect of the matter: for cowardice flies from perils of death, for the avoidance of which the necessity of preserving life offers the greatest inducement. But intemperance is in the matter of pleasures, the seeking after which is not so necessary to the preservation of life: because intemperance turns rather upon certain adventitious delights and desires than upon desires and delights that are natural. But the greater the necessity which the motive to sin seems to carry with it, the lighter is the sin. And therefore intemperance is a more grievous vice than cowardice on the part of

[1] Cf. *Ethics and Natural Law*, pp. 49, 50: I-II. q. 30. art. 3. q. 77. art. 5. (Trl.)

the object or matter which is its motive. Also on the part of the man himself who sins: in the first place, because the more the sinner is in possession of his faculties, the more grievous is his sin: hence sins are not imputed to people out of their senses. But fears and severe griefs, especially where there is danger of death, bewilder a man's wits: whereas the pleasure that prompts to intemperance has no such effect. Secondly, because a sin is more grievous as it is more voluntary; but intemperance has more of a voluntary character about it than cowardice, in two ways. In one way, because what is done through fear has its principle in an impulse from without: hence it is not absolutely voluntary, but partly voluntary and partly involuntary; whereas what is done for pleasure is absolutely voluntary. In another way, because the proceedings of the intemperate man are more voluntary in detail, though less voluntary in general. For no one would wish to be intemperate; but a man is allured by the particular attractions of pleasure that make him intemperate. Wherefore for the avoidance of intemperance the great remedy is not to dwell on the consideration of particular attractions in detail. But as concerns cowardice it is the other way about: for the particular acts that force themselves upon one, as throwing away one's arms and the rest, are less voluntary, but the general purpose is more voluntary, which is to save one's life by flight. But that is absolutely the more voluntary proceeding, which is more voluntary in the particular details that attach to the action in the doing. And therefore intemperance, being absolutely more voluntary than cowardice, is the greater vice.[1]

§ 1. As it is the greater virtue not to be overcome by the stronger temptation, so it is the less vice to be overcome by the stronger, and the greater vice to be vanquished by the weaker.

ARTICLE IV.—*Is the vice of intemperance especially shameful?*

R. Shame is reckoned to be the opposite of honour and glory. Now honour is due to excellence, and glory denotes brilliancy and lustre. Intemperance then is especially shameful for two reasons. First, because it is most opposed to the excellence of man, being in the matter of the pleasures that are common to us with brute beasts. Secondly, because it is most opposed to the lustre and beauty of man, inasmuch as in the pleasures that intemperance pursues there appears less of the light of reason, whence comes all the lustre and beauty of virtue: hence also such pleasures are said to be especially things for slaves.

§ 1. As Gregory says: "To vices of the flesh there attaches less shame, but greater infamy."

§ 2. The general prevalence of sin diminishes the turpitude and infamy of certain vices in the opinion of men, but not in the nature of the vices themselves.

[1] Intemperance, it must be remembered, here means not drunkenness only, but impurity,—in fact, all sensual vice. (Trl.)

QUESTION CXLIII.

OF THE PARTS OF TEMPERANCE IN GENERAL.

ARTICLE I.—*Does Tully suitably assign as the parts of temperance, continence, clemency, and decorum?*

R. The possible parts of a virtue are of three sorts, *integral, subjective,* and *potential.* The conditions that must concur to the virtue are called *integral* parts of the virtue. Thus there are two integral parts of temperance: *sense of shame,* by which one shuns the turpitude that is contrary to temperance; and *sense of propriety,* by which one loves the beauty of temperance.

By the *subjective* parts of a virtue are understood its species. Now diversity of species in virtues goes according to diversity of matter or object. Temperance then is about delights of touch, which are divided into two kinds. Some are connected with nutrition; and in regard of these, for the matter of eating, is *abstinence,* and for the matter of drink, *sobriety.* Some are connected with the reproductive faculty; and in regard of these there is *chastity,* concerned with the primary pleasure of the act of reproduction itself, and *modesty,* about the attendant circumstances of pleasure in kisses, touches, and embraces.

By the *potential* parts of a primary virtue are meant the secondary virtues, that observe in some other matters, in which it is not so difficult, the same mode of discretion that the primary virtue observes in some primary matter. Now it belongs to temperance to moderate the delights of touch, which are most difficult to moderate. Hence any virtue whatsoever that puts in practice moderation in any matter, and restrains appetite in its tendency in any direction, may be set down for a part of temperance, as a virtue attached thereto. There are three modes of this practice of moderation: one in interior motions of the soul, another in exterior motions and acts of the body, and a third in exterior things. In the soul there are found three movements of tendency, besides the motion of sensual desire which is checked and moderated by temperance. There is first the motion of the will under the impulse of passion; and this motion is checked by *continence*, the effect of which virtue is that, though the man suffers immoderate sensual desires, yet the will is not overcome. Another interior movement of tendency is the movement of hope, and of fiery daring following upon hope; and this movement is moderated or checked by *humility*. The third is the movement of anger tending to revenge, which is checked by *meekness* or *clemency*.

As regards bodily movements and actions, the check of moderation is imposed by *decorum*. Regarding exterior things a twofold moderation is to be observed: first, that superfluities be not sought:

and for this there is assigned *content;* secondly, in not seeking things too dainty and far-fetched: and thereunto *simplicity* is assigned.

QUESTION CXLV.

OF PROPRIETY.

ARTICLE III.—*Does propriety differ from utility and pleasurableness?*

R. Propriety is found in the same subject with utility and pleasurableness, but differs from them in the way we look at things. For a thing is said to be *proper* as having a certain beauty according to the ordering of reason. But what is ordered according to reason is naturally suited to man; and every being takes a natural pleasure in what suits it; and therefore propriety is naturally pleasurable to man. Still not everything that is pleasurable is proper: because a thing may be suitable in point of sense and not in point of reason. Such a pleasurable thing is in disregard of the reason in man that perfects his nature. Virtue also itself, being in itself proper, is referred to something else as to an end, namely, to happiness. And thus propriety and utility and pleasurableness are the same in subject. But they differ according to the way that we look at them: for a thing is called *proper*, as having a certain excellence worthy of honour on the score of spiritual beauty;[1] it is called *pleasurable* as setting desire at rest; it is called *useful* as being referred to something else. Nevertheless *the pleasurable* is of wider extension than *the useful* and *the proper:* for everything that is useful and proper is in some sort pleasurable, but not everything pleasurable is useful and proper.

QUESTION CXLVI.

OF ABSTINENCE.

ARTICLE I.—*Is abstinence a virtue?*

R. Abstinence by its name implies a subtraction of food. Therefore the name of abstinence may be taken in two ways: in one way, as denoting simply the subtraction of food, and in this way abstinence denotes neither a virtue nor an act of virtue, but something indifferent; in another way, it may be taken as abstinence regulated by reason, and then it signifies either a habit of virtue or an act.

§ 2. Moderation in food as to quantity and quality belongs to the art of medicine, where there is question of the health of the body, but to

[1] In the previous article, St. Thomas says that "propriety is the same as spiritual beauty." This sense of *proper* appears in the English Bible and in Shakspeare, *e.g.* (Hebrews xi. 23): "Moses was a proper child," where the Rheims version has "comely babe." And we still speak of "a proper man of his hands." The value of this article is apparent in the question of utilitarianism. Utilitarianism is simply a denial of the element of beauty as anything distinct from utility. (Trl.)

abstinence where there is question of interior affections as referred to the standard of rational good. Hence Augustine says: "It makes no matter at all to virtue what food or how much one takes, provided he do it according to the decencies of the society that he lives with, and of his own character, and according to the needs of his health; but what does matter to virtue is the ease and serenity of mind with which he goes without these creature comforts, when it is right or necessary to go without them."

§ 3. It belongs to temperance to bridle delights that overmuch allure the soul to go after them, as it belongs to fortitude to strengthen the soul against fears that repel it from the good of reason. And therefore as the praise of fortitude consists in a certain excess, and from this all the parts of fortitude take their name; so also the praise of temperance consists in a certain defect, or stopping short, and from this temperance itself and all its parts have their name. Hence also abstinence, which is a part of temperance, has its name from defect, or stopping short: and yet it stands in the golden mean, inasmuch as it is according to right reason.

ARTICLE II.—*Is abstinence a special virtue?*
R. Moral virtue preserves the good of reason against the assaults of passion; and therefore where there is found a special way in which passion withdraws us from the good of reason, there is need there of a special virtue. But the pleasures of the

table are naturally apt to withdraw a man from the good of reason, both on account of their greatness, as also on account of the necessity of taking food, which man needs for the preservation of life, of which he has the strongest desire. And therefore abstinence is a special virtue.

§ 3. The use of clothes is an introduction of art, but the use of food is of nature; and therefore there rather ought to be a special virtue for moderation in food than for moderation in dress.[1]

QUESTION CXLVII.

OF FASTING.

ARTICLE I.—*Is fasting an act of virtue?*

R. An act is virtuous by being directed by reason to some proper good. And this is the case with fasting. For fasting is taken up principally for three ends. First, to repress the concupiscences of the flesh; hence the Apostle says, "In fastings, in chastity,"[2] because by fastings chastity is preserved. Secondly, it is taken up that the mind may be more freely raised to the contemplation of high things; hence Daniel,[3] after a three weeks' fast, received a revelation from God. Thirdly, to satisfy for sin; hence it is said: "Be converted to me with all your heart, in fasting and in weeping and in mourning."[4]

[1] In q. 143. St. Thomas has mentioned *content* and *simplicity* as dealing, among other things, with moderation in dress. (Trl.)
[2] 2 Cor. vi. 5, 6.   [3] Daniel x. 2—12.   [4] Joel ii. 12.

§ 2. The golden mean of virtue is taken, not according to quantity, but according to right reason. Now reason judges that sometimes for some special cause a man should take less food than would be proper for him in his ordinary state, as for the avoidance of disease, or for the readier performance of some bodily labour.[1] And much more does right reason direct this for the avoidance of spiritual evils and the attainment of spiritual goods. Still right reason does not sanction so great a diminution of food as that the support of nature becomes impossible; because as Jerome says: " There is no difference between killing yourself in a long time and in a short:[2] because he offers a holocaust out of rapine, who immoderately afflicts his body either with too great want of food or with shortness of sleep." In like manner also right reason does not make such a diminution of food as to render the man incapable of doing the work that is his duty. Hence Jerome says: " A rational man loses dignity, when he prefers either fasting to charity, or watching to having his wits about him."

§ 3. The natural fast, whereby a man is said to be fasting before he eats, consists in a mere negation, and therefore cannot be set down as an act of virtue, but only that fast whereby one for a reasonable purpose abstains in some degree from food. Hence

---

[1] *e.g.*, a jockey in training. (Trl.)

[2] That is, if your end in view is to kill yourself; otherwise a man may go and live in an unhealthy country, when he knows that such a sojourn will shorten his days; and *a pari* of corporal austerities. (Trl.)

the former is called *the fast of fasting;* but the latter *the fast of the faster,* as of an agent acting for a purpose.

ARTICLE III.—*Is fasting of precept?*

R. As it belongs to secular princes to deliver legal prescriptions determinant of natural law on points that affect the public interest in secular matters, so it belongs to ecclesiastical prelates to make statutory enactments for the common advancement of the faithful in spiritual goods. Now fasting is useful for the blotting out and restraining of sin, and for the raising of the mind to spiritual things; and every one is by natural reason bound to make such use of fasting as is necessary for himself to the above ends. And therefore fasting in general falls under precept of the law of nature; but the determination of time and manner of fasting falls under precept of positive law, which is laid down by the prelates of the Church.[1]

§ 1. Absolutely considered, fasting is not of precept; but it is of precept to every one who needs such a remedy. And because the generality of men do need such a remedy, as well because "in many things we all offend,"[2] as also because "the flesh lusteth against the spirit,"[3] it was therefore convenient that the Church should create certain statutory fasts to be observed by all alike,—not as subjecting to precept what is absolutely matter of

[1] See I-II. q. 94. art. 3. note. (Trl.)
[2] St. James iii. 2.   [3] Galat. v. 17.

supererogation, but as determining in particular what is necessary in general.

§ 3. The fasts that are of precept are not contrary to the liberty of the faithful people, but rather are useful for preventing the slavery of sin, which is repugnant to spiritual liberty, of which it is said: "For you, brethren, have been called unto liberty; only make not liberty an occasion of the flesh."[1]

ARTICLE IV.—*Are all bound to observe the fasts of the Church?*

R. General statutes are set forth according as they suit the generality; and therefore the legislator in framing them has his eye on what happens generally and for the most part. But if from any special cause anything is found in any one that is inconsistent with the observance of the statute, the legislator does not intend to bind such a person to observing it. Here however we must proceed with discrimination. For if the cause be evident, the man may lawfully by himself omit the observance of the statute, especially where custom intervenes, or where he cannot easily have recourse to a superior. But if the cause be doubtful, one ought to have recourse to the superior who has power to dispense in such matters.

§ 1. The commandments of God are commandments of the natural law, which are of themselves necessary to salvation. But the enactments of the Church are on points that are not of themselves

[1] Galat. v. 13.

of necessity to salvation, but only by the institution of the Church. And therefore obstacles may arise, in consideration of which some persons are not bound to observe fasts thus commanded.

§ 2. In children there is most evident cause for not fasting, as well on account of the weakness of nature, for which they want frequent food and not much at a time, as also because they want much food for the necessity of growth. And therefore so long as they are in the growing stage, which is generally to the end of the third seven years, they are not bound to the observance of the Church's fasts. It is suitable however that even during this time they should exercise themselves in fasting, more or less, according to the measure of their age. Sometimes however when great tribulation threatens, for a sign of stricter penance fasts are proclaimed even for children.

§ 3. As regards travellers and work-people, a distinction it seems should be made. If the travelling and the toil of labour can conveniently be put off or diminished without detriment to bodily health, and to the exterior good estate that is requisite for the preservation of bodily or spiritual life, then the fasts of the Church are not to be omitted on that ground. But if there is an urgent necessity of travelling at once, and making long days' journeys, either for the preservation of bodily life, or for anything necessary to spiritual life, and the fasts of the Church cannot be observed at the same time, a man is not bound to fast, because it does not seem to have been the intention of the Church in enacting fasts, thereby to hinder other pious and more necessary proceedings. Still it seems that in such cases recourse should be had to the dispensation of the superior, except where a custom happens to obtain: because from the mere fact of prelates dissembling they seem to consent.

§ 4. The poor who can get enough to suffice them for one meal, are not excused by their poverty from the fasts of the Church: from which however they appear to be excused who beg alms bit by bit, and cannot get all at once enough for their keep.

QUESTION CXLVIII.

OF GLUTTONY.

ARTICLE I.

§ 2. The vice of gluttony does not reside in the substance of the food, but in the appetite ill-regulated by reason. And therefore if one exceed in quantity of food, not through appetite, but thinking it necessary for oneself, that is not a piece of gluttony, but of inexperience.

ARTICLE III.—*Is gluttony the greatest of sins?*

R. The gravity of a sin may be considered in three ways. First and foremost, according to the matter of the sin; and in this way sins in the matter of the things of God are the greatest. Secondly, on the part of the sinner; and in this way the sin of gluttony is rather extenuated than aggravated, as well in consideration of the necessity of taking food, as also on account of the difficulty of discerning and regulating what is suitable on such occasions. Thirdly, on the part of the effect consequent; and in this respect the vice of gluttony has some magnitude, inasmuch as divers sins are occasioned thereby.

ARTICLE IV.—*Are the species of gluttony distinguished according to these five conditions: too soon, too expensively, too much, too eagerly, too daintily?*
R. Gluttony means inordinate appetite in eating. Now in eating there are two things to consider, the food that is eaten, and the eating thereof. And consequently there may be a twofold inordinateness of appetite: one in respect of the food itself that is taken; and thus in respect of the substance or species of the food one seeks dishes that are *expensive;* in respect of the quality one seeks dishes too elaborately prepared, that is, *daintily;* in respect of quantity one exceeds in eating *too much.* The other inordinateness is in the taking of the food, either by anticipating the due time of eating, which is *too soon;* or by not observing due mode and manner in eating, which is *too eagerly.*

ARTICLE VI.—*Are the daughters of gluttony duly assigned as five: inept mirth, buffoonery, uncleanness, much talking, and dulness of mind for intellectual things?*
R. Those vices are counted among the daughters of gluttony, that follow from immoderate delight

in eating and drinking. And they may be either on the part of the soul or on the part of the body. On the part of the soul they come in four ways: and first on the part of the reason, the edge of which is dulled by immoderation in meat and drink; and in this respect *dulness of perception in intellectual things* is put down as a daughter of gluttony; as, on the contrary, abstinence helps to the gathering of wisdom, according to the text: " I thought in my heart to withdraw my flesh from wine, that I might turn my mind to wisdom."[1] Secondly, in respect of the appetite, which is in many ways disordered, the guidance of reason slumbering under the immoderate load of meat and drink; and in this respect is set down *inept mirth*. Thirdly, for inordinateness of word; and for that is set down *much talking*. Fourthly, for inordinateness of action; and for that is set down *buffoonery*, that is, jocularity springing from defect of reason, which cannot restrain its words, nor its exterior gestures either. On the part of the body there is ranked *uncleanness*.

[1] Eccles. ii. 3.

QUESTION CXLIX.

OF SOBRIETY.

ARTICLE II.

§ 1. Food and drink alike may hinder the good of reason, overwhelming it in excess of pleasure; and on that score abstinence is concerned alike with food and drink. But intoxicating liquor hinders reason in a special manner, and therefore requires a special virtue.

ARTICLE III.—*Is the use of wine altogether unlawful?*

R. No food or drink considered in itself is unlawful, according to the sentence of our Lord, who says: "Not that which goeth into the mouth defileth a man."[1] And therefore to drink wine, ordinarily speaking, is not unlawful. But it may be rendered unlawful incidentally; sometimes from the condition of him who drinks, because he is easily hurt by wine, or because he is bound by a special vow not to drink wine; sometimes from the manner of drinking, because one exceeds due measure; sometimes on the part of others, who are scandalized thereby.[2]

[1] St. Matt. xv. 11.   [2] See q. 43. (Trl.)

§ 1. Wisdom may be had in two ways. In one way, according to the common measure, sufficiently for salvation; and for this measure of wisdom it is not requisite that one should abstain altogether from wine, but only from the immoderate use of it. In another way, wisdom may be had in some degree of perfection; and for that it is requisite in some persons for the perfect perception of wisdom that they should be total abstainers from wine, where conditions of place and person so require.

§ 2. The Apostle[1] does not say that it is good to abstain from wine absolutely, but only in the case of some being scandalized at our use of it.

§ 3. Christ withdraws us from some things as being entirely unlawful, from other things as being hinderances to perfection; and in this way He withdraws some from wine on a motive of zeal for perfection, as He withdraws others from riches and such like things.

ARTICLE IV.—*Is sobriety more requisite in greater personages?*

R. Virtue has regard to two things: on the one hand, to the contrary vices which it excludes, and to the appetites which it curbs; and on the other hand, to the end to which it leads. Thus then there may be two reasons for which a given virtue is more requisite in certain persons. One reason would be because in some persons there is greater proneness to the desires that need to be curbed by virtue, and to the vices that are put away by virtue.

[1] Romans xiv. 21.

And in this way sobriety is especially required in young men and in women. Hence, according to Valerius Maximus, among the ancient Romans women used not to drink wine. The other reason for sobriety being more requisite in certain persons, is because it is more necessary to their special work. Wine taken in immoderate quantities is a marked hinderance to the use of reason; and therefore upon old men, whose reason ought to be active for the instruction of others, and upon bishops, or ministers of the Church, who ought devoutly to apply to spiritual duties, and upon kings, whose wisdom ought to be their subjects' guide—sobriety is especially enjoined.

QUESTION CL.

OF DRUNKENNESS.

ARTICLE I.—*Is drunkenness a sin?*

R. Drunkenness, meaning the mere loss of reason that comes of drinking much wine, does not denote any guilt, but a penal loss consequent on guilt. Taken in another way, drunkenness may mean the act by which one incurs this loss. That act may cause drunkenness from the excessive strength of the wine beyond what the drinker looked for. Thus understood again, drunkenness may happen without sin. But the act may cause drunkenness in another way, from the inordinate desire and use of wine; and in that way drunkenness is set down to be a sin, and is contained under gluttony as the species under the genus.

ARTICLE II.—*Is drunkenness a mortal sin?*

R. The guilt of drunkenness consists in an immoderate use and desire of wine. This may come into operation in three ways: in one way, without the person knowing that the drink is immoderate and intoxicating; and at that rate drunkenness may be without sin. In another way, when the person perceives the drink to be immoderate, but does not reckon it strong enough to make him drunk; and in that way drunkenness may be with venial sin. In a third way, it may happen that the person perceives very well that his drink is immoderate and intoxicating, and yet had rather get drunk than abstain from drink. Such a man is properly called a drunkard; because mortal sins receive their species, not from what happens incidentally beside the intention of the agent, but from what is of itself intended.[1] And thus drunkenness is a mortal sin, because thereby a man willingly and knowingly deprives himself of the use of reason, by which he acts according to virtue and avoids sin; and so he sins mortally by putting himself in the danger of sinning. For Ambrose says: "We say that drunkenness is a thing to be avoided, as putting it out of our power to guard ourselves against the commission of crime: for the things that we are on our guard against when sober, we do in ignorance through

[1] Cf. I-II. q. 78. art. i. § 2. (Trl.)

drink." Hence, ordinarily speaking, drunkenness is a mortal sin.

§ 1. The circumstance of its being habitual makes drunkenness a mortal sin, not by the mere iteration of the act, but because it is impossible for a man to be an habitual drunkard without getting drunk knowingly and willingly, as he has frequent experience of the strength of the liquor and of his own liability to intoxication.

§ 3. The measure of meat and drink is to be fixed to suit the health of the body; and therefore as what is the right measure for a man in health is often too much for a sick man, so also it may be that what is too much for a man in health is the right measure for one that is sick. And thus when one eats or drinks a great quantity by medical advice for the purposes of an emetic, the food or drink so taken is not to be considered to be in excess. Still it is not necessary for the drink to be intoxicating to act as an emetic, because even warm water will serve that purpose: and therefore this would furnish no excuse for drunkenness.[1]

ARTICLE III.—*Is drunkenness the most grievous of sins?*

R. A thing is said to be evil as being a taking away of good. Hence the greater the good taken

---

[1] It looks as though St. Thomas would allow drinking even to intoxication for medical purposes, if it were necessary, but can see no such necessity. By implication here he justifies the use of anæsthetics, allowing one to lose his reason for a time with a grave cause where there is no danger of sin. (Trl.)

away, the more grievous the evil. But divine good is greater than human good. And therefore the sins that are directly against God are more grievous than the sin of drunkenness, which is directly opposed to the good of human reason.

§ 1. Man has a special proneness to sins of intemperance, because desires and delights of this sort are connatural to us; and in this respect sins of this sort are particularly dear to the devil, as Chrysostom says, "Nothing is so dear to the devil as drunkenness and dissipation:" not because they are more grievous than other sins, but because they are more frequent among men.

§ 2. The good of reason is hindered in two ways: in one way by what is contrary to reason; in another way by what takes away the use of reason. But there is more evil in what is contrary to reason than in what takes away for a time the use of reason.

ARTICLE IV.—*Does drunkenness excuse from sin?*
R. There are two elements in drunkenness, the loss ensuing and the act preceding. On the part of the loss ensuing, which is a loss of the free use of reason, drunkenness has the quality of excusing from sin, as causing involuntariness by ignorance. But on the part of the act preceding there seems need of a distinction. For if from that act drunkenness ensued without sin, then the further sin that ensues is totally excused from guilt. But if the act preceding was culpable, at that rate one is not totally excused from the ensuing sin, as that is made

voluntary by the voluntariness of the preceding act, inasmuch as the agent was engaged on an unlawful action at that time, and thence came to fall into the sin that ensued. Still the sin that ensues is diminished with the diminution of its voluntary character.

QUESTION CLI.

OF CHASTITY.

ARTICLE I.

§ 1. Chastity resides in the soul as in its subject, but the matter thereof is in the body. For it belongs to chastity that, according to the judgment of reason and the choice of the will, a person should use with moderation the bodily members.

ARTICLE II.—*Is chastity a general virtue?*

R. The name of chastity is taken in two ways: in one way properly, and in that way it is a special virtue having a special matter, namely the desires of sexual pleasure. In another way, the name of chastity is taken metaphorically. For as it is in the union of bodies that sexual pleasure consists, which is the proper matter of chastity and of the opposite vice of luxury, so in the spiritual union of the mind with certain objects there arises a delight, which is the matter of a spiritual chastity, metaphorically so called, or of a spiritual fornication, also metaphorically so called. For where the mind of man takes delight in spiritual union with that object with which it ought to be united, namely with God, and abstains from the delight of union with other objects contrary to the due requirement of divine order, such delight and such abstinence is called *spiritual chastity*, according to the text: "I have espoused you to one husband, that I may present you as a chaste virgin to Christ."[1] But if, contrary to the due requirement of divine order, the mind takes delight in a union with other objects, it will be called *spiritual fornication*, according to the text: "Thou hast prostituted thyself to many lovers."[2] And taking it in this way, chastity is a general virtue, because by every virtue the mind of man is withdrawn from the delight of union with unlawful objects.

ARTICLE IV.—*Does modesty belong specially to chastity?*

R. Modesty is especially concerned with the signs of sexual affection, as looks, kisses, and touches; but chastity regards rather the sexual act itself. And therefore modesty is referred to chastity, not as a virtue distinct from it, but as the expression of a circumstance of chastity. Sometimes however one is put for the other.

[1] 2 Cor. xi. 2.   [2] Jerem. iii. 1.

QUESTION CLII.

OF VIRGINITY.

ARTICLE II.—*Is virginity unlawful?*

R. In human acts, that is vicious which is against right reason. Now right reason carries this with it, that a man should use means to the end in the measure that suits the end. But the good of man is threefold: one sort consisting in exterior goods; another in the goods of the body; and the third in the goods of the soul, among which the goods of the contemplative life are better than the goods of the active life, as the Philosopher proves.[1] Of these goods, exterior goods are referred to goods of the body; goods of the body to goods of the soul; and furthermore the goods of the active life to the goods of the contemplative life. It belongs therefore to rightness of reason that one should use exterior goods in the measure that suits the body; and so of the rest. Hence if one were to abstain from having certain possessions, which he otherwise might lawfully hold, practising this abstinence for the good of his bodily health, or even for the better contemplation of truth, that is no vicious abstinence, but quite in keeping with right reason. And

[1] See *Ethics and Natural Law*, pp. 9, 10. (Trl.)

in like manner, supposing one abstains from bodily pleasures to have more freedom for the contemplation of truth, that again belongs to rightness of reason. But it is for this that religious virginity abstains from all sexual pleasure, that it may more freely apply itself to divine contemplation. For the Apostle says: "The unmarried woman and the virgin thinketh on the things of the Lord, that she may be holy both in body and spirit."[1] Hence it remains that virginity is not anything vicious, but rather commendable.

§ 1. A commandment has the character of a debt. But there are two sorts of debts: one debt that must be paid by one individual; and a debt of that sort cannot be ignored without sin; another debt that has to be paid by a community: and to the payment of that debt not every individual in the community is bound. For there are many needs in a community, and one individual cannot meet them all; but they are met by the community in this way, that one meets one need and another another. So then the precept of the law of nature given to man about eating must needs be fulfilled by every individual: otherwise the individual could not be maintained. But the precept given about generation, "Increase and multiply,"[2] regards the whole community of mankind. Now this community has need, not only of corporal multiplication, but also of spiritual increase. And therefore it is sufficient provision for human society, if some lay out their strength in carnal generation, while others, abstain-

[1] 1 Cor. vii. 34.   [2] Genesis i. 28.

ing from that, apply themselves to the contemplation of divine things, for the beauty and welfare of the whole human race: even as in an army some guard the camp, some carry the standards, some fight with swords, all which offices are so many debts to the community, but debts that cannot be discharged all by one man.[1]

ARTICLE III.—*Is virginity a virtue?*

R. The formal and completely constituting element in virginity is the purpose of perpetual abstinence from sexual pleasure; which purpose is rendered praiseworthy by the end in view, inasmuch as it is taken up to find free scope for divine things. But the material element in virginity is the integrity of the flesh, void of all experience of sexual pleasure. But where there is a special matter of goodness, having a special excellence, there is found there a special character of virtue: as appears in munificence, which has to do with large expenditure, and is thereby a special virtue distinct from liberality, which deals in general with all use of money. But the keeping oneself void of experience of sexual pleasure has a degree of excellence and praise above keeping oneself free of the inordinate enjoyment of sexual pleasure. And therefore virginity is a special virtue, standing to chastity as munificence to liberality.

§ 1. Men have from their birth what is the material element in virginity, namely, the integrity of the flesh void of experience of sexual acts, but

[1] *Ethics and Natural Law*, pp. 264—266. (Trl.)

they have not what is the formal element in virginity, namely, the purpose of preserving this virginity for God's sake;[1] from which purpose it is that virginity derives its character of virtue. Hence Augustine says: "We do not extol in virgins the fact of their being virgins, but the fact of their being virgins dedicated to God by religious continence."

§ 3. Virtue may be repaired by penance so far as the formal element of the virtue goes, but not for the material element. For if a munificent man has wasted his riches, penance for his sin does not restore them to him again; and in like manner he who has lost his virginity by sin does not recover by penance the matter of virginity, but he recovers the purpose of virginity. As for the matter of it, there is one thing that cannot be restored, not even by miracle, namely, it cannot be that he who once has experienced sexual pleasure should come to the condition of never having experienced it: for God cannot make what is done undone.

§ 4. Virginity, as it is a virtue, means a purpose, strengthened by vow, of perpetually preserving one's integrity. For Augustine says: "By virginity the integrity of the flesh is vowed, consecrated, and preserved to the Creator of the soul and of the flesh." Hence virginity as a virtue is never lost except by sin.[2]

[1] Cf. the difference between *the fast of fasting* and *the fast of the faster*, q. 147 art. 1. § 3. (Trl.)

[2] That is, supposing the vow to be indispensable, which as a fact no vow is, though this point was not made out in St. Thomas's day. (Trl.)

ARTICLE IV.—*Is virginity more excellent than marriage?*

R. Divine good is better than human good: as well because the good of the soul is preferable to the good of the body, as also because the good of the contemplative life is preferable to the good of the active. But virginity is ordained to the good of the soul in the contemplative life, which is to "think on the things of the Lord:" whereas marriage is ordained to the good of the body, the bodily multiplication of the human race, and belongs to the active life, because husband and wife, living in the married state, are under necessity to think of "the things of the world."[1] And therefore beyond doubt virginity is to be preferred to conjugal continence.

§ 2. Though virginity is better than conjugal continence, still it may be that a married person is better than a virgin for two reasons. First, in regard of chastity itself, if the married person is more ready at heart to keep his virginity, if it were proper for him to do so, than the person who is actually a virgin. Hence Augustine instructs a virgin to say: "I am not better than Abraham, but better is the chastity of the unmarried than the chastity of the married." And he adds the explanation: "For what I do now, Abraham would have done better, if it had had to be done then; and what those saints of old did, that would I do now, if it were to be done." Secondly, because perchance he who is not a virgin has some virtue more excellent than virginity. Hence Augustine says: "Whence does

[1] 1 Cor. vii. 34.

the virgin know, all solicitous as she be for the things that belong to the Lord, whether perchance through some weakness of purpose, unknown to herself, she be yet unripe for martyrdom, while that married woman, to whom she was forward to prefer herself, is already capable of drinking the chalice of the Lord's Passion?"

ARTICLE V.—*Is virginity the greatest of virtues?*
R. When we call a thing most excellent, we may mean in one way that it is most excellent of its kind; and in that way virginity is most excellent of the kind of chastity: for it transcends the chastity both of the widowed and of the married state. And because beauty is eminently the attribute of chastity, therefore to virginity is attributed the most excellent beauty. Hence Ambrose says: "Who can conceive greater beauty than that of the virgin, who is loved by the King, approved by the Judge, dedicated to the Lord, consecrated to God?" In another way a thing is called most excellent absolutely; and in that way virginity is not the most excellent of virtues. For the end always excels the means to the end; and the more effectually a thing bears on the end, the better it is. But the end that renders virginity commendable is application to divine things. Hence the theological virtues, and even the virtue of religion, the act whereof is occupation with divine things, are preferred to virginity. Again, they put forth more energy in striving to adhere to God, who lay down their lives for that purpose, as the martyrs do; or who sacri-

fice their own will and all that they can have, as they do who live in monasteries, rather than virgins who sacrifice to this end sexual enjoyment.

§ 3. The virgins "follow the Lamb wheresoever he goeth,"[1] because they imitate Christ, not only in integrity of mind, but also in integrity of flesh; and therefore they follow the Lamb in more things than others do. Still it is not necessary that they should follow Him closer than others, because other virtues than virginity make a closer adherence to God by imitation of Him in the qualities of the mind. The "new canticle" that the virgins alone sing, is the joy that they have for having kept the integrity of their flesh.

QUESTION CLIII.

OF THE VICE OF LUXURY.

ARTICLE II.—*Can there be no sexual act without sin?*

R. Sin in human acts is what is against the order of reason. Now it is the function of that order to refer everything suitably to its own proper end. And therefore it is not a sin for man to make a reasonable use of things for the end to which they were made, in due mode and order, provided that end be something truly good. But as the preservation of the corporal nature of an individual is something truly good, so also is the preservation of the

[1] Apoc. xiv. 4.

nature of the human species an excellent good thing. Now as the use of food is directed to the preservation of the life of one man, so is the use of sexual intercourse directed to the preservation of the whole race of mankind. And therefore as the use of food can be without sin, when it is done in due mode and order as is proper for the welfare of the body, so the use of sexual intercourse can be without sin, done in due mode and order as is proper to the end of human generation.

§ 2. Abundance of pleasure in an act, when the act is directed according to reason, is not contrary to the golden mean of virtue. And besides, it matters not to virtue how much pleasure the exterior sense feels: that depends upon bodily disposition: what does matter is, how the inward desire stands affected to such pleasure. Nor from the fact that simultaneously with such pleasure reason can have no free play for the consideration of spiritual things, can it be shown that the act in question is contrary to virtue. Mere occasional interruption of the act of reason for some purpose according to reason, is not contrary to virtue: otherwise it would be contrary to virtue to go to sleep.

ARTICLE III.—*Can the luxury that is about sexual acts be a sin?*

R. The more necessary a thing is, the greater the need of the order of reason being observed in its regard; and consequently, the greater the vice, if the order of reason be there set aside. But the use of sexual intercourse is very necessary to the common good, being the preservation of the human race; and therefore here the observance of the order of reason is especially to be insisted on, and anything contrary to the order of reason in this matter will be vicious. But it is the nature of luxury to exceed the mode and order of reason in the matter of sexual pleasures; and therefore without doubt luxury is a sin.

ARTICLE IV.—*Is luxury a capital vice?*

R. A capital vice is a vice which has an end highly provocative of desire, so that by desire thereof a man is led to the commission of many sins, all of which are said to arise from that vice as from their main and principal source. But the end of luxury is a pleasure most attractive to the sensitive appetite, as well for the quantity of the pleasure as for the connaturalness of the desire. Hence plainly luxury is a capital vice.

ARTICLE V.—*Are the daughters of luxury duly stated to be—blindness of mind, inconsiderateness, headlong haste, inconstancy, self-love, hatred of God, affection for the present world, horror or despair of the world to come?*

R. When the inferior powers are strongly affected towards their objects, the consequence is that the superior powers are interfered with and thrown into disorder in their acts. But the vice of luxury strongly moves the inferior or concupiscible appetite to its object, that is, to pleasure, and consequently throws the higher powers, the reason and will, into very great disorder. Now there are four acts of reason when anything has to be done. The first is simple understanding, apprehending some end as good; and this act is hindered by luxury, according to the text: "Beauty hath deceived thee, and lust hath perverted thy heart."[1] And to this account is set down *blindness of mind*. The second act is counsel of the means to be taken to the end; and this also is hindered by lustful desire. Hence Terence says, speaking of lustful love: "You cannot guide by counsel a thing that admits neither of counsel nor of any restraint." And to this account is set down *headlong haste*, which means the withdrawal of counsel. The third act is judgment of the thing to be done; and this is hindered by luxury: for it is said of the licentious old men: "They perverted their own mind, that they might not remember just judgments."[2] And to this account is set down *inconsiderateness*. The fourth act is the command of reason for the thing to be done, which also is hindered by luxury, inasmuch as the assault of passion prevents the man from executing what he formerly resolved to do. Hence Terence says of some one who gave out that he was going to leave his mistress: "These words one little false tear will quench." There follow two inordinate acts on the part of the will. One of them is the desire of the end; and to this account is set down *self-love* in the matter of the pleasure that is inordinately sought, and on the

[1] Daniel xiii. 56.   [2] Daniel xiii. 9.

·other hand, *hatred of God*, as forbidding the coveted
pleasure. The other act is the desire of the means
to the end; and to this account is set down *affection
for the present world*, in which one wishes to enjoy
his pleasure; and on the other hand is set down
despair of the world to come, because the man too
much engrossed in carnal pleasures has no care
to arrive at spiritual joys, but loathes them.

§ 1. As the Philosopher says: "Intemperance
most of all destroys prudence;" and therefore it
is the vices opposed to prudence that most of all
arise from luxury, which is the chief species of
intemperance.

QUESTION CLIV.

OF THE PARTS OF LUXURY.

ARTICLE II.—*Is simple fornication a mortal sin?*

R. Without any doubt it is to be held that
simple fornication is a mortal sin. In proof whereof
we must observe that every sin is mortal, that is
committed directly against human life. But simple
fornication involves an inordinateness that tends to
the hurt of the life of the child, who is to be born
of such intercourse. For we see in the case of all
animals in which the care of male and female is
requisite for the rearing of the offspring, that there
is not among them promiscuous intercourse, but
the male is limited to one or more females, as in
all birds: whereas it is otherwise with animals in

which the female alone is sufficient to rear what she bears. But it is manifest that for the education of man there is required, not only the care of the mother by whom he is nourished, but much more the care of the father, by whom he has to be trained and defended, and advanced in all good gifts as well interior as exterior. And therefore promiscuity is against the nature of man: the intercourse of the male with the female must be with a fixed and certain person, with whom the man must stay, not for a short period, but for a long time, even for a lifetime. Hence it is natural in the human species for the male to be anxious to know his own offspring for certain, because he has the education of that offspring; but this certainty would be destroyed if there were promiscuous intercourse. This fixed assignment of the person of the female is called *matrimony*, which is said accordingly to be an institution of natural law. But because sexual intercourse is directed to the common good of the whole human race, and common good is subject to the determination of law, it follows that the union of male and female, which is called matrimony, has to be determined by some law. The way in which it is determined amongst us, is discussed in the treatise on the Sacrament of Matrimony. Hence, as fornication is promiscuous intercourse, being beside and out of wedlock, it is contrary to the good of the offspring that is to be educated: it is therefore a mortal sin. And a mortal sin it remains, even though the committer of fornication makes sufficient provision for the education of the child: for the determination of the law is taken according to what commonly happens, and not by what may happen in a particular case.[1]

ARTICLE III.

§ 1. The evil desire that aggravates sin consists in the inclination of the will. But evil desire in the sensitive appetite diminishes sin: because the stronger the passion under the impulse of which one sins, the less grievous is the sin. And such is the nature of the strength of the evil desire in this case, and very great it is. Hence Augustine says: "Of all the struggles of Christians, harder than the rest are the conflicts of chastity, where the fighting has to be done daily, and victory is rare." And Isidore says: "It is by the luxury of the flesh more than by anything else that the human race is made subject to the devil," the reason being, that it is harder to overcome the violence of this passion.

ARTICLE IV.—*Do touches and kisses amount to a mortal sin?*

R. A thing is said to be a mortal sin in two ways: in one way, *of its own kind;* and in this way kissing, embracing, or touching, are not acts that of their own nature imply mortal sin: for they may be done without passion, either in compliance with the custom of the country, or for some necessity

---

[1] St. Thomas's principle throughout comes to this: *An act which of its own nature is the initial act of paternity, must never be done in a way that is intrinsically incompatible with the rest of the office of a father.* See further, *Ethics and Natural Law*, pp. 263—272. (Trl.)

or reasonable cause. In another way a thing is said to be a mortal sin *for the motive that prompts it*: as he who gives alms to induce another to heresy, sins mortally by his unwholesome intention. Now not only consent to the act, but consent to the pleasure also of mortal sin, is itself a mortal sin. And therefore, since fornication is a mortal sin, and much more other species of luxury, it follows that consent to the pleasure of such a sin is a mortal sin, and not only consent to the act. And therefore, in so far as kisses and embraces of this sort are acts done for this sort of pleasure, it follows that they are mortal sins; and it is in that regard only that they are called lustful. Hence such acts, inasmuch as they are lustful acts, are mortal sins.

§ 2. Though kisses and touches do not of themselves hinder the good of human offspring, yet they proceed from lust, which is the root of such hinderance; and thence they derive the character of mortal sin.

ARTICLE V.—*Is nocturnal pollution a sin?*

R. Nocturnal pollution may be considered in two ways: in one way in itself; and in that way it does not bear the character of sin. For every sin depends on the judgment of reason: since even the first motion of sensuality has not the character of sin except inasmuch as it is capable of being checked by the judgment of reason; and therefore, when the judgment of reason is taken away, the character of sin is taken away. Now in the sleeping state the reason has not a free judgment. For there is no sleeper who does not take fantastic images of realities for the realities themselves.[1] And therefore what a man does asleep, not having the free judgment of reason, is not imputed to him to blame, as neither is that which a madman does.

In another way nocturnal pollution may be considered relatively to its cause. That cause may be in the first place bodily, when humour superabounds in the body. If then the superabundance of humour be from a culpable cause, as from excess in eating or drinking, than the nocturnal pollution has a guiltiness from its cause.[2] But if the superabundance of humour be from no culpable cause, then the nocturnal pollution is culpable neither in itself nor in its cause.

Another cause of nocturnal pollution may be psychical and interior, when it happens in consequence of some thinking done before in waking hours. Such thinking is sometimes purely specu-

---

[1] St. Thomas here refers back to p. 1. q. 84. art. 8. § 2., where amongst other things he writes of light sleep: "Not only the imagination remains free, but even common consciousness is in part set free, so that the man judges in his sleep that what he sees are dreams, as if he could then distinguish between realities and phantoms. But still common consciousness remains in some degree impeded. And therefore, though the man distinguishes some appearances from realities, yet in some he is always deceived. Thus then by the way that the consciousness is set free and the imagination in sleeping, the judgment of the intellect becomes free, not entirely however. Hence they who make syllogisms when they are asleep, always find on waking that they have been at fault on some point." (Trl.)

[2] Not however the guiltiness of luxury, unless the cause itself be of the kind of luxury, as instanced below. (Trl.)

lative, as when one makes carnal sins matter of scientific discussion; sometimes it is attended with a certain feeling either of attraction or horror. Nocturnal pollution however is more likely to happen, when the thought of carnal vices that occasions it has been attended with some attraction to such pleasures, because there remains thereof some vestige and inclination in the soul of the sleeper. Hence the Philosopher says that "the dreams of good men are better than those of the common run;" and Augustine, that "through the good disposition of the soul some of its merits appear in sleep." Thus again nocturnal pollution may derive a guiltiness from its cause. Sometimes however it follows from mere speculative thinking of carnal vices, even when attended with horror for them; and then it has no guiltiness, neither in itself nor in its cause. Thus it appears that nocturnal pollution is never a sin, but sometimes is the consequence of a sin preceding.

ARTICLE VIII.—*Is adultery a determinate species of luxury distinct from the rest?*

R. In adultery there is a twofold sin against chastity and the good of human generation: first, inasmuch as the adulterer cohabits with a woman not joined with him in wedlock, thus neglecting what is requisite for the good education of his own offspring; again, because he cohabits with a woman that is joined in wedlock with another man, thus hindering the good of another man's offspring. In the same way of the married woman that is corrupted by adultery. Hence it is said of her: "She hath offended against her husband,"[1] as her act makes against his certainty of her offspring: "She hath gotten her children of another man," which is against the good of her own offspring. Hence adultery is a determinate species of luxury.

ARTICLE XII.—*Is unnatural vice the greatest sin of all the species of luxury?*

R. The worst corruption in every kind is the corruption of the principle on which all the rest depends. Now the principles from which reason starts are the principles established by nature: for reason, supposing those things that nature has determined, disposes of other things according as is fitting; and this appears both in speculation and in practice. And therefore, as in matters of speculation the most grievous and most shameful error is in things of which man has knowledge furnished him by nature, so in matters of practice the most grievous and shameful action is that which goes against what is determined according to nature. Since then in unnatural vice man transgresses what is determined according to nature concerning the use of sexual pleasures, it follows that sin in this matter is most grievous. The next most heinous form is *incest,* which is against the natural reverence due to those who are bound to us by ties of kindred.

[1] Ecclus. xxiii. 33.

QUESTION CLV.

OF THE POTENTIAL PARTS OF TEMPERANCE;
AND FIRST OF CONTINENCE.[1]

ARTICLE I.—*Is continence a virtue?*

R. The name of *continence* is taken in two several ways by different authors. Some take the name to mean abstinence from all sexual pleasure. In this sense virginity is perfect continence, and widowhood secondary continence. But others call *continence* resistance to evil passions in a case where they are violent; and this is the way that the Philosopher takes *continence*. This continence has something of the character of virtue, inasmuch as reason makes a firm stand against the passions, not to be led away by them. Still it does not attain to the perfect standard of moral virtue, according to which even the sensitive appetite is subject to reason, so that violent passions contrary to reason do not arise therein. And therefore the Philosopher says that "continence is not a virtue, but an intermediate condition," inasmuch as it has something of virtue, and in some respect falls short

[1] St. Thomas's view of continence will prove scarcely intelligible to the reader who is not master of the contents of a note subjoined to I-II. q. 58. art. 3. (Trl.)

of virtue. Taking however virtue in the wider sense of the term, to mean any principle whatever of praiseworthy acts, we may say that continence is a virtue.

§ 2. Man is properly that which he is according to reason.

ARTICLE III.—*Is the concupiscible faculty the subject of continence?*

R. Every virtue, whatever subject it resides in, makes that subject differ from the disposition that it has when under the opposite vice. But the concupiscible faculty is precisely in the same state in the continent as in the incontinent man: because in both the one and the other it breaks out into violent evil desires. Hence it is plain that the subject of continence is not the concupiscible faculty. In like manner also the reason is in the same state in both: because both the continent and the incontinent man has his reason straight and right as it should be; and each of them, when he is not under passion, has a purpose of not yielding to unlawful desires. The first difference between them is found in their choice of action: because the continent man, violent as are his passions, chooses to withstand them for reason's sake: while the incontinent man chooses to yield to his, for all the contradiction of reason. And therefore the subject in which continence resides must be that power of the soul whose act is choice; and that is the will.

ARTICLE IV.—*Is continence better than temperance?*

R. Taking continence to mean the resistance of reason to strong evil desires, temperance is much better than continence: because the good of virtue is praiseworthy from being according to reason; and the good of reason is more robust in the temperate man, in whom even the very sensitive appetite is subject, and as it were broken in, to reason, than in the continent man, whose sensitive appetite makes violent resistance to reason by evil passions. Hence continence stands to temperance as the imperfect to the perfect.

§ 2. There are two possible causes for the strength or weakness of passion. Sometimes the cause is corporal: as some from their physical constitution have stronger inclinations than others; and again some have opportunities of pleasure more apt to inflame desire than others have. Arising from such a cause, weakness of passion diminishes merit; while strength of passion increases it. But sometimes weakness of passion is traceable to a praiseworthy spiritual cause, namely, to intensity of charity, or to strength of reason, as is the case with the temperate man. And in this way weakness of passion increases merit by reason of the cause that it is due to.

§ 3. The will stands nearer to reason than does the sensitive appetite. Hence the good of reason, which is what is praiseworthy in virtue, is shown to be greater by its reaching, not only to the will, but also to the concupiscible faculty, as is the case with the temperate man,—greater than it would be if it reached only to the will, as is the case with him who is merely continent.

QUESTION CLVI.
OF INCONTINENCE.

ARTICLE I.—*Does incontinence belong to the soul or to the body?*

R. Everything is attributed rather to that which is its ordinary cause than to that which merely affords it occasion. But whatever there is on the part of the body, merely affords occasion for incontinence. It may happen from the disposition of the body that violent passions arise in the sensitive appetite; but passions, however violent, are not a sufficient cause of incontinence, but only an occasion: for while the use of reason lasts, man can always resist his passions. And therefore the ordinary cause of incontinence is on the part of the soul, which does not resist the passions by the use of reason.

§ 3. The concupiscence of the flesh in the incontinent man overcomes the spirit, not of necessity, but by some negligence of the spirit not resisting vigorously.

ARTICLE II.

§ 1. Man can avoid sin and do good, not however without the divine assistance, according to the text:

"Without me you can do nothing."[1] Hence man's need of the divine assistance in order to be continent, does not exclude incontinence from being a sin, because, as is said, "What we can do by our friends, we can in a manner do of ourselves."

ARTICLE III.—*Does the incontinent man sin more than the intemperate?*[2]

R. Sin, according to Augustine, lies principally in the will: for "it is by the will that we sin or live aright." And therefore, where there is greater inclination of the will to sin, there is more grievous sin. But in the intemperate man the will is inclined to sin by its own choice, that proceeds from a habit acquired by custom:[3] whereas in the incontinent man the will is inclined to sin by some passion. And because passion quickly passes off, whereas a habit is a quality difficult to change, it follows that the incontinent man repents at once, when the fit of passion is over, which happens not with the intemperate man: nay, the latter is even glad to have sinned, because the act of sin by habit has become connatural to him. Hence it is said of such that they "are glad when they have done evil, and rejoice in most wicked things."[4] Hence it is clear

---

[1] St. John xv. 5.

[2] The *intemperate man* here does not mean the mere drunkard, but the man who has a confirmed habit of any or all of the vices that are directly opposed to the cardinal virtue of temperance, and who sins by habit and on principle, whereas the *incontinent man* sins by the impulse of one hour and is sorry for it the next. (Trl.)

[3] On habit and custom, see *Ethics and Natural Law*, p. 67. (Trl.)

[4] Prov. ii. 14.

that the intemperate man is much worse than the incontinent, as the Philosopher also says.[1]

§ 1. Ignorance of the understanding sometimes precedes the inclination of the appetite, and causes it; and where that is the case, the greater the ignorance, the less the sin, which even may be totally excused inasmuch as ignorance causes involuntariness. In another way, conversely, ignorance on the part of the reason follows the inclination of appetite; and the greater such ignorance, the more grievous the sin, because it argues a stronger inclination of appetite. Now the ignorance as well of the incontinent as of the intemperate man arises from the fact of the appetite being inclined somehow, whether by passion as in the incontinent, or by habit as in the intemperate. But greater ignorance is hereby caused in the intemperate than in the incontinent. This appears in one way in point of duration, because in the incontinent the ignorance lasts only while the passion lasts, like the access of a fever; but the ignorance of the intemperate lasts continually on account of the permanence of the habit: hence it is likened, as the Philosopher says, to consumption or any chronic disease. There is

[1] The reference is to the famous chapter of the *Nicomachean Ethics*, VII. viii., which chapter, with this Article of St. Thomas, well reveals the folly of the old Jansenist treatment of relapsing penitents, as though such people were all *intemperate*, whereas they are, most of them, merely *incontinent*. The *intemperate* man does not come to confession, except from motives of hypocrisy, when the way of the world about him takes him there. The words *incontinent* and *intemperate* here of course are used, not in their common English meaning, but in the technical sense of St. Thomas and Aristotle, for which see once more I-II. q. 58. art. 3. § 2. note. (Trl.)

another way in which the ignorance of the intemperate is the greater, and that is in respect of the matter of which he is ignorant. For the ignorance of the incontinent man is in respect of some particular object of choice, which he here and now takes to be worthy of choice; but the intemperate man labours under ignorance touching his very end and aim, judging it to be a good thing to yield himself to his lusts without restraint. Hence the Philosopher says that "better is the incontinent man than the intemperate, because in the former the best thing, namely, the principle, is saved," to wit, a right estimate of the end and aim of life.

§ 2. For the cure of the incontinent mere knowledge is not sufficient, but there is required the inward aid of grace mitigating concupiscence, and also an application of the external remedy of admonition and correction; by which means the man begins to resist his passions, and such resistance weakens passion. And by the same means the intemperate man also may be cured, but his cure is more difficult for two reasons. The first is regarding his reason, which has got warped in its estimate of the final end and aim, which end and aim is in practice what a principle is in demonstrative science. But it is more difficult to bring back to the truth one who errs in a matter of principle; and in like manner in practical things, it is more difficult to bring back one who errs in respect of the end and aim of life. The second reason regards the inclination of the appetite, which in the intemperate man is a thing of habit, and that is hard to remove; but the inclination of the incontinent man comes of passion, which can be more easily repressed.

§ 3. The lust of the will, which increases the sin, is greater in the intemperate than in the incontinent. But the lust of concupiscence of the sensitive appetite is at times greater in the incontinent, who never sins except under grave concupiscence; whereas the intemperate man sins even under slight concupiscence, and at times anticipates concupiscence.

ARTICLE IV.—*Is the man who is incontinent of anger, worse than him who is incontinent of concupiscence?*

R. The sin of incontinence may be considered in two ways. In one way, in respect of the passion whereby reason is overcome; and in this way incontinence of concupiscence is more disgraceful than incontinence of anger, because the motion of concupiscence has a greater inordinateness than the motion of anger. And this for four reasons: first, because the motion of anger is in some way partaker in reason, inasmuch as the angry man is striving to avenge an injury done him, a course that reason in some sort dictates, yet not altogether, because he does not seek the due mode and manner of vengeance: whereas the motion of concupiscence is entirely according to sense, and nowise according to reason. Secondly, because the motion of anger follows more upon a bodily constitution prone to anger than concupiscence follows upon a bodily disposition thereto: but what comes of a physical disposition of the body is accounted more pardonable. Thirdly, because anger seeks to go to work more openly, but concupiscence seeks lurking-places and comes in by stealth. Fourthly, because under concupiscence a man acts with pleasure; but under anger he acts as it were under the coercion of an antecedent annoyance. In another way, the sin of incontinence may be considered in respect of the evil into which one falls by departing from reason; and in this way incontinence of anger is generally the more grievous, because it leads to the hurt and damage of one's neighbour.

QUESTION CLVII.

OF CLEMENCY AND MEEKNESS.

ARTICLE I.—*Are clemency and meekness quite the same thing?*

R. Moral virtue deals with passions and actions. Now interior passions are mainsprings of exterior actions, or obstacles to the same. And therefore the virtues that regulate the passions concur in some sort to the same effect as the virtues that regulate actions, though they differ in species from them. Thus to justice it properly belongs to restrain a man from theft, to which he is inclined by that inordinate love and desire of money which is checked by liberality;[1] and therefore liberality concurs with justice to the effect of abstinence from theft. And so in the matter before us, the passion of anger provokes one to inflict too severe a penalty; while it is the direct office of clemency to tend to diminish penalties, which office may be made ineffectual by excess of anger. And therefore meekness, as curbing the impetuosity of anger, concurs to the same effect as clemency; and yet the two differ from one another, inasmuch as clemency goes to moderate the external punishment, while meekness properly diminishes the passion of anger.

ARTICLE II.

§ 2. Clemency works for the diminution of penalties, not bringing them below the standard fixed by right reason, but still below the standard of the general law which legal justice observes: clemency however, in view of particular considerations, diminishes the penalties, and decrees that the man is not to be further punished.

ARTICLE III.

§ 1. One thing is the diminution of penalties according to the intention of the legislator, though not according to the words of the law; and this belongs to equity. Another thing is a moderation of temper withholding a man from using his full power to inflict penalties; and this properly belongs

---

[1] St. Thomas has told us (q. 117. art. 2. § 1.): "The interior passions"—of love and desire of money—"are the immediate matter of liberality: but the external thing, money, is the object of those passions." (Trl.)

to clemency. And this moderation of temper comes from a certain sweetness of disposition, moving one to abhor all that can give pain to another. Hence Seneca says, "Clemency is a gentleness of spirit." Conversely, sternness seems to be the quality of a mind that makes no scruple of putting others to pain.

ARTICLE IV.—*Are clemency and meekness virtues of the first rank?*

R. There may be virtues of the first rank, which are so not absolutely and in all respects, but relatively and in a certain sort. Now clemency and meekness cannot be virtues absolutely of the first rank, because their merit consists in removing men from evil by diminishing anger or punishment, whereas it is more perfect to attain to good than to be free from evil. And therefore the virtues of faith, hope, and charity, and even prudence and justice, which absolutely lead to good, are absolutely greater virtues than clemency and meekness. But relatively clemency and meekness may well claim a certain pre-eminence among all the virtues that resist impulses to evil. For the impetuosity of anger, which is mitigated by meekness, is a particular hinderance to the mind of man from freely judging of the truth: and therefore meekness particularly makes a man master of himself; while clemency in abating penalties seems to come very near to charity, which is the chief of virtues, prompting us to do good to our neighbours and prevent evil to them.

§ 1. Meekness prepares a man for the knowledge of God by removing obstacles to that knowledge, first, by making him master of himself through the abatement of anger; and again, inasmuch as it is a point of meekness not to contradict the words of truth, as many men do contradict them, under the excitement of anger.

QUESTION CLVIII.

OF IRASCIBILITY.

ARTICLE I.—*Is it lawful to get angry?*
R. Evil may be found in the passions sometimes by the mere *species* of the passion, as determined by its object. Thus envy from its species involves evil: for it is sadness at another's good, of itself an irrational thing; and therefore the mere mention of envy points at once to something evil. But this is not the case with anger, or the craving for vengeance: for vengeance may be sought either well or ill. In another way, evil is found in a passion in respect of the *quantity*, that is, the excess or defect of the passion. In this way evil may be found in anger, when one is angry overmuch or too little, beside the mark of right reason. But if one is angry according to right reason, then to get angry is praiseworthy.

§ 2. Anger may stand to reason either *antecedently*, and so draw reason from its right course, and hence have a character of evil, or *consequently*, moving the sensitive appetite according to the order of reason against vices; and this anger is good, and is called the *anger of zeal*. Hence Gregory says: "The greatest care must be taken that anger, which is taken up for an instrument of virtue, come not to have dominion over the mind, nor rule as mistress there; but like a handmaid ready to serve, let her know her place at the back of reason's chair." Anger such as this, although in the execution of the deed it does to some extent impede the judgment of reason, still does not destroy the rectitude of reason. Hence Gregory says that "the anger of zeal troubles the eye of reason, but the anger of vice quite blinds it." But it is not against the idea of virtue that the deliberation of reason should be interrupted, while the execution of what has been determined by reason is going on; since art also would be impeded in its action, if it had to deliberate about the thing to be done when it ought to be doing it.

§ 3. To seek vengeance in order to work evil on him who has to be punished, is unlawful; but to seek vengeance in order to work the correction of vice and the maintenance of the good of justice, is praiseworthy; and to this end the sensitive appetite can tend, inasmuch as it is moved by reason. And while vengeance is accomplished according to the order of judicial procedure, it is accomplished by God, whose minister the authority is that punishes.[1]

[1] Cf. above, q. 108. art. 1. (Trl.)

§ 4. To the text, "Thou being master of power judgest with tranquillity,"[1] it is to be said that we can and ought to liken ourselves to God in seeking after what is good; but in the mode of seeking after it we cannot liken ourselves to Him at all: because in God there is no sensitive appetite as there is in us, the movement of which ought to second the action of reason.[2]

ARTICLE II.

§ 1. In passion considered absolutely, there is no character of merit or demerit, praise or blame. But according as passion is regulated by reason, it can bear the character of something meritorious and praiseworthy; and contrariwise as it is not regulated by reason.

§ 3. The movements that forestall the judgment of reason are not in a person's power universally, so that none such shall ever arise; though reason can hinder any such movement taken singly, if it arises. And in this way it is said that the movement of anger is not in a person's power, not so far, that is to say, as that none shall arise. Since however the movement is in some sort in the person's power, it does not entirely lose the character of sin, if it be inordinate.

§ 4. The irascible faculty in man is naturally subject to reason; and therefore its act is natural to man so far as it is according to reason; and so far as it is beside the order of reason it is against the nature of man.

[1] Wisdom xii. 18.   [2] Cf. I-II. q. 24. art. 2. (Trl.)

Article IV.—*Is anger a very grievous sin?*

R. If we look at the object of desire that the angry man has before him, anger seems to be the least of sins: for anger desires some penal evil in the light of something good, namely, as vengeance; and therefore, in respect of the evil that it desires, the sin of anger goes with those sins which desire the evil of a neighbour, to wit, with envy and hatred. But hatred seeks simply the evil of another as such: the envious man seeks the evil of another through desire of his own glory; while the angry man seeks the evil of another in the light of a just vengeance. Hence it appears that hatred is more grievous than envy, and envy than anger. But in respect of inordinateness of manner, anger goes beyond other sins for the violence and rapidity of its movement. Hence Gregory says: "Kindling with anger the heart flutters, the body trembles, the speech suffers impediment, the face glows, the eyes flash, the visage is unrecognizable, the tongue sets up a clamour, but mind can put no construction on what it says."

Article VI.—*Should anger have a place among the capital vices?*

R. That is called a capital vice, from which many vices take their origin. Now anger has the property of originating many vices in two ways: first, on the part of its object, which is something highly desirable, as vengeance is sought in the light of something just and proper, and attractive by its intrinsic fitness; and then again from the impetuosity of the onset of anger, whereby it casts the mind headlong to the doing of all disorder. Hence clearly anger is a capital vice.

§ 3. To the words of the gloss, "Irascibility is the gate of all vices: when that is shut, rest will be given to the virtues within: when that is open, the spirit will sally forth to the commission of all crime," it is to be said that anger is called *the gate of vices* incidentally, as removing the obstacle to their free course, that is, impeding the judgment of reason. It is at the same time directly and ordinarily the cause of certain special sins, which are called its *daughters*.

ARTICLE VII.—*Are the daughters of anger duly assigned to be six: brawling, swelling of spirit, contumely, clamour, indignation, and blasphemy?*

R. Anger may be considered in three ways: first, as it is in the heart; and in that way there are born of anger two vices: one on the part of him against whom the man is angry, and whom he reckons an unworthy person to offer him such a slight, and in view of this there is set down *indignation;* the other on the part of the angry man himself, inasmuch as he goes thinking out divers methods of revenge, and his mind is filled with such thoughts, and in view of this there is set down *swelling of spirit*. In another way, anger is considered as it is in the mouth; and in that way a twofold inordinateness proceeds: one inasmuch as the man shows his anger in his way of speaking, and in view of that is set down *clamour*, which means disorderly and confused speech; the other inordinateness consists in breaking out into injurious words, either against God, and that will be *blasphemy*, or against one's neighbour, and that will be *contumely*. In a third way, anger is considered as proceeding to deeds, and so from anger there arise *brawls*, by which are understood all hurts by deed done in anger to a neighbour.

ARTICLE VIII.—*Is there any vice, the opposite of irascibility, arising from lack of anger?*

R. If anger is taken for a simple motion of the will, whereby one inflicts punishment, not out of passion, but on principle, lack of anger in that sense is undoubtedly a sin. Otherwise, taking anger for a motion of the sensitive appetite, attended with passion and bodily symptoms, we must say that in man such a motion necessarily follows upon the simple motion of the will; because naturally the inferior appetite follows the move of the superior appetite, unless something comes in the way. And therefore the motion of anger cannot altogether be wanting in the sensitive appetite, except by the cessation or weakening of the motion of the will. Consequently the absence of the passion of anger is as much a vice as is the failure of the movement of the will to punish according to the judgment of reason.

§ 1. He who is totally devoid of anger when he ought to be angry, imitates God indeed in respect of the absence of passion, but not in respect of this, that God punishes on principle.

§ 2. The passion of anger is useful, as are all other motions of the sensitive appetite, to the end that man may more promptly fulfil what reason dictates: otherwise to no purpose would the sensitive appetite be in man, whereas nature does nothing in vain.

QUESTION CLIX.

OF CRUELTY.

ARTICLE I.

"The opposite of clemency is cruelty, which is nothing else than sternness in the exaction of penalties."[1]

§ 1. Rational abatement of penalties is an act of equity, but the sweetness of disposition that prompts such abatement belongs to clemency: so also excess of punishment, so far as the outward act goes, is an act of injustice; but as for the austerity of temper that makes one forward to lay on increase of punishment, that excess belongs to cruelty.

§ 2. Mercy and clemency agree in both of them shrinking from and abhorring the making of another miserable: but to mercy it belongs to relieve misery by the bestowal of kindness; to clemency to diminish misery by abatement of penalties. And because cruelty means excess in the exaction of penalties, cruelty is more directly opposed to clemency than to mercy.

[1] Seneca, *De Clementia*, ii. 4.

ARTICLE II.—*Does cruelty differ from savagery, or brutality?*

R. The name of *savagery*, or *brutality*, is so called from the likeness that it bears to wild beasts, who are also called *savage*. For these sort of animals do hurt to men in order to feed on their bodies, not for any cause of justice, since the consideration of that belongs to reason only. And therefore, properly speaking, it is called *brutality*, or *savagery*, when in inflicting punishments a man considers not any fault of the person who is punished, but has regard merely to his own delight in the torture of his fellows. This is clearly a case of brutality: for such delight is not human but brutal, coming either from evil custom or from corruption of nature, as do other similar bestial proclivities. Cruelty, on the other hand, has regard to the fault that is in the party that is punished, but exceeds due measure in punishing. And therefore cruelty differs from savagery, or brutality, as human malice differs from that which is bestial.

QUESTION CLXI.

OF HUMILITY.

ARTICLE I.—*Is humility a virtue?*

R. There is this about arduous good, that it has something in it to attract the appetite, namely, the quality itself of goodness; and something to repel, namely, the difficulty of attaining that which is so attractive. On the former ground there arises the motion of hope, on the latter the motion of despair. Again, in the movements of appetite that come as impulses urging us forward, there must be a moral virtue moderating and curbing: but in regard of those movements that are by way of drawing back and shrinking, there must be a moral virtue to strengthen and urge us on. And therefore two virtues are necessarily concerned with the appetite for arduous good : one to check and curb the mind, that it run not to excess after high things, and this is the work of the virtue of humility; another to strengthen the mind against despair, and urge it on to the prosecution of great enterprises according to right reason, and this is magnanimity. Evidently therefore there is such a virtue as humility.

§ 3. Humility checks the appetite, that it tend not to great things beyond right reason: while magnanimity urges the spirit on to great endeavours according to right reason. It appears then that magnanimity is not opposed to humility, but the two agree in this, that they are both according to right reason.

§ 4. The Philosopher[1] intended to treat of virtues according as they are referred to the end of civil life, in which life the subjection of one man to another is determined by order of law, and is matter of legal justice. But humility, as it is a special virtue, particularly regards the subjection of man to God, for whose sake also he humbles himself in submission to other men.

ARTICLE II.—*Is humility concerned with the appetitive faculty?*

R. It belongs properly to humility that a man should repress himself, and not reach out to what is above him. To this end it is necessary that he should know the measure in which he falls short of what is above his strength. And therefore the knowledge of one's own shortcoming belongs to humility, serving as a guiding rule to appetite; but humility essentially resides in the appetite itself.

[1] Aristotle in his *Ethics* makes no mention of humility: indeed that virtue hardly has a name in classical Greek. The Philosopher tells us (*Ethics*, IV. c. iii. n. 4), with something of a sneer: "The man who is good for little, and rates himself accordingly, is sensible, but not magnanimous." Such a one stands in contrast with the magnanimous man, the man who is worth a great deal and knows it, the Alexander or Napoleon of his day, who (in Aristotle's conception of him) has no notion of abasing himself before any man, and whom to attempt to govern were like "claiming to rule over Jupiter." *Politics*, III. c. xiii. n. 25. (Trl)

And therefore it is the proper office of humility to direct and control the motion of the appetitive faculty.

§ 3. Humility seems principally to imply subjection of man to God; and therefore Augustine, who by "poverty of spirit"[1] understands humility, sets it down to the gift of fear, whereby man reveres God.

ARTICLE III.—*Ought a man in humility to take all men for his superiors?*

R. In man two things may be considered: what there is of God, and what there is of man. Of man there is whatever points to defect; but of God is all that makes for salvation and perfection, according to the text: "Destruction is thy own, O Israel; thy help is only in me."[2] Now humility properly regards the reverence whereby a man is subject to God. And therefore every man ought to count himself, for what there is of his own, inferior to his neighbour for what there is of God in that neighbour. But humility does not require one to count what there is of God in himself inferior to what he can see of God in another. For they who partake of the gifts of God know that they have them, according to the text: "That we may know the things that are given us from God."[3] And therefore, without prejudice to humility, men may prefer the gifts they have themselves received to the gifts of God that they see bestowed on others, as the Apostle says: "In other generations it was not

---
[1] St. Matt. v. 3. [2] Osee xiii. 9. [3] 1 Cor. ii. 12.

known as now it is revealed to his holy apostles."[1] In like manner humility does not require that any man should deem what is his own in himself inferior to that which is of man in his neighbour: otherwise everybody would have to reckon himself a greater sinner than everybody else; whereas the Apostle says, without prejudice to humility: "We by nature are Jews, and not of the Gentiles sinners."[2] But a man may reckon that there is some good in his neighbour which he has not himself got, or some evil in himself that is not in another man; and on that score he may in humility esteem himself inferior to another.

§ 2. If we prefer what there is of God in our neighbour to what there is of our own in ourselves, we cannot be betrayed into falsehood.

§ 3. Humility, like other virtues, resides principally in the soul. And therefore a man in inward act may hold himself inferior to another; but in the outward acts of humility, as in the acts of other virtues, due moderation is to be observed, that they may not tend to the detriment of our neighbour. But if you do what you ought to do, and others take thence occasion to sin, that is not imputable to your humble behaviour: because you have given no scandal, however much another may be scandalized.

ARTICLE IV.—*Is humility a part of temperance?*

R. In assigning parts to the virtues, the principal thing to consider is the likeness in the mode of

[1] Ephes. iii. 5.   [2] Galat. ii. 15.

virtue. Now the mode of temperance, from which it chiefly has praise, is the curbing or repression of the impetuosity of passion. And therefore all virtues that curb or repress impetuous affections, or put a check upon conduct, are set down as parts of temperance. But as meekness represses the movement of anger, so humility represses the movement of hope, which is a motion of the spirit tending to great things. And therefore, as meekness is set down for a part of temperance, so also is humility.

§ 2. Parts are assigned to the primary virtues, not as they agree in subject or matter, but as they agree in their formal mode of being. And therefore, though the subject in which humility resides be the irascible faculty, yet the virtue is put down as part of temperance on account of its mode.

§ 3. Though magnanimity and humility agree in matter, yet they differ in mode; on which account magnanimity is set down as part of fortitude, and humility as part of temperance.

ARTICLE V.—*Is humility chiefest of virtues?*

R. The good of human virtue lies in the order of reason, which order obtains principally in reference to the end. Hence the theological virtues, that have the ultimate end for their object, stand above all others. The order of reason, in the second place, obtains in regard of means to the end. This reference lies essentially in the reason itself that makes it: by participation it lies in the appetitive faculty that is referred to the end by reason. The reference of the appetitive faculty to the end is in general the work of justice, especially of legal justice.[1] Now humility makes a man thoroughly submit to the award of legal justice on all points alike; while every other virtue produces this submission on some particular matter. And therefore, after the theological virtues, and after the intellectual virtues which regard reason itself, and after justice, legal justice especially, humility ranks above the rest of the virtues.[2]

§ 2. The first step in the acquisition of virtues is in one way the removal of obstacles; and in this way humility is the first step, as expelling pride, and rendering man subject and open to receiving the influx of divine grace, emptying the tumour of pride. Hence it is said: "God resisteth the proud, and giveth grace to the humble."[3] And in this respect humility is called the foundation of the spiritual edifice. But the first positive step in the acquisition of virtues is drawing near to God; and the first drawing near to God is by faith, according to the text: "He that cometh to God must believe."[4] And in this respect faith is laid down for a foundation in a nobler style than humility.

§ 4. The reason why Christ has particularly commended humility to us, is because thereby is removed the chief obstacle to man's salvation. For man's salvation consists in tending to things

[1] It should be remembered that the *appetitive faculty* includes the will, which is called the *rational appetite*. (Trl.)
[2] Religion (q. 81. art. 6.) and obedience (q. 104. art. 3.) are ranked above the other moral virtues, and consequently above humility. But they are both of them potential parts of justice. (Trl.)
[3] St. James iv. 6.   [4] Hebrews xi. 6.

heavenly and spiritual, from which he is hindered by striving to magnify himself in earthly things. And therefore, for the removal of this obstacle, our Lord has shown by examples of humility how external grandeur should be despised. And thus humility is a predisposition to man's free approach to spiritual and divine goods. As then perfection is better than a predisposition thereto, so charity and other virtues, by which a man positively tends to God, are preferred to humility.

ARTICLE VI.—*Are the twelve degrees of humility duly marked in the scheme of Blessed Benedict?*

R. Humility resides essentially in the appetite, and consists in man's curbing the impetuosity of his spirit so that it shall not tend inordinately to great things; at the same time it finds its rule in the cognitive faculty, in the knowledge that keeps a man from esteeming himself above his real worth: and the principle and root of both these growths is reverence for God. Now from a disposition of humility within there proceed certain outward signs in words and deeds and gestures, as in the case of other virtues, for "a man is known by his look, and a wise man, when thou meetest him, is known by his countenance."[1] And therefore in the aforesaid degrees of humility there is set down something that belongs to the root of humility, which is the *twelfth* degree, to the effect that a man should fear God, and be mindful of all His commandments. There is also set down something appertaining to

[1] Ecclus. xix. 26.

appetite, to avoid inordinate striving after excellence, and that in three particulars. One is that a man should not follow his own will; and that is the *eleventh* degree. Another is that he should regulate his will according to the will of his superior; and that is the *tenth* degree. A third is that he should not desist from this for the hardships and severities that he meets with; and this is the *ninth* degree. There are also set down some points appertaining to the man's thought and recognition of his own shortcomings; and that in three ways. One is recognition and acknowledgment of his own shortcomings; and that is the *eighth* degree. The second is, upon consideration of one's own deficiencies, to esteem oneself insufficient for greater posts, and that is the *seventh* degree. The third is to prefer others to oneself in this regard; and that is the *sixth* degree. There are also set down some points appertaining to outward signs: one of which is that a man should not in his works withdraw himself from the common way; and that is the *fifth* degree. Two others are concerning words: that a man should not be hasty to anticipate the time to speak; and that is the *fourth* degree; nor exceed measure in his speech: and that is the *second* degree. Two others are taken up with exterior behaviour: namely, in repressing the raising of the eyes, which is the *first* degree; and in checking laughter and other signs of foolish mirth, which is the *third* degree.

QUESTION CLXII.

OF PRIDE.

ARTICLE I.—*Is pride a special sin?*

R. The sin of pride may be considered in one way in its own proper species which it has in regard of its proper object; and in this way pride is a special sin, because it has a special object: for it is an inordinate desire to excel. In another way it may be considered as redounding upon other sins: and in this way it has a certain general agency, inasmuch as all sins may arise out of pride. That they may do in two ways: either in the regular and ordinary course, inasmuch as other sins are directed to the end of pride, which is to excel, and everything that is inordinately desired may be reduced to excellence; or again indirectly or incidentally by removal of the obstacle, inasmuch as by pride man despises the divine law by which he is restrained from sinning, according to the text: "Thou hast broken my yoke, thou hast burst my bands, and thou saidst, I will not serve."[1] We must observe, however, that the general agency of pride goes thus far, that all vices may at times arise out of pride, but not so far as that all vices always do arise

[1] Jerem. ii. 20.

out of pride. For although all the commandments of the law may be transgressed in any variety of sin by contempt, which is a piece of pride, yet the commandments are not always transgressed out of contempt, but sometimes out of ignorance, sometimes out of weakness. And hence it is that, as Augustine says, "many things are wrongly done, that are not done in pride."

§ 3. A sin may spoil a virtue in one way by being directly contrary to the virtue; and in this way pride does not spoil every assignable virtue, but only humility, as every other special sin spoils the special virtue opposed to it, by working the contrary effect. There is another way in which a sin spoils a virtue, by abusing the said virtue; and in this way pride spoils every virtue, inasmuch as it takes occasion of growing proud from the virtues, as it does from all other points of excellence.

ARTICLE III.—*Is the irascible faculty the subject in which pride resides?*

R. To find the subject of any virtue or vice we must inquire after the proper object of it. For the object of any habit or act cannot be different from the object of the power wherein they both reside. But the proper object of pride is arduous matter. Hence pride must belong somehow to the irascible faculty. But the irascible faculty may be looked at in two ways. In one way properly, as it is part of the sensitive appetite, of which sensitive appetite, anger, properly understood, is a passion. In another way the irascible faculty may be taken in a wider sense of the term to extend even to the intellectual appetite; to which appetite anger is sometimes attributed, in the sense in which we ascribe anger to God and to the angels, not as a passion, but as a judgment of justice passing sentence. If then the arduous matter, which is the object of pride, were merely something sensible to which the sensitive appetite could tend, then pride would needs be in the irascible faculty, which is part of the sensitive appetite. But because the arduous matter that pride regards is found alike in sensible and in spiritual things, we must say that the subject of pride is the irascible faculty, not merely properly so called, as it is part of the sensitive appetite, but taken in a wider sense, as it is found in the intellectual appetite. Hence pride is placed also in the devils.

§ 1. The knowledge of truth is twofold: one purely speculative; and this knowledge pride hinders indirectly, by taking away the cause that gives it birth. For the proud man neither subjects his intellect to God, so as to gather the knowledge of truth from Him, according to the text, " Thou hast hidden these things from the wise and prudent,"[1] that is, from the proud who think themselves wise and prudent, "and revealed them to little ones," that is, to the humble; nor again does he condescend to learn from men, though it is said, "If thou wilt incline thine ear," that is, listen humbly, "thou shalt receive instruction."[2] There is another knowledge of the truth that is practical, and such

[1] St. Matt. xi. 25. [2] Ecclus. vi. 34.

knowledge is directly hindered by pride, because proud men, delighting in their own excellence, scorn the excellence of truth. As Gregory says: "Though the proud understand and grasp sundry recondite truths, they cannot experience the sweetness of them; and though they know how the truth stands, they are ignorant of how it tastes." Hence it is said: "Where humility is, there also is wisdom."[1]

ARTICLE IV.

§ 1. True judgment may be corrupted in two ways. One way is in the general, and in that way true judgment on matters of faith is corrupted by unbelief. Another way in which true judgment may be corrupted is in regard of some particular object of choice: and this is no case of unbelief. Thus any one who commits fornication, judges for the time being that it is good for him to commit that sin; and yet he is not an unbeliever, as he would be if he were to say in general that fornication is a good thing. So again it is a piece of unbelief to say in general that there is any good gift that is not of God, or that grace is given to men for their deserving; but for a man to be moved by an inordinate seeking of his own excellence, so to glory in his own good parts as if he had them of himself, or of his own deserving, is a piece of pride and not of unbelief, properly speaking.[2]

ARTICLE V.—*Is pride a mortal sin?*
R. Pride is opposed to humility, and humility

[1] Prov. xi. 2.   [2] Cf. I-II. q. 77. art. 2. (Trl.)

properly regards the subjection of man to God: hence contrariwise pride properly regards the want of this subjection, in that one lifts himself up above the limit prefixed for him according to the divine rule or measure, contrary to what the Apostle says: "We will not glory beyond our measure, but according to the measure of the rule which God hath measured to us."[1] And therefore it is said: "The beginning of the pride of man is to fall off from God;"[2] because the root of pride is taken to be in this, that a man somehow is not subject to God and to the rule of His guidance. But clearly this want of subjection to God bears the character of mortal sin, for that is what turning away from God comes to: consequently pride is a mortal sin of its kind. But as in other matters that are mortal sins of their kind, there are some movements which by reason of their incompleteness are only venial sins, because they get the start of the judgment of reason, and are without its consent, so also in the matter of pride it happens that some movements of pride are only venial sins, while reason consents not to them.[3]

ARTICLE VI.—*Is pride the most grievous of sins?*
R. There are two elements in sin: the turning

[1] 2 Cor. x. 13.   [2] Ecclus. x. 14.
[3] Understand this of the absence of perfect consent: for without some sort of consent or voluntary negligence of the reason, that is, of the rational appetite, or will, there can be no actual sin whatever, not even venial for "the will, which is the origin of voluntary acts good and bad, is the origin of sins." I-II. q. 74. art. 1. Cf. I-II. q. 74. art. 10. note; II-II. q. 154. art. 5. beginning. (Trl)

to the good that perishes, which *turning to* is the material element in sin; and the turning away from the good that perishes not, which *turning away* is the formal and completely constituent element of sin. On the side of the turning to the perishable, pride has not the attribute of being the greatest of sins: because the height which the proud man inordinately affects, has not of its own nature the greatest possible opposition to the good of virtue. But on the side of the turning from the imperishable, pride has the utmost grievousness: because in other sins man turns away from God either through ignorance, or through weakness, or through desire of some other good; but pride involves a turning away from God merely because one will not be subject to God and to His rule. Hence Boethius says, that "while all vices fly from God, pride alone sets itself against God;" on which ground it is especially said that "God resisteth the proud."[1] And therefore the turning away from God and from His commandments, which is a sort of appanage of other sins, belongs to pride as part and parcel of itself, since the act of pride is a contempt of God. And because what is part and parcel of a thing, always takes precedence over what is a mere appanage of the same, it follows that pride is of its kind the most grievous of sin, because it exceeds them all in that turning away from God, which is the formal and crowning constituent of sin.

§ 1. The movement of pride creeping on imperceptibly has no very great grievousness before it is

[1] St. James iv. 6.

overtaken by the judgment of reason. After reason has caught and found it out, then it is easily avoided, as well on the consideration of one's own weakness, according to the text, "Why is earth and ashes proud?"[1] as also on consideration of the greatness of God, according to the text, "Why doth thy spirit swell against God?"[2] as also from the imperfect nature of the goods of which man is proud, according to the text, "All flesh is grass, and all the glory thereof as the flower of the field;"[3] and again, "All our works of justice are as filthy rags."[4]

§ 2. In respect of what it *turns to*, pride is not the greatest of sins, as neither is humility the greatest of virtues. But in respect of what it *turns away from*, it is the greatest of sins, as adding greatness to other sins; for it is precisely by its proceeding from pride, that the sin of unbelief is rendered more grievous than it would be if it arose from ignorance or infirmity.

§ 3. As in syllogisms leading to an impossible conclusion, sometimes the error is brought home to one by his being landed in a more manifest absurdity; so also to bring their pride home to them, God punishes some by letting them fall into sins of the flesh, which, though they are less sins, yet contain a more manifest unsightliness. Hence again appears the grievousness of pride. For as a wise physician suffers his patient to fall into a disease of milder type for the cure of a more

[1] Ecclus. x. 9. [2] Job xv. 13. [3] Isaias xl. 6.
[4] Isaias lxiv. 6.

grievous malady, so the greater grievousness of the sin of pride is shown by the fact that, for the cure of it, God permits men to rush headlong into other sins.

ARTICLE VII.

§ 3. There need not be the same order of progress in virtues as in vices. For vice is the corrupter of virtue; and what is first in generation is last in corruption. And therefore as faith is the first of virtues, so unbelief is the last of sins, to which man is brought at times by other sins. Hence on the text, "Rase it, rase it, even to the foundation thereof;"[1] the gloss says, that by the heaping up of vices loss of faith gradually comes on; and the Apostle says, that "some rejecting a good conscience have made shipwreck concerning the faith."[2]

§ 4. Pride is the cause of the grievousness of other sins. We find accordingly, prior to pride, some lighter sins committed out of ignorance or weakness; but among grievous sins pride is the first, as being the cause that makes other sins grievous.

ARTICLE VIII.—*Should pride be set down for a capital vice?*

R. Considering the universal influence of pride upon all vices, Gregory has not numbered it among the other capital sins, but has ranked it as queen and mother of vices. Hence he says: "When

[1] Psalm cxxxvi. 7. [2] 1 Timothy i. 19.

the queen of vices, pride, has fully overcome and captured a heart, she presently hands it over to be laid waste by her generals, the seven principal vices, whence multitudes of other vices have their origin."

§ 2. Pride is not the same thing as vainglory, but is the cause of vainglory. For pride seeks inordinately after excellence; but vainglory seeks the manifestation of that excellence.

QUESTION CLXVI.

OF STUDIOUSNESS.

ARTICLE I.—*Is knowledge properly the matter of studiousness?*

R. Study properly implies a vigorous application of the mind to some object. Now the mind is not applied to an object otherwise than by knowing or trying to know it. Hence the mind is first applied to knowledge, and secondarily to those things whereunto man is led by knowledge. And therefore study primarily regards knowledge, and in the second place any actions besides, to the doing of which we are guided by knowledge. But the virtues have properly assigned to them that matter, with which they are first and primarily conversant, as fortitude is conversant with perils of death, and temperance with the pleasure of touch. And therefore studiousness is properly said to be about knowledge.

Article II.—*Is studiousness a part of temperance?*

R. To temperance it belongs to moderate the movement of appetite, that it run not to excess after natural desires. Now as man in his bodily nature desires naturally the pleasures of food and of sex, so in his soul he naturally desires knowledge: hence the Philosopher says that "all men naturally desire to know." The moderation of this desire belongs to the virtue of studiousness. Consequently studiousness is a potential part of temperance, being attached to it as a secondary to a primary virtue.

§ 3. On the side of the soul man is inclined to desire knowledge; and being so, he must put a laudable restraint on the craving, so as not to push his investigation of things beyond the bounds of moderation. On the other hand, man is inclined on the side of his bodily nature to shun the labour of searching after knowledge. In the first respect then studiousness consists in applying the curb; and in this respect it is set down to be a part of temperance. But in the second respect, the merit of this virtue lies in vigorous application to the pursuit of knowledge: and hence it has its name.

QUESTION CLXVII.

OF CURIOSITY.

ARTICLE I.—*Can there be curiosity in the matter of intellectual knowledge?*

R. The knowledge of truth on the one hand, and the craving and eagerness to know the truth on the other, are not to be esteemed alike. Knowledge of truth is in itself good, though it may be evil incidentally by reason of something that follows upon it, either because one is proud of his knowledge, as the text has it, " Knowledge puffeth up,"[1] or inasmuch as a man uses his knowledge of truth to sin. But the craving or eagerness to know truth may be either right or wrong. It is wrong if the efforts made after knowledge are directed to it on that side on which it is incidentally fraught with evil; for example, in the case of those whose study of science is directed to gain a vantage-ground for pride. Hence Augustine says: "There are those who abandoning virtues, and knowing not what God is, and how great is the majesty of the Nature that never changes, think that they are doing something great by curiously and intently investigating this whole mass of material things that we call the

[1] 1 Cor. viii. 1.

universe. So great is the pride hence generated, that they fancy themselves actually to dwell in the heavens about which they dispute so much."

In another form vice may show itself as an inordinateness in the craving and eagerness to learn the truth. That may be in four ways. One way is when this eagerness withdraws a person from another pursuit, which is his bounden duty. Hence Jerome says: "We see priests leaving the gospels and prophets, to read comedies and sing the love-verses of pastoral poetry." In another way, when one is eager to learn from an unlawful source, as in those who inquire of evil spirits about things to come: and this is superstitious curiosity. The third way is when one seeks to learn the truth about creatures without reference to the due end, which is the knowledge of God. Hence Augustine says: "We must not gratify a curiosity, idle and sure to be thrown away over the study of creatures; but we must make of that study a ladder to ascend to immortal and everlasting goods." A fourth way is inasmuch as one is eager to know that truth which lies above his ken; for thereby men easily fall into errors. Hence it is said: "Search not the things that are too high for thee, and search not into things above thy ability, and in many of his works be not curious: for the suspicion of them hath deceived many and hath detained their minds in vanity."[1]

§ 1. The good of man consists in the knowledge of truth; but the sovereign good of man does not

[1] Ecclus. iii. 22—26.

consist in the knowledge of any and every truth, but in the perfect knowledge of the higher truth. And therefore there may be an element of vice in the knowledge of some truths, inasmuch as desire of that knowledge is not duly directed to the knowledge of the sovereign truth, wherein sovereign blessedness consists.

§ 2. The knowledge of truth in itself is good; but it may be abused to an evil end, or inordinately desired: for even the desire of a good thing needs to be duly regulated.

§ 3. Though the study of philosophy in itself is lawful and praiseworthy, still because some philosophers abuse it to assail the faith, the Apostle says: " Beware lest any man cheat you by philosophy and vain deceit, according to the traditions of men, and not according to Christ."[1]

ARTICLE II.—*Has the vice of curiosity place in the matter of sensible knowledge?*

R. The knowledge that comes by the senses is ordered to two ends: in man; as in other animals, it is ordered to the end of maintenance of the body; because by means of this knowledge men and other animals avoid what is hurtful, and seek out what is necessary for their sustenance; again, in man it is specially ordered to minister to intellectual knowledge, whether speculative or practical. To apply oneself then to the eager knowing of sensible things may be vicious in two ways: in one way, inasmuch as the sensible knowledge so gained is not directed

[1] Coloss. ii. 8.

to anything useful, but rather turns a man away from some profitable inquiry;[1] in another way, inasmuch as sensible knowledge makes for some evil end, as the looking at a woman makes for lust, and diligent inquiry into others' doings makes for detraction.

§ 2. The looking on at public shows becomes criminal, in so far as such representations render a man prone to the vices either of luxury or cruelty.

QUESTION CLXVIII.

OF MODESTY, OR DECORUM, IN THE OUTWARD MOVEMENTS OF THE BODY.[2]

ARTICLE I.—*Is there any virtue in the outward movements of the body?*

R. Moral virtue consists in man's performances being directed by reason. But manifestly the exterior movements of man are open to the direction of reason; for the exterior members move at the command of reason. Hence there is a moral virtue that consists in the due ordering of these movements.

---

[1] To prevent our taking this too rigidly, see the next Question, art. 2. In no author more than in St. Thomas, and nowhere in St. Thomas more than in his moral writings, is it important to read one passage in the light of another, and to accord particular utterances to the general tenor of the author's mind. (Trl.)

[2] A different virtue from the modesty (*pudicitia*) spoken of II-II. q. 151. art. 4. (Trl.)

§ 1. Outward movements are signs of inward dispositions, according to the text, "The attire of the body, and the laughter of the teeth, and the gait of the man, show what he is;"[1] and Ambrose says, "The movement of the body is the voice of the soul."

§ 4. The paying of special attention to the arrangement of outward movements is blameworthy, if it means that the outward movements are so feigned as not to tally with the inward dispositions. But enough special attention ought to be paid to ensure the correction of anything inordinate in our movements. Hence Ambrose says: "Away with artificiality, but secure propriety."

ARTICLE II.—*Can there be any virtue in games and sports?*

R. As man needs bodily rest to refresh his body, which cannot labour continually, because its strength is limited and proportioned to finite toil, so with the mind the case is the same for the same reason. And therefore, when the mind exerts itself beyond its measure, it labours and is fatigued thereby, especially because in the operations of the soul the body labours also, inasmuch as the intellectual soul uses powers that work by means of bodily organs. But sensible goods are connatural to man; and therefore, when the mind soars above the things of sense, and is intent upon the works of reason, the result is a certain psychical fatigue, whether it be the works of practical or of speculative reason that

[1] Ecclus. xix. 27.

the man is intent upon: more however if he be intent upon the works of contemplation, because thereby he soars higher above sensible things; though possibly in some exterior works of the practical reason greater labour of the body is involved. But as bodily fatigue is thrown off by rest of the body, so must psychical fatigue be thrown off by rest of the mind. Now the mind's rest is pleasure or delight. And therefore a remedy must be applied to psychical fatigue by some pleasure, and the intense application to rational pursuits must be for the time intermitted. Thus we read of blessed John the Evangelist, that when some persons were scandalized to find him at play with his disciples, he told one of them, who had a bow, to shoot an arrow, and so again and again, and then asked him if he could go on doing that always. The other answered that if he tried to do it always, the bow would break. Hence blessed John drew the moral, that in like manner man's head would break, if his mind was kept for ever on the strain. But sayings or doings of this sort, wherein nothing is sought beyond amusement, are spoken of as things said or done in *sport* or *jest*. And therefore we must at times make use of such things to rest the mind. In doing so there are three precautions to be observed. The first and principal is, that the aforesaid amusement be not sought for in actions or words that are unseemly or hurtful. The second is, that the gravity of the mind be not altogether relaxed. Hence Tully says: "In our very jests let some glimpse of a virtuous character shine out." The third precaution here as in all other human actions is, that whatever is said or done should be in keeping with the person, the season, and the place, as Tully says that it should be "worthy of the time and of the man." Now a habit working according to reason is a moral virtue; and therefore in the matter of games and sports there can be a virtue, which the Philosopher calls *eutrapelia* (sprightliness).[1]

§ 1. Jests ought to suit the matter in hand and the person speaking. Hence Tully says: "When the audience are tired, it is not without utility for the orator to start some new and ridiculous topic, provided the dignity of the subject does not bar every avenue to a jest." Hence Ambrose, when he says, "I consider that not only extravagant jokes but all jokes are to be avoided," does not exclude joking universally from conversation, but from the pulpit. Hence he says before: "Though jests be at times proper and pleasing, yet they are out of keeping with the ecclesiastical rule. For, not finding them in Holy Scripture, how can we use them?"[2]

§ 2. Chrysostom's saying, "Not God but the devil is the giver of sport," is to be understood of those who use sports and games inordinately, and especially of those who make it the end of their life to play and amuse themselves, as is said of some, "They have counted our life a pastime;"[3] against

---

[1] In his *Rhetoric*, II. 12, Aristotle defines *eutrapelia* as πεπαιδευμένη ὕβρις, "a cultivated variety of horseplay." (Trl.)

[2] Understand—in the pulpit. (Trl.)   [3] Wisdom xv. 12.

whom Tully says, "We are not so brought into being by nature as that sport and jest should be accounted the end of our existence; rather we are meant to be on serious thoughts intent, and on grave and weighty purposes."[1]

§ 3. Things done in jest in their kind are not directed to any end; but the pleasure that comes of doing them is directed to the recreation and rest of the mind. Hence Tully says: "It is lawful to use play and jesting, but only as we use sleep and other manners of repose, then when we have acquitted ourselves of our grave and serious duties."

ARTICLE III.

§ 3. Sport and play are necessary to the business of human life. Now for all purposes that are useful to society certain lawful callings may be appointed. And therefore the calling of stage-players, being directed to afford solace to men, is not in itself unlawful, nor are they in the state of sin, provided they practise their playing moderately, employing no unlawful words or actions therein, and not carrying their playing into the midst of occupations or seasons where it has no place. And though in the social order they fulfil no other office in reference to other men, yet with regard to themselves and to God they have other serious and virtuous occupations, praying, and ordering their passions and actions, and at times also giving alms to the poor. Hence they who contribute moderately to their support do not sin, but do an act of justice, giving

[1] Cf. *Ethics and Natural Law*, p. 60. (Trl.)

them the hire of their service. But if any individuals run to excess, wasting their substance on such persons, or support those stage-players who act unlawful plays, they sin as fostering them in their sin. In this sense Augustine says: "To give one's money to stage-players is a huge vice, not a virtue," —unless some stage-player happened to be in extreme need, in which case he would have to be relieved, for Ambrose says: "Feed the man dying of hunger: whoever you are that are able to save a man by giving him food, you have slain him if you have not fed him."

ARTICLE IV.—*Is there any sin in being too little disposed to sport and play?*

R. Everything that is against reason in human things is faulty. Now it is against reason for any one to make himself burdensome to others, making no fun himself and stopping other people's fun. Hence Seneca says: "Behave so wisely as that none may account thee stern, nor despise thee as making thyself cheap." But they who have too little disposition to sport and play, say nothing laughable themselves, and frown upon others saying such things, not admitting the moderate playfulness of others. And therefore these persons are at fault, and are called "hard and clownish," as the Philosopher says. But because sport is useful for rest and pleasure, and pleasure and rest are not things to be sought for their own sake in human life, but as aids to work, therefore defect in the disposition to sport and play is less of a vice than excess in the same. Hence the Philosopher says: "A little pleasure is enough in life for seasoning, as a little salt to meat."

§ 1. Sport and play are forbidden to penitents, because mourning is enjoined upon them for their sins. Nor is this a piece of vice in the way of defect: for it is according to reason that in their case the measure of sport and play should be cut down.

QUESTION CLXIX.

OF MODESTY IN DRESS.

ARTICLE I.—*Can there be virtue and vice in matters of toilet?*

R. In the exterior things that man uses there is no vice, but only on the part of man himself who uses them immoderately. This immoderation may appear in two ways: one way is in comparison with the standard of custom in the social circle in which the person moves. Hence Augustine says: "Offences against manners are to be avoided according to the different fashion of manners. The convention of society, sanctioned by custom or by law, is not to be violated by the private whim of any citizen or stranger: for ungainly is every part that is not in agreement with the whole to which it belongs." In another way there may be immoderation arising from the inordinate affection of him who uses exterior things, when a man comes to luxuriate too much in such things, whether his use of them be according to the custom of the society in which he lives, or go beyond that custom. Hence Augustine says: " In the use of things there must be no luxury: for luxury not only abuses wickedly the custom of society in the sphere in which it lives, but often even goes beyond that custom, and breaking out into the foulest excesses, openly shows the shame that it formerly concealed behind the veil of customary observance."

On the side of defect there may be a twofold inordination, one in the way of negligence and refusal to take any trouble to make one's outward man what it should be; the other is making these very deficiencies of toilet a matter of vainglory.

§ 2. They who are in positions of dignity, or again the ministers of the altar, wear more costly robes than other men, not for their own glorification, but to signify the excellence of their office or of divine worship: and therefore there is no fault in their so doing. Nor yet does he who wears a meaner dress than his fellows, always sin. For if he does it for the maceration of the flesh, or the humiliation of the spirit, it is an act of the virtue of temperance. The wearing of a mean dress is particularly proper in those who exhort other men by word and example to penance, as the Prophets did, of whom the Apostle says: " They wandered about in sheep-skins."[1]

[1] Hebrews xi. 37.

ARTICLE II.—*Is indulgence of the love of dress a mortal sin in women?*

R. As regards female dress the same points are to be attended to as have been noted above concerning toilet generally; and moreover there is one other special fact to be observed, that is given in the text: "And behold a woman meeteth him in harlot's attire, prepared to deceive souls."[1] However, a married woman may lawfully lay herself out to please her husband, lest he despise her and form other connections. Hence it is said: "She that is married thinketh on the things of the world, how she may please her husband."[2] And therefore, if a married woman dresses well to please her husband, she may do so without sin. But those women who neither have nor want to have husbands, or who are in a state that binds them not to marry, cannot without sin seek to please the eyes of men to make them fall in love with them, because that is to furnish their neighbour with an incentive to sin. And if they dress themselves with this express purpose, that people may fall in love with them, they sin mortally: but if it is done out of thoughtlessness, or vanity and love of display, it is not always a mortal sin, but venial sometimes. Some ladies however in this situation may be excused from sin, when their dressing is not done out of vanity, but in compliance with a fashion to the contrary of what has been laid down: though such a fashion is not praiseworthy.[3]

[1] Prov. vii. 10. [2] 1 Cor. vii. 34.
[3] To illustrate St. Thomas by a later Doctor of the Church, we quote from the *Life of St. Jane Frances*, Quarterly Series, p. 37:

§ 2. Women's painting of themselves is a species of counterfeit that cannot be without sin.[1] Such painting however is not always fraught with mortal sin, but only when it is done for lasciviousness or in contempt of God. It is further to be observed that it is one thing to counterfeit a beauty not possessed, and another thing to conceal an ugliness arising from any cause, as from sickness or other such incident : for that concealment is lawful.[2]

§ 4. In any art of manufacturing articles that men cannot use without sin, workmen making such things would thereby sin, as directly supplying others with an occasion of sin: thus it would be if one were to manufacture idols or articles of idolatrous worship. But any art that there may be, the products of which can be used by men either for good or for evil, as in the case of swords and arrows, is not a sinful art to practise; and only such arts as this ought to be called *arts*.[3] Where

---

"One day at dinner, when the Bishop (St. Francis de Sales) had his usual place next her as mistress of the house, he observed that her dress was more fashionably made than usual. Taking an opportunity when he could not be overheard, the Bishop said to her in a low voice : ' Madame, should you like to marry again ? ' ' No, indeed, my lord,' she instantly replied. ' Then you should pull down your flag,' he said, smiling, but in such a way that she could not take offence. Madame de Chantal perfectly understood him, and when she took her place at dinner the next day, her dress was docked of certain little trimmings and coxcombries which had given it the appearance of smartness." (Trl)

[1] See q. 111. art. 1. (Trl.)

[2] So, says the Angelic Doctor, the lady may paint—if she is ugly. (Trl.)

[3] The rule here given regulates the compounding and sale of poisons. (Trl.)

however the products of any art are for the most part turned to evil use, arts in that case, though not unlawful in themselves, are to be exterminated from the city by the official act of the Sovereign. Since then women may lawfully adorn themselves, either to maintain the becoming level of their state, or even somewhat to improve upon it, and please their husbands, it follows that the makers of finery for this purpose do not sin in the practice of their art, except it be possibly by inventing sundry superfluous and curious novelties.[1]

[1] Here ends St. Thomas's long examination of virtues and vices, which has occupied the whole of the *Secunda-Secunda* so far, besides the general treatment of the matter in *Prima-Secunda*, qq. 55—88. The remainder of the *Secunda-Secunda*, here presented, is mainly a treatise on the religious state, which, as a state, is the culmination of moral excellence, and the exposition of it a fitting last word from *Aquinas Ethicus*. (Trl.)

QUESTION CLXXXII.

OF THE COMPARISON OF THE ACTIVE LIFE WITH THE CONTEMPLATIVE.

ARTICLE I.—*Is the active life better than the contemplative?*

R. A thing may well be in itself more excellent, and yet in some respect be surpassed by another thing. We must say then the contemplative life is, absolutely speaking, better than the active. Which the Philosopher proves by eight reasons: of which the first is, because the contemplative life becomes a man in respect of the most excellent element in his nature, namely, his understanding. The second is, because the contemplative life can be more continuous, though not in its highest act. The third is, because the delight of the contemplative life is greater than that of the active. The fourth is, because in the contemplative life man is more self-sufficient and needs fewer things. The fifth is, because the contemplative life is loved for its own sake, while the active life is directed to something ulterior to itself. The sixth is, because the contemplative life consists in a certain stillness and rest, according to the text: "Be still and see that I am God."[1] The seventh is, because the contem-

[1] Psalm xlv. 11.

plative life is formed upon divine things, but the active life upon human things. The eighth is, because the contemplative life is life according to that which is proper to man, namely, the intellect, whereas in the operations of the active life the lower powers concur, which are common to us with dumb animals. A ninth reason is added by our Lord,[1] which is explained by Augustine: "From thee shall one day be taken away the burden of necessity, but the sweetness of truth is eternal." Relatively however, and in some particular case, the active life is rather to be chosen for the necessity of our present time, as also the Philosopher says: "Philosophy is better than riches, but riches are better to a man in need."

§ 1. Not only the active life belongs to prelates, but they ought also to be excellent in the contemplative life. Hence Gregory says: "Let the bishop be foremost in action, and high above all in contemplation."

§ 3. Sometimes for some necessity of the present life one is called away from contemplation to the works of the active life, yet not in such a way as to be obliged entirely to abandon contemplation. And thus it is clear that when one is called from the contemplative life to the active, it is not done in the way of subtraction, but in the way of addition.

ARTICLE II.—*Is the active life of greater merit than the contemplative?*

R. The root of merit is charity. Now since

[1] St. Luke x 42.

charity consists in the love of God and of our neighbour, and the love of God is in itself more meritorious than the love of our neighbour, it follows that what belongs more directly to the love of God, is more meritorious of its kind than what directly belongs to the love of our neighbour for God. But the contemplative life directly and immediately appertains to the love of God, whereas the active life is more directly ordered to the love of our neighbour, being "busy about much serving."[1] And therefore of its kind the contemplative life is of greater merit than the active. But it may happen that one individual merits more in the works of the active life than another in the works of the contemplative, if through an abounding love for God, to the end that His will may be fulfilled, and for His glory, this person endures to be separated from the sweetness of divine contemplation for a time: as did the Apostle,[2] as Chrysostom expounds: "His whole heart was so flooded with the love of Christ, that even that which was otherwise his greatest desire, to be with Christ, he could bring himself to set aside for the good pleasure of Christ."

§ 1. Outward labour works to the increase of our accidental reward; but the increase of merit, touching our essential reward, lies principally in charity, one sign of which is outward labour endured for Christ; but a much more express sign of it is the neglect of all that belongs to this life to devote oneself with delight to divine contemplation alone.

§ 3. A sacrifice is spiritually offered to God

[1] St. Luke x. 40.   [2] Romans ix. 3.

when anything is rendered to Him. But of all the goods of man God most willingly accepts the good that consists of the soul of man, that it be offered to Him in sacrifice. A man should offer himself to God, first his own soul, according to the text, "Have pity on thine own soul, pleasing God;"[1] then the souls of others, according to the text, "He that heareth, let him say, Come."[2] But the closer one unites his own or another's soul to God, the more acceptable is the sacrifice to God: hence it is more acceptable to God that one should apply his own and other souls to contemplation than to action. Therefore Gregory's saying, "No sacrifice is more acceptable to God than zeal of souls," is not a preference of the merit of the active before that of the contemplative life, but a declaration that it is more meritorious to offer to God one's own and other souls than any exterior gifts whatsoever.

ARTICLE III.—*Is the contemplative life hindered by the active life?*

R. The active life may be considered either as meaning the zealous exercise of exterior functions; and from that point of view it is manifest that the active life hinders the contemplative, inasmuch as it is impossible for any man to be at once occupied with exterior actions and at the same time apply himself to divine contemplation: or the active life may be considered as composing and ordering the passions, and in this respect the active life helps

[1] Ecclus. xxx. 24.   [2] Apoc. xxii. 17.

contemplation, which is hindered by the disorder of the passions.

Article IV.

§ 3. On the saying of Gregory, "Often they who might have contemplated God in peace and quiet, have fallen and given way under the burden of occupations; and others who, had they had occupation, would have lived well and profitably to mankind, have perished under the sword of their own peace and quiet,"— it is to be remarked that persons of strong passionate inclinations, which prompt them to impetuous action, are, absolutely speaking, better fitted for an active life, owing to the restlessness of their spirit. Hence Gregory says: "Some are so restless, that if they get rest from labour, they labour all the more grievously: because the more liberty and free time they have for their own thoughts, the worse storms they endure in their hearts." Others again have naturally a purity and peace of soul fitting them for contemplation; and if these persons are totally set aside for active occupations, they will suffer loss.

QUESTION CLXXXIII.

OF OFFICES AND VARIOUS STATES OF MEN IN GENERAL.

ARTICLE I.—*Does state (status) essentially denote the condition of liberty or slavery?*[1]

R. State (*status*, "a standing") properly speaking signifies a special position, wherein a thing is set aside according to the manner of its nature, and established in a sort of immobility. For it is natural to man for his head to be erect and his feet planted firm on the ground, and the rest of the intervening members arranged in due order; which is not the case when the man is lying down, or sitting, or reclining, but only when he is standing straight up; nor again is he said to *stand* if he is moving, but only when he is at rest. Hence with reference to men the incidents about them that are extrinsic and easily variable do not constitute *a state;* for

[1] *Status* is a technical term of Roman Law. "The *status* of men means that by which they are partakers in a certain right. And since slaves are partakers in no civil right, they are said on that account to have no *status:* therefore when they come to be freemen, they are not considered to change their *status*. Cases of *status* are those in which a freeman is claimed as a slave, or a slave as a freeman. All freemen are said to change their *status*, who lose either their liberty, or their citizenship, or their rights in a particular family." Vicat, *Vocabularium Juris Utriusque*, s.v. (Trl.)

instance, one's being rich or poor, in dignity or in a plebeian condition. Hence also in the Civil Law it is said that in the case of a man losing his seat in the Senate it is his *dignity* rather than his *state* that is taken from him. That alone is considered to belong to a man's *state*, which regards the obligation of his person, as he is his own master or in the power of another, and that not for any light or easily changeable cause, but on some permanent ground; or in other words, something which forms part of the notion of liberty or slavery. Hence state (*status*) properly regards liberty or slavery, whether in spiritual or in civil matters.

§ 3. An *office* is so called in relation to action: *rank* or *grade*, in regard of order of superiority or inferiority. But to the notion of *state* there is requisite immobility as regards the condition of the person.

ARTICLE II.—*Ought there to be in the Church a variety of offices or states?*

R. The variety of states and offices in the Church points in the first place to the perfection of the Church. For as in the order of nature that perfection which exists in God simply and uniformly, cannot exist in creatures except in various forms and in many manners; so also the fulness of grace that is united in Christ the Head, overflows upon His members in manifold variety, that the body of the Church may be whole and perfect. And this is what the Apostle says: "And he gave some apostles, and some prophets, and other some evangelists, and other some pastors and doctors, for the perfecting of the saints."[1] Secondly, it is matter of necessity for the necessary work of the Church. For different men must be set aside for different work, that all may be done more expeditiously and without confusion: as the Apostle says, "In one body we have many members, but all the members have not the same office."[2] Thirdly, this is part of the dignity and beauty of the Church, a beauty which consists in order: hence it is said, "When the Queen of Saba saw all the wisdom of Solomon, and the apartments of his servants, and the order of his ministers, she had no longer any spirit left in her;"[3] and the Apostle says: "In a great house there are not only vessels of gold and of silver, but also of wood and of earth."[4]

§ 3. As in the natural body the different members are kept together in unity by the virtue of the quickening spirit, on the departure of which the members of the body break up; so also in the body of the Church peace between the different members is kept by the virtue of the Holy Ghost, who quickens the whole body of the Church. Hence the Apostle says: "Careful to keep the unity of the Spirit in the bond of peace."[5] A man departs from this unity of the Spirit by seeking the things that are his own; as even in the earthly State peace is destroyed by the citizens severally seeking their own private interests. Other-

---

[1] Ephes. iv. 11.   [2] Romans xii. 4.
[3] 3 Kings x. 4, 5.   [4] 2 Timothy ii. 20.   [5] Ephes. iv. 3.

wise the variety of offices and of states furthers the preservation of peace by giving more people an interest in public business.

ARTICLE IV.—*Does the difference of states answer to the difference between beginners, proficients, and perfect?*

R. State (*status*) is in regard of freedom or bondage. In spiritual things there is a twofold bondage and a twofold freedom. There is one bondage of sin, and another bondage of justice. In like manner there is a twofold freedom, one from sin and one from justice: as the Apostle says, "When you were servants of sin, you were free men to justice; but now being made free from sin, you are become servants to God."[1] It is the bondage of sin or of justice, when one is bent either upon evil by the habit of sin, or upon good by the habit of justice. In like manner also freedom from sin is when one is not overcome by the inclination to sin; and freedom from justice is when the love of justice does not hold one back and make one slow to do evil. But because natural reason inclines a man to justice, and sin is against natural reason, it follows that freedom from sin is true freedom; and such freedom goes along with the bondage of justice: because both by the one and the other the man tends to what becomes a man. In like manner real bondage is the bondage of sin; and that goes along with freedom from justice: for hereby a man is hindered from what properly

[1] Romans vi. 20, 22.

befits him. But it is by human effort that man is rendered the bondsman either of justice or of sin: as the Apostle says, "To whom you yield yourselves servants to obey, his servants you are whom you obey, whether it be of sin, unto death, or of obedience, unto justice."[1] Now in every human effort we may take a beginning, a middle, and an end. Consequently the state of spiritual bondage and freedom[2] is marked off into three parts: the beginning, which is the state of beginners; the middle, which is the state of proficients; and the end, which is the state of the perfect.

QUESTION CLXXXIV.

OF WHAT RELATES TO THE STATE OF PERFECTION IN GENERAL.

ARTICLE I.—*Is the perfection of Christian life to be looked for in charity especially?*

R. Everything is said to be perfect inasmuch as it attains to its proper end, which is the ultimate perfection of the thing. But it is charity that unites us to God, the ultimate end of the human mind, because "he that abideth in charity abideth in God, and God in him."[3] And therefore it is by charity especially that the perfection of Christian life is measured.

[1] Romans vi. 16.
[2] That is, bondage of justice and freedom from sin. (Trl.)
[3] 1 St. John iv. 16.

ARTICLE II.—*Can any one be perfect in this life?*
R. The perfection of Christian life consists in charity. Now perfection implies what we may call a "universal thoroughness:" for that is perfect to which nothing is wanting. We may consider therefore perfection in three forms. One absolute, or total, as well on the part of the person loving as on the part of the object loved; so that God should be loved as much as He is lovable. Such perfection is not possible to any creature: God alone is capable of it, in whom good is found in its entirety and in its essence. There is another perfection where the totality is absolute on the part of the person loving, in that the whole power of his affection is ever absolutely fixed upon God; and such perfection is not possible on the way to Heaven, but will be realized on our arrival in our heavenly home. There is a third perfection that is neither total as regards the object loved nor total on the part of the person loving. It does not involve a continual actual yearning after God, but only an exclusion of whatever is inconsistent with the motion of love towards God. So Augustine says: "The poison of charity is cupidity; and perfection is the absence of all cupidity."[1] And such perfection can be had in this life, and that in two ways; in one way to the extent of excluding from the heart all that is

---

[1] What St. Augustine calls *cupidity*, St. Ignatius calls *inordinate affection*. The "absence of all cupidity" is called by St. Philip Neri, and after him by Cardinal Newman, *detachment*. St. Ignatius calls it *indifference*. Other names for it are *spiritual poverty, liberty of spirit, purity of heart;* and lastly, St. Thomas calls it on its positive side, *devotion*, II-II. q 82. (Trl.)

contrary to charity, as is mortal sin; and without such perfection charity cannot be: consequently this perfection is of necessity to salvation. The other way goes to the extent of excluding from the heart, not only all that is contrary to charity, but also all that hinders the entire concentration of the heart upon God. Charity can exist without this perfection, as it exists in beginners and in proficients.

§ 2. They who are perfect in this life are said to "offend in many things"[1] by venial sins that follow from the infirmity of the present life; and in this respect there hangs about them some imperfection as compared with the perfection of our heavenly home.

§ 3. As the state of the present life does not suffer a man always to tend actually to God, so neither does it allow of his love actually going out upon all his neighbours individually; but it is enough that it goes out upon them all alike in general, and upon individuals habitually and in preparedness of mind.[2] We may observe also in the love of our neighbour a twofold perfection, as in the love of God: one without which charity cannot be, which means that man must harbour in his heart nothing contrary to the love of his neighbour; the other without which charity can be. The latter perfection shows itself, first, in *extension*, so that not only friends and acquaintances are

[1] St. James iii. 2.
[2] That is, he habitually holds himself in readiness to do kindness to any individual that needs it. (Trl.)

loved, but even strangers, and furthermore enemies:[1] for this, as Augustine says, is "the mark of the perfect sons of God." Secondly, in *intensity*, as evinced by what a man is prepared to cast aside for the sake of his neighbour, when it comes not only to sacrificing exterior goods, but braving bodily afflictions and death to boot, as it is said: "Greater love than this no man hath, that a man lay down his life for his friend."[2]

ARTICLE III.—*Does perfection consist in the precepts or in the counsels?*

R. Of itself and essentially the perfection of Christian life consists in charity; principally in the love of God, and secondarily in the love of our neighbour. But the love of God and of our neighbour does not fall under precept in any fixed measure, in such a way as to leave anything beyond an assignable quantity a matter of counsel. This is evident from the form of the precept, "Thou shalt love God with thy whole heart:" for *whole* and *perfect* are the same. Moreover, in the case of the end, no measure is applied, but only in the case of means to the end.[3] Hence it appears that perfection consists essentially in the precepts. But secondarily and instrumentally perfection consists in the counsels, which like the precepts are directed to charity, but not all in the same way. For the other precepts that there are besides the precepts of charity, are directed to the removal of things

[1] See II-II. q. 25. art. 8. (Trl.)
[2] St. John xv. 13.   [3] Cf. II-II. q. 27. art. 6. (Trl.)

contrary to and incompatible with charity; while the counsels are directed to the removal of certain things that are obstacles to the act of charity, and yet are not contrary to charity, as marriage, occupation with secular business, and the like. Hence in the *Conferences of the Fathers* the Abbot Moses says: " Fasts, watchings, meditation on the Scriptures, nakedness, and the deprivation of all goods, are not perfection, but instruments of perfection: for the end consists not *in* them, but *through* them we arrive at the end: by these steps we strive to ascend to the perfection of charity."

§ 1. In those words of our Lord one thing is laid down as the way to perfection: "Go, sell what thou hast and give to the poor;"[1] and another thing is added in which perfection consists: "And come, follow me."

§ 2. Since what falls under precept may be fulfilled in different manners, he is not a transgressor of the precept who does not fulfil it in the most excellent manner, but it is enough that he fulfils it in any manner whatever. Now the lowest degree of divine love is that nothing be loved above it, or contrary to it, or on a level with it. He who falls short of this degree of perfection, nowise fulfils the precept.

§ 3. As man has from birth a certain perfection of his nature, that which belongs to the essence of his species; and there is another perfection to which he is brought by growth: so there is a perfection of charity, belonging to the very species of

[1] St. Matt. xix. 21.

charity, which is that God should be loved above all things, and nothing be loved against God. There is again even in this life another perfection of charity, to which one arrives by a process of spiritual growth, when a man abstains from even lawful things, to be more free to devote himself to acts of service to God.

ARTICLE IV.—*Is every one who is perfect in a state of perfection?*

R. State (*status*) properly points to a man's condition as freeman or slave. Now there may be spiritual liberty or slavery either in respect of what goes on internally or of what goes on externally. And because "man seeth those things that appear, but the Lord beholdeth the heart,"[1] hence it is that, as regards a man's interior disposition, the condition of his spiritual state is discerned by the judgment of God; but for what goes on externally, his spiritual state is fixed according as he stands to the Church. And so it is that we are now speaking of states, considering the beauty that arises in the Church from the diversity of states and conditions therein. Now we must observe that among men, for one to attain to the state of liberty or slavery, there is requisite in the first place some binding or releasing: for the mere fact of one man serving another does not make him a slave, because even free men do service, as it is written: "By charity of the spirit serve one another;"[2] nor is a man made free by the mere fact of ceasing to serve, as

[1] 1 Kings xvi. 7. [2] Galat. v. 13.

we see in the case of runaway slaves: but he is properly a slave who is bound to serve; and he is free, who is released from servitude. Secondly, it is requisite that the binding above-mentioned be done with some solemnity, as some solemnity is gone through in other transactions that are meant to stand and endure perpetually amongst men. Thus then one is properly said to be in a state of perfection, not from the eliciting of the act of perfect love, but from binding oneself with some solemnity to the practices of perfection. It happens also that some bind themselves to what they do not observe, and others fulfil what they have not bound themselves to: as was the case with those two sons, one of whom "said, I will not; and afterwards he went: the other said, I go, sir; and he went not."[1] And therefore there may be some perfect people who are not in a state of perfection; and some in a state of perfection who yet are not perfect.

ARTICLE V.—*Are religious and prelates in a state of perfection?*

R. To a state of perfection there is requisite a perpetual obligation to the practices of perfection, attended with some solemnity. Both of these requisites are found in religious and in bishops. For religious bind themselves by vow to keep aloof from worldly things, that otherwise they might lawfully have used, that by renouncing such things they may be more free to apply their minds and

[1] St. Matt. xxi. 28—30.

hearts to God, in which application the perfection of the present life consists. Their offering is also attended with a certain solemnity of profession and benediction. In like manner also bishops bind themselves to the practices of perfection by taking up the pastoral office, part of which office is that the shepherd should "lay down his life for his sheep."[1] Hence the Apostle says to Timothy: "Thou hast confessed a good confession before many witnesses;"[2] that is, "in his ordination," as the interlinear gloss there says. Also a ceremony of consecration goes along with the above-mentioned profession, according to the text: "Stir up the grace of God, which is in thee by the imposition of my hands,"[3] which the gloss explains of the grace of the episcopate.

§ 2. Men take up a state of perfection, not as professing themselves to be perfect, but as professing that they are aiming at perfection. Hence one who takes up a state of perfection is not guilty of a lie or a piece of pretence by not being perfect, but only if he revokes his purpose of aiming at perfection.

ARTICLE VIII.—*Are parish priests and archdeacons in positions of greater perfection than religious?*

R. A comparison of superior excellence has no place among persons on the side on which they agree, but on the side on which they differ. Now in parish priests and archdeacons we may consider

[1] St. John x. 15. [2] 1 Timothy vi. 12. [3] 2 Timothy i. 6.

three things: their state, their order, and their office. For their state, they are seculars; for their order, they are priests or deacons; for their office, they have the cure of souls. If therefore we set up on the other side one who is in state a religious, in order a deacon or priest, and in office has cure of souls, as is the case with many monks and canons regular, he excels on the first point, and on the other two points he will be equal. But if the second individual differs from the first in state and office, while agreeing with him in order, as is the case with religious priests and deacons who have no cure of souls, it is plain that the second will be more excellent than the first in state, inferior in office, and equal in order. We must consider therefore which superior excellence is higher, that of state or that of office. In this comparison there are two things to attend to, goodness and difficulty. If therefore the comparison be made in point of goodness, in that respect the state of religion carries it over the office of parish priest or archdeacon: because the religious binds himself for his whole life to the study of perfection; but the parish priest or archdeacon does not bind himself for his whole life to the cure of souls, as a bishop does; nor has he the principal care of his subjects, as a bishop has; but only certain details of the cure of souls are committed to the office of parish priests and archdeacons. And therefore the comparison of the religious state to their office is like comparing the universal to the particular, or a holocaust to a sacrifice, which is less than a holocaust.[1] But this comparison is to be understood as referring only to the kind of the work: for in respect of the charity of the worker it happens sometimes that a work, less of its kind, is more meritorious by being done on a motive of greater charity.

But if we consider the difficulty of living well in religion, and that of living well in the office of the cure of souls, in that comparison it is more difficult to live well with cure of souls, owing to exterior dangers: yet at the same time religious life is more difficult in regard of the kind of work itself, from the restrictions of regular observance.

But if a religious be also without order,[2] as is the case with lay-brothers, in that case it is clear that the superior excellence of order carries it in dignity, because by holy order one is appointed to the august ministries whereby Christ Himself is served in the Sacrament of the Altar: and for this there is required greater interior sanctity than is required even by the religious state. Hence, other things being equal, a clerk in holy orders sins more grievously, if he does anything contrary to sanctity, than a religious who has received no sacred order; although a lay-brother in religion is bound to regular observances, to which they in holy orders are not bound.

---

[1] St. Thomas tacitly assumes that the study of perfection in a religious furnishes him with occupation of at least equal value with that which the cure of souls furnishes to the parish priest. For the assumption he might refer us back to q. 182. art. 2. (Trl.)

[2] Not in holy orders. (Trl.)

§ 6. The difficulty that comes of the arduousness of the work, adds to the perfection of the virtue. But the difficulty that arises from exterior obstacles, sometimes even diminishes the perfection of the virtue, as when one has not enough love of virtue to be willing to avoid what are obstacles to virtue, according to the advice of the Apostle: "Every one that striveth for the mastery refraineth himself from all things."[1] But at other times it is a sign of more perfect virtue, as when obstacles to virtue occur of a sudden, or by some unavoidable cause, and yet the man swerves not from virtue for all that. Now in the state of religion there is greater difficulty from the arduousness of the works; but in the case of persons living in the world in any condition, the difficulty is greater that arises from obstacles to virtue, obstacles which religious have providently stepped out of the way of once for all.

[1] 1 Cor ix 25.

QUESTION CLXXXVI.

OF THE THINGS IN WHICH THE RELIGIOUS STATE PROPERLY CONSISTS.

ARTICLE I.—*Does religion mean a state of perfection?*

R. What is the attribute of many things in common, is eminently attributed to that to which it belongs in a more excellent way. Thus the virtue which preserves firmness of soul in the most difficult conjunctures, claims to itself the name of fortitude; and the virtue that tempers the greatest pleasures claims the name of temperance. But religion is a virtue whereby one presents something to the service and worship of God. And therefore they are called eminently *religious*, who hand over the dominion of themselves to the divine service, offering as it were a holocaust to God. Hence Gregory says: "There are some who reserve nothing to themselves, but immolate to Almighty God the sense, tongue, life and substance, which they have received." But the perfection of man consists in a total adhesion to God; and in this way religious life stands for a state of perfection.

§ 2. To religion there belong not only offerings of sacrifice, and other such acts which are proper to religion, but also the acts of all virtues, in so far as they are referred to God's service and honour. And thus if one sets aside his whole life to the divine service, his whole life belongs to religion; and in this way, from the religious life which they lead, they are called religious who are in the state of perfection.

§ 4. The religious state is instituted principally for the gaining of perfection by means of certain exercises whereby the obstacles to perfect charity are removed. Much more are the occasions of sin cut off, sin being the total destruction of charity. Hence, as it is part of penance to cut off the causes of sin, it follows that the religious state affords a most convenient place for penance.

ARTICLE II.—*Is every religious bound to all the counsels?*

R. A thing appertains to perfection in three ways: first, *essentially*, and in this way the perfect observance of the precepts of charity appertains to perfection. In another way, a thing appertains to perfection *consequently*, as do the acts which follow from the perfection of charity, as meeting a curse with a blessing,[1] and the fulfilment of other such directions: for whereas these directions are matters of precept in readiness of heart to fulfil them when necessity requires,[2] the fulfilling of them

[1] St. Luke vi. 28.

[2] *E.g.*, sometimes the only practical way of overcoming the temptation to meet a curse with a curse, which would be sinful, is to force ourselves to answer with a blessing; and then the blessing may be said to be *necessary*. Cf. II-II. q. 72. art. 3. (Trl.)

where there is no necessity is the fruit of a superabundance of charity. In a third way, a thing appertains to perfection *as an instrument* and predisposing cause; such things are poverty, continence, abstinence, and the like.

The perfection of charity itself is the scope and aim of the religious state. And the said state is a training and exercise for the arriving at perfection: whereunto people may arrive by different exercises, as a cure may be wrought by different medicines. Now in him who is working towards an end, it is not a necessary condition that he should have already reached the end: what is requisite is that he should be taking some way that leads to the end. Therefore he who adopts the religious state is not bound to have perfect charity, but he is bound to make it his aim and endeavour to have perfect charity. And in the same way he is not bound to fulfil those directions, the fulfilment of which is consequent upon the perfection of charity, but he is bound to turn his face towards the fulfilment of them, the contrary of which he does by despising them: hence he does not sin if he omits them, but sins if he despises them. In like manner again he is not bound to all the exercises by which perfection is arrived at: but he is bound to those which are definitely mapped out for him according to the rule of which he has made profession.

§ 1. He who goes into religion does not profess to be perfect, but professes to be aiming at the attainment of perfection; as he who enters the school does not profess to be learned, but professes to study for the acquirement of learning. Hence Augustine says: "Pythagoras would not profess himself to be a sage, but a lover of wisdom."[1] And therefore a religious is not an offender against his profession if he is not perfect, but only if he despises the idea of aiming at perfection.

§ 2. As all are bound to love God with their whole heart, and yet there is one entirety of perfection that cannot be omitted without sin, and another that may be omitted without sin, provided it be without contempt; so also all men, as well religious as seculars, are bound in some sort to do whatever good they can, for it is said to all alike, "Whatsoever thy hand is able to do, do it earnestly,"[2] and yet there is a measure of fulfilment of this precept sufficient to avoid sin, which is, if a man do what he can as the condition of his state requires, provided he do not despise the idea of doing better, for by such contempt the mind is set and rooted against spiritual progress.

§ 3. There are certain counsels the neglect of which would involve a man's whole life in secular business: these counsels are matter of the essential vows of religion; and to them all religious are bound. There are other counsels of better courses of action in certain particulars, which may be omitted without a man's life being involved in

---

[1] Pythagoras first took the name of *philosopher*, or *lover of wisdom* (Trl.)

[2] Eccles. ix. 10.

secular concerns; hence religious need not be bound to all such particulars.[1]

ARTICLE III.—*Is poverty a requisite of religious perfection?*

R. The state of religion is an exercise and training by which men arrive at the perfection of charity. For this it is necessary totally to withdraw the affection from worldly things: for Augustine says, speaking to God, "He loves thee less, who loves aught with thee that he loves not for thee." Now by the possession of worldly goods a man's mind is allured to love them. Hence for the acquirement of the perfection of charity the first foundation is voluntary poverty, which means that a man should live without anything of his own, as our Lord says: "If thou wilt be perfect, go sell what thou hast."[2]

§ 5. The state of bishops is not directed to the gaining of perfection, but rather proceeds on the strength of perfection already possessed to the governing of others, and ministering to them, not only in spirituals, but in temporals also; which is a work of the active life, in which many things occur that have to be done through the instrumentality of riches. And therefore of bishops, whose profession is the government of the flock of Christ, it is not required that they go without anything of their own, as it is required of religious, whose profession it is to be in training for the acquirement of perfection.

---

[1] This opens out the possibility of one Order being severer than another; and of *strict* or *mitigated observance*, without any corruption. (Trl.)   [2] St. Matt. xix. 21.

ARTICLE IV.—*Is perpetual continence requisite for the perfection of religious life?*

R. The religious state requires the withdrawal of the obstacles that stand in a man's way and prevent him from giving himself entirely to the divine service. Such an obstacle is the commerce of the sexes, as well on account of the quantity of the pleasure and increase of concupiscence by its frequent repetition, as also on account of the solicitude which it occasions in a man about the management of wife and family and temporal affairs.

ARTICLE V.—*Does obedience appertain to the perfection of religious life?*

R. The religious state is a training or exercise in aiming at perfection. Now persons in training or exercise, to arrive at any end, must follow some one's direction, and be trained or exercised at his discretion, as scholars under a master. And therefore religious must be subject to some one's training and command for what concerns religious life. Hence it is said: "In the life of monks, the word is subjection and pupillage." Therefore obedience is requisite for religious perfection.

§ 3. The subjection of religious is principally to bishops, who stand to religious as givers to receivers of perfection, or as initiators to initiated, as may be seen from Dionysius.[1] Hence neither hermits nor religious superiors are excused from obedience to bishops; and if they are exempt wholly

[1] The same word in Greek means to *initiate* and to *perfect*. (Trl.)

or in part from the jurisdiction of the diocesan bishops, they are still bound to obey the Sovereign Pontiffs, not only in matters common to them with other Christians, but also in things that especially belong to the discipline of religious life.

§ 4. The vow of obedience in religion extends to the laying out of a man's whole life, and thus has a certain universality, though it does not extend to all particular acts. For some acts do not belong to religion, because they deal not with things belonging to the love of God and our neighbour. Such acts are the stroking of the beard, the raising of a straw from the earth, and the like; these do not fall under vow nor under obedience.[1]

§ 5. The necessity that is of constraint makes an action involuntary, and excludes the notion of praise and merit; but the necessity that follows obedience is not a necessity coming of constraint, but of free-will, inasmuch as a man wills to obey, though otherwise, perhaps, looking at the thing commanded as it is in itself, he would not be willing to accomplish it. And therefore, because by the vow of obedience a man subjects himself for God's sake to the necessity of doing some things that are not

---

[1] We are told (I-II. q. 18. art. 9.) that acts like these are not properly moral or human acts, but lie outside the sphere of morality. On the extent of religious obedience, see further, II-II. q. 104, art. 5. § 3. *Suarez on the Religious State*, c. 10, n. 8 (trl. Humphrey), says: "In religious bodies obedience is not vowed absolutely and without limit, but according to the Rule of each Order. The common doctrine of the schools, of theologians as well as canonists, is that a superior cannot oblige a religious to that which is foreign to, or lies altogether outside his Rule." Vol. II. p. 24. (Trl.)

pleasant in themselves, on that account the things that he does are more acceptable to God, even though they be less considerable, because there is nothing greater that man can give to God than for His sake to submit his own will to the will of another.

ARTICLE VI.—*Is it requisite for religious perfection that poverty, chastity, and obedience, should be made matters of vow?*

R. It belongs to religious to be in a state of perfection. Now for a state of perfection there is required an obligation to the practices of perfection; and that obligation to God is effected by vow. But poverty, continence, and obedience belong to the perfection of Christian life; and therefore the religious state requires that a man be bound by vow to these three things. Hence Gregory says: "When a man has vowed to Almighty God his whole having, his whole living, and his whole liking, that is a holocaust."

§ 2. Religious perfection requires that a man should render to God, as Gregory says, his "whole living" or life. But a man cannot in act render his whole life to God, because life is not all of it at once, but passes in successive moments. Hence a man cannot render his whole life to God otherwise than by the obligation of a vow.

§ 3. To the words of Augustine, "Of our tributes of service those are the more grateful which, though it were allowable for us not to pay them, still we do pay for love's sake," it is to be said that, among other tributes allowable for us not to pay, is the tribute of our own liberty, which a man holds dearer than all other things. And therefore when a man of his own accord deprives himself of the liberty of abstaining from what belongs to the service of God, he renders a most grateful tribute to God. Hence Augustine says: "Repent not of the vow you have made; nay, rejoice to have no longer allowed you, what might have been allowed you to your loss. Happy necessity, that compels to the better course."

ARTICLE VII.—*Is it proper to say that in these three vows religious perfection lies?*

R. The religious state may be considered either as an exercise of aiming at the perfection of charity, or as a rest to the human mind from exterior solicitudes, as the Apostle says: "I wish you to be without solicitude;"[1] or as a holocaust whereby one offers oneself and all that one has to God. And accordingly the religious state is set up in its integrity by these three vows. First, as regards the exercise of perfection, it is required that a man should put away from himself entirely all that could possibly hinder his whole heart from going out to God, wherein the perfection of charity consists. There are three such possible hinderances: the covetousness of external goods, which is removed by the vow of poverty; the craving for sensual pleasure, especially that of a sexual character, which is cut off by the vow of continence; and the

[1] 1 Cor. vii. 32.

inordination of the human will, which the vow of obedience excludes. In like manner the restlessness of worldly solicitude turns principally on three things: on the management of external goods, which solicitude the vow of poverty takes away; on the government of wife and children, which care is cut off by the vow of continence; and on the laying out of one's own conduct, which care is cut off by the vow of obedience, whereby a person commits himself to the disposal of another. In like manner it is also a holocaust, whereby one offers all that one has to God: first, the good of exterior things by the vow of poverty; secondly, the good of the body by the vow of continence, which is a renunciation of the greatest pleasures of the body; thirdly, the good of the soul by obedience, which is an offering to God of one's own will. And therefore the religious state is suitably set up in its integrity by these three vows.

§ 2. All the other observances of religious orders are reducible to the above-mentioned three principal vows. Thus any means instituted for the procuring of a livelihood, as labour, begging, and the like, are reducible to poverty, for the maintenance of which religious procure their livelihood by these means. Other means by which the body is macerated, as fastings, watchings, and such like observances, are reducible to the keeping of the vow of continence. And any means instituted in religious orders regarding human acts, whereby one is directed to the end of religion, that is, to the love of God and of one's neighbour—such as reading, praying, visiting of the sick—are comprehended under the vow of obedience, which concerns the will, as that power directs its acts to an end which is at another's discretion.

§ 4. As for the honour that is paid to God and to all the saints for their virtue, according to the Psalm, "To me thy friends, O God, are made exceedingly honourable,"[1] it does not belong to religious to renounce that honour in aiming at the perfection of virtue. But the honour that is paid to exterior excellence they do renounce, by the very fact of their quitting the secular life: hence no special vow is required for this renunciation.

ARTICLE VIII.—*Is the vow of obedience chief of the three vows of religion?*

R. The vow of obedience is the chief of the three vows of religion for three reasons, first, because by the vow of obedience a man offers something greater to God, namely, his own will, which is a better gift than his own body, which he offers by continence, and than exterior things, which he offers by the vow of poverty. Hence what is done on a motive of obedience is more acceptable to God than what is done of one's own will. Hence Jerome says to the monk Rusticus: "Thou art not to be left to thy own discretion; do not what thou wilt; eat what thou art bidden; have what thou hast received; wear what is given to thee." Hence even fasting is not acceptable to God if attended with self-will, according to the text: "Behold, in

[1] Psalm cxxxviii. 17.

the day of your fast your own will is found."[1] Secondly, because the vow of obedience contains under itself the other vows, while they do not contain it: for though a religious is bound by vow to observe continence and poverty, yet these things fall also under obedience, to which it belongs to observe many other things besides continence and poverty. Thirdly, because the vow of obedience properly extends to acts that lie close to the end, scope, and aim of religion: now the nearer a thing comes to the end, the better it is. Hence also the vow of obedience is the more essential to religion; for if without the vow of obedience one were to observe even by vow voluntary poverty and continence, he would not for all that belong to the religious state, which state has the preference even over virginity observed by vow.

ARTICLE IX.

§ 3. One offends by *contempt*, when his will refuses to be subject to the ordinance of the law or rule, and thence proceeds to act against the law or rule. Conversely, when by some particular cause, as concupiscence or anger, one is led to act against the provisions of the law or rule, he does not sin by contempt, even though he sin repeatedly. But frequency of sinning disposes and induces to contempt, according to the text: "The wicked man when he is come into the depth of sins, contemneth."[2]

[1] Isaias lviii 3.   [2] Prov. xviii. 3.

ARTICLE X.—*Does the religious sin more grievously than the secular for the same kind of sin?*

R. The sin that is committed by religious may in three ways be more grievous than sin of the same species committed by seculars. First, if it be against a vow of religion: thus fornication in a religious is against the vow of continence, and theft against the vow of poverty, and not only against the precept of the divine law. Secondly, if the religious sins out of contempt: because this seems to be greater ingratitude for the divine benefits by which he has been raised to the state of perfection. Hence the Lord complains: "What is the meaning that my beloved hath wrought much wickedness in my house?"[1] Thirdly, the sin of religious may be greater on account of the scandal, because more people have their eyes on his life. But if a religious, not out of contempt but out of weakness or ignorance, commits some sin that is not against the vow of his profession, and commits it without any scandal, he sins more lightly for the same kind of sin than the secular: because his sin, if it is venial, is as it were swallowed up in the multitude of good works that he does; and if it is mortal, he more easily rises from it again. Hence on the text, "When he shall fall, he shall not be bruised,"[2] Origen says: "If the unjust[3] sins, he repents not, and has no mind to correct his sin; but the just man has a mind for his own amendment

---

[1] Jerem. xi. 15.   [2] Psalm xxxvi. 24.
[3] The unjust here is "intemperate;" the just man sinning is "incontinent," according to the terminology of q. 156. art. 3. (Trl.)

and correction; as he who had said, 'I know not the man,' afterwards when he was looked upon by the Lord, knew how to weep bitter tears; and he who had seen the woman from the roof, and lusted after her, knew how to say, 'I have sinned and done evil before thee.'" The religious is also aided by his fellows to rise again, according to the text: "If one fall, he shall be supported by the other: woe to him that is alone, for when he falleth, he hath none to lift him up."[1]

§ 3. The just do not easily sin out of contempt, though they sometimes fall into sin out of ignorance or weakness, from which they are easily raised up. But if they do come to sin out of contempt, they become the worst and the most incorrigible of all, according to the text: "Thou hast broken my yoke, thou hast burst my bands, and thou saidst: I will not serve. On every high hill and under every green tree thou didst prostitute thyself."[2] And Augustine says: "From the time that I began to serve God, as I have hardly found better men than those who have advanced to goodness in monasteries, so I have not found worse than those who have fallen in monasteries."

[1] Eccles. iv. 10.   [2] Jerem. ii. 20.

QUESTION CLXXXVII.

OF THE THINGS PROPER FOR RELIGIOUS TO DO.

ARTICLE I.—*Is it lawful for religious to preach and teach?*

R. A thing is said to be *unlawful* for a person in two ways: in one way, because he has in his being some element contradicting and conflicting with that which is said to be *unlawful* for him. Thus it is lawful for no man to sin, because every man has within himself reason and an obligation to the law of God, elements with which sin is in conflict. And in this way it may be said to be unlawful for such and such a one to preach or teach, because he has something in himself inconsistent with these functions, the inconsistency arising either from a precept, as persons irregular by ecclesiastical enactment are not allowed to ascend to holy orders, or from sin, as the text has it: "To the sinner God hath said, Why dost thou declare my justices?"[1] But preaching and teaching are not unlawful for religious in this way: both because there is nothing in their vows and precept of their rule obliging them to abstain from these functions, and also because they are not unfitted for them by

[1] Psalm xlix. 16.

any sin that they have committed, but rather are made fit and proper persons by the exercise of holiness which they have taken up. It is foolish to say that a person's advance in holiness makes him less fit to exercise spiritual functions. Foolish therefore is the opinion of those who pretend that the religious state is of itself an impediment to the exercise of such employments.[1]

In another way a thing is said to be *unlawful* for a person, not on account of any contradictory or conflicting element in his being, but for the lack of power in him: thus it is not lawful for a deacon to celebrate mass, because he has not the order of priesthood; and it is not lawful for a simple priest to pass sentence, because he has not the authority of a bishop. But there is a difference here: for matters of order cannot be committed but to him who has the order; as the celebration of mass cannot be committed to a deacon unless he becomes

---

[1] Pius VI in 1794, in his Bull *Auctorem Fidei*, nn. 80—84, condemns as "false, pernicious, scandalous," various utterances of the Jansenist Synod of Pistoia in opposition to this portion of St. Thomas, *e.g.*, that "the state of Regulars from its nature cannot be reconciled with the care of souls;" that "it could be wished that St. Thomas in defending them had written with less heat and greater accuracy:" that members of the one religious order which these reformers would still tolerate in the Church, were "not to be admitted to holy orders." that among their occupations there should be "a due portion kept inviolate for labour of the hands:" that "vows of chastity, poverty, and obedience shall not be admitted as a general and standing rule: if any one wishes to make those vows, all or some of them, he shall ask advice and leave of the Bishop, who shall never permit the vows to be perpetual, nor to be made for more than one year at a time," &c. (Trl.)

a priest: but matters of jurisdiction can be committed to those who have not ordinary jurisdiction, as the pronouncing of sentence is committed by a bishop to a simple priest. And in this way it is said to be not lawful for monks and other religious to preach and teach, because the religious state does not empower them to do such things. They may however do them if they receive order or ordinary jurisdiction, or again if powers of jurisdiction be committed to them.[1]

ARTICLE III.—*Are religious bound to work with their hands?*

R. Manual labour is directed first and foremost to getting a livelihood: hence it was said to the first man, "In the sweat of thy brow thou shalt eat thy bread."[2] Secondly, it is directed to the removal of idleness: hence it is said, "Send him to work that he be not idle, for idleness hath taught much evil."[3] Thirdly, it is directed to the maceration of the body and the curbing of concupiscence: hence it is said: "In labours, in fastings, in watchings, in chastity."[4] So far then as manual labour is directed to gaining a livelihood, it falls under necessity of precept as a means necessary to the said end: for what is ordained to an end, has its necessity from the end, being necessary inasmuch

---

[1] This last sentence must mean "if they receive holy orders, and jurisdiction whether ordinary or delegated." (Trl.)
[2] Genesis iii. 19.   [3] Ecclus. xxxiii. 28, 29.
[4] 2 Cor. vi. 5, 6.

as the end cannot be gained without it.[1] And therefore he who has not anything else to live upon, is bound to manual labour, whatever be his condition,—understanding by manual labour all services to human society by which a man may lawfully make a livelihood, whether with hands, feet, or tongue. But so far forth as manual labour is ordained for the removal of idleness or the maceration of the body, it does not fall under necessity of itself, because the flesh may be reduced by other means, as by watchings and fastings; and idleness may be removed by meditations on Holy Scripture and praises of God.

§ 1. The precept set forth by the Apostle, "Work with your own hands as we commanded you,"[2] is a precept of natural law; and all alike are bound by this precept, both religious and seculars, as by all other precepts of the natural law. Still not every man sins that does not work with his hands; because not all individuals are bound to those precepts of the law of nature which regard the good of many, but it is enough that one sets himself to one office, another to another,—some artisans, some husbandmen, some judges, some

---

[1] The necessity here described would be spoken of by a modern theologian as *necessitas medii* in contradistinction to *necessitas præcepti*. I do not find in St. Thomas the convenient word *medium*, "means," which figures so much in modern school Latin. He says always, with Aristotle, *ea quæ sunt ad finem*. However (I-II. q. 8. art. 3 § 3.) we read: "In the execution of a work, what makes for the end (*ea quæ sunt ad finem*) is as the intervening ground (*media*), and the end as the terminus." (Trl.)

[2] 1 Thess. iv. 11.

teachers, and the like, as the Apostle has it: "If the whole body were the eye, where would be the hearing? if the whole were the hearing, where would be the smelling?"[1]

§ 5. The Apostles' working with their hands was sometimes a matter of *necessity*, sometimes of *supererogation*. Of *necessity*, when they could not find sustenance from others: hence on the text, "We labour working with our own hands,"[2] the gloss says, "because nobody gives us anything." Of *supererogation*, as appears by 1 Cor. ix. 12—15, where the Apostle says that he has not used the power that he had of living by the Gospel. This supererogation he practised, first, to take away the occasion of preaching from the false apostles, who preached for temporal profits only;[3] secondly, to avoid burdening those to whom he preached;[4] thirdly, to give an example of working to the idle.[5] But the Apostle did not act thus in the places where he had opportunity of preaching every day, as at Athens, as Augustine notes. Religious are not bound to imitate the Apostle on this point, as they are not bound to all works of supererogation. Hence neither did the other Apostles work with their hands.

ARTICLE IV.—*Is it lawful for religious to live on alms?*

R. It is lawful for any man to live on what is his *own*, or on what is *due* to him. Now a thing

---

[1] 1 Cor. xii. 17.   [2] 1 Cor. iv. 12.   [3] 2 Cor. xi. 12.
[4] 2 Cor. xii. 13.   [5] 2 Thess. iii. 8.

becomes a person's *own* by the liberality of a giver. And therefore the religious or clerics on whose monasteries or churches endowments are bestowed by the munificence of princes or other faithful, may live thereupon without labouring with their hands; and yet it is certain that they live by alms. Hence in like manner whatever movable goods are bestowed on religious by the faithful, they may lawfully live thereupon: for it is folly to say that one may receive great possessions in alms, and not a piece of bread or a little money. But because these benefits are considered to be bestowed on religious, to the end that they may be more free to apply to acts of religion, of which acts they who supply their temporal needs desire to have a share, the use of the above-mentioned gifts would be rendered unlawful to them if they were to desist from the acts of religion, because in that case, so far as in them lay, they would defraud the purpose of the donors.

As for a thing being *due* to another, that comes to be in two ways. In one way by necessity, which makes all things common, as Ambrose says. Therefore if religious suffer necessity, they may lawfully live on alms. This necessity may be from bodily weakness, preventing them from gaining a livelihood by manual labour; or because what they do so gain is insufficient; or because in their former life they were not accustomed to manual labour, delicately nurtured persons being unable to stand such toil. In another way a thing becomes a man's *due*, because he renders some service to bodies or to souls. And on this count religious may live on alms as their due in four ways: first, if they preach by the authority of prelates empowering them to do so; secondly, if they are ministers of the altar,[1] because the Sacrifice of the Altar, wherever it is celebrated, is common to the whole people of the faithful; thirdly, if they are students of Holy Scripture for the common benefit of the whole Church; fourthly, if they give to the monastery the temporal goods that they had, they may live on the alms offered to the monastery. But if there be any religious who without necessity, and without doing any good, want to live in ease and idleness upon the alms that are given to the poor, that is an unlawful line to take.

ARTICLE V.—*Is it lawful for religious to beg?*
R. If we consider begging as it is on the part of the agent, the act has a certain abjection attaching to it. For they count as the most abject of mankind, who are not merely poor, but so needy as to be obliged to receive their living from others. Thus for humility's sake some laudably beg, as others take up other works that carry a certain abjection with them, taking this to be the most effectual remedy against pride, which they wish to extinguish, either in themselves, or in others by their example. In another way we may consider begging in regard of what is got by begging; and thus there may be two inducements to the practice: one, the desire of having riches, or a livelihood

[1] 1 Cor. ix. 14.

without working for it, and in that way begging is unlawful. The other inducement is necessity or utility: necessity, when one cannot live otherwise ; utility, when one wants to carry out some useful work which cannot be carried out without the alms of the faithful, as a bridge, or a church, or as we see scholars begging that they may be able to apply to the study of wisdom for the public good. And thus it is lawful for religious, as for seculars, to beg.

ARTICLE VI.

§ 3. According to our Lord's teaching,[1] in works of holiness men ought to do nothing for display. Now display comes easiest when one does something new and strange. Hence the advice: "Let him who is at prayer do nothing strange to fix the gaze of men, crying out, or smiting his breast, or stretching out his hands." Still not every novelty that fixes men's eyes upon the doer of it, is reprehensible: for it may be even well done. Hence Augustine says: "When a man in the profession of Christianity fixes the eyes of all the world upon himself by an unusual squalor and meanness in his dress, supposing him to do so of choice and not of necessity, then from the rest of his works we may know whether he does it from contempt of toilet luxuries or from a desire of notoriety." But this desire of notoriety seems especially removed from the thoughts of religious, who wear a mean habit as a sign of their profession, which is to despise the world.

[1] St. Matt. vi. 16, 18.

QUESTION CLXXXVIII.

OF THE VARIETY OF RELIGIOUS ORDERS.

ARTICLE I.—*Is there only one religious order?*
R. The state of religion is an exercise whereby one is trained to the perfection of charity. Now there are different works of charity to which a man may apply himself; and there are different sorts of exercises. And therefore religious orders may differ in one way according to the variety of the purposes which they are ordained to serve; thus one order may be for giving hospitality to pilgrims, another for visiting and ransoming captives. In another way there may be a variety of religious orders according to the various sorts of exercises which they follow: thus the body is chastised in one order by abstinence, and in another by manual labour. But because the end is the main point everywhere, the variety of orders in respect of the variety of the ends of their several institutes is greater than that which arises from variety of exercises.

§ 1. The common element in every religious order is the duty of entirely devoting oneself to the service of God. Here there is no variety: it is not as though in one order a man might keep back some part of himself, and in another not; but the variety arises from the various ways in which it is possible to serve God, and the various manners of disposing oneself thereto.

§ 4. The multitude of religious orders might create confusion, if various orders were destined to the prosecution of the same end, and that by the same means, where there was no need and no use for so many. For the prevention of this there is a salutary provision, that no new religious order be instituted without the approval of the Sovereign Pontiff.

ARTICLE II.—*Can a religious order be instituted for the works of the active life?*

R. The religious state is ordained for the end of charity, which extends to the love of God and of our neighbour. The contemplative life, which desires to occupy itself with God alone, is directly taken up with the love of God: whereas the active life, which ministers to our neighbour's needs, is directly taken up with the love of our neighbour. And as it is on the motive of charity that our neighbour is loved for God, so also the service done our neighbours redounds on to God, according to the text: "As long as you did it to one of these my least brethren, you did it to me."[1] Hence inasmuch as these services rendered to our neighbour are referred to God, they are called *sacrifices* in the text: "Do not forget to do good and to impart: for by such sacrifices God's favour is obtained."[2]

[1] St. Matt. xxv. 40. [2] Hebrews xiii. 16.

And because it properly belongs to religion to offer sacrifice to God, it follows that some religious orders are fitly and suitably ordained to the employments of the active life.

§ 1. In the employments of the active life solitude is preserved, not to the effect that the man does not converse with men, but to this effect, that he is solely intent upon serving God. In religious thus engaged in view of God, their action is inspired by contemplation of divine things. Hence they are not altogether deprived of the fruit of the contemplative life.

§ 2. All religious are in the same condition with monks as regards their entire dedication to the divine service, the observance of the essential vows of religion, and abstinence from secular business. But there is no need of likeness on other points, proper to the monastic profession, which is specially directed to the contemplative life.[1]

ARTICLE III.—*Can there be a religious order destined for military service?*

R. A religious order may be instituted not only for the works of the contemplative life, but also for the works of the active life, in so far as they have to do with the helping of our neighbours and the service of God, but not for the obtaining of any worldly end. But the duty of a soldier may be directed, not merely

---

[1] Exclusive of the Military Orders, the four kinds of religious known to canonists are Canons Regular, Clerks Regular, Monks, and Friars. (Trl.)

to the helping of private persons, but even to the defence of the entire commonwealth: hence it is said of Judas Machabeus that he "fought with cheerfulness the battle of Israel."[1] Such fighting also may be directed to the preservation of divine worship: hence Simon says, "You know what great battles I and my brethren and the house of my father have fought for the laws and the sanctuary."[2] Hence a military religious order may suitably be instituted, not for any worldly end, but for the defence of the divine worship and the public safety.

§ 1. To the text, "I say to you not to resist evil,"[3] it is to be said that there are two ways of not resisting evil: one way by forgiving the wrong done to oneself, and that may be a point of perfection, when it is expedient so to behave for the salvation of others; the other way is by patiently enduring the injuries done to others, and that is an imperfect and even a vicious course, if one can well resist the wrong-doer. Hence Ambrose says: "The fortitude that in war preserves our country from barbarians, or at home defends the weak, is full justice." Our Lord says in the same place: "Of him that taketh away thy goods, ask them not again;"[4] and yet if one were not to ask back the goods belonging to others, when they were his concern to keep, that would be sinful: for a man may laudably give away his own, but not another's. Much less are the interests of God to be neglected.

---

[1] 1 Mach. iii. 2. [2] 1 Mach. xiii. 3. [3] St. Matt. v. 39.
[4] St. Luke vi. 30.

Article IV.—*Can a religious order be instituted to preach or hear confessions?*

R. It is a greater thing to defend the faithful against the errors of heretics, and against the temptations of devils, than to maintain the cause of the faithful people with material arms. And therefore it is most fitting and proper for an order to be instituted for preaching and other functions that go towards the saving of souls.

§ 2. As some religious orders are instituted for military service, to wage war not of their own authority, but by the authority of the Church or of princes: so also religious orders are instituted to preach and hear confessions, not by their own authority, but by the authority of prelates, superior and inferior, to whom that duty officially belongs; and thus to be subordinate to prelates in such a ministry is proper to such a religious order.

Article V.—*Is it right for a religious order to be instituted for purposes of study?*

R. The study of letters befits religious in three ways. First, as to the contemplative life, which is doubly aided by the study of letters, in one way directly by the illumination of the intellect, in another way indirectly by removing the dangers of contemplation, that is, the errors which in the contemplation of divine things frequently befall those who are ignorant of the Scriptures. Secondly, the study of letters is necessary for religious who are destined for preaching and other such functions. Nor is it any argument to the contrary, to say that the Apostles were sent to preach without any study of letters: because, as Jerome says, "What others usually gather from training and daily meditation in the law of God, was suggested to them by the Holy Ghost." Thirdly, the study of letters is becoming in a religious order for a purpose that is common to every religious order, namely, for avoiding the wantonness of the flesh. Hence Jerome says to the monk Rusticus: "Love the science of the Scriptures, and thou shalt not love the vices of the flesh." For the labour of study turns away the mind from wantonness, and wears down the flesh.

§ 3. To apply to other branches of learning than that which is "according to godliness,"[1] is not proper to religious, whose whole life is made over to acts of the service of God, except so far as other branches of learning are conducible to sacred learning.[2]

ARTICLE VII.—*Does the holding of property in common diminish the perfection of a religious order?*

R. Perfection does not consist essentially in poverty, but in the following of Christ. Poverty is

---

[1] Titus i. 1.
[2] This holds of what may be called the *esoteric* studies of religious, those proper to perfect them in their own state. But the members of an educational order nowadays have to study many things, the bearing of which on sacred learning is remote enough, not more remote however than the art of war, which was the study of the Templars and Hospitallers. (art. 3.) A military order forms a precedent for a good deal. (Trl.)

a sort of instrument or exercise for arriving at perfection. It is so, inasmuch as the taking away of riches is the removal of three chief obstacles to charity, which are the solicitude that riches bring; the love of riches, which is increased by possession of them; and the vainglory or elation that is born of riches. Of these three the first cannot be entirely separated from riches, be they great or small; for a man must be to some extent solicitous about acquiring or preserving exterior goods; nor is all solicitude forbidden by our Lord, but only that which is superfluous or noxious. But the other two, namely, love of riches, and elation or glorying on the score of riches, follow upon riches, only when they are abundant. Yet it makes a difference in the matter, whether the riches, be they abundant or be they moderate, are held as private property or in common. For solicitude about private property is part of that private and particular love, with which a man loves himself in the temporal order; but solicitude about the common estate is part of that love of charity, which "seeketh not its own," but looks to the common good. And because religious life is ordained to the perfection of charity, which perfection consists in loving God to the contempt of oneself, the having anything of one's own is inconsistent with the perfection of religious life; but solicitude about goods held in common stock may belong to charity, even though a higher act of charity, such as divine contemplation or the instruction of one's neighbour, be hindered thereby. Hence it appears that to have superabundance of wealth in common stock is an obstacle to perfection, though it does not totally exclude it: but to have of exterior goods in common stock, sufficient for a simple life, is no hinderance to religious perfection, if we consider poverty in regard of the common end of all religious orders, which is a free and untrammelled application to acts of the service of God. But if we consider it in regard of the special ends that religious orders severally have set before them, then in reference to this or that end in view a greater or a lesser poverty is befitting in a religious order; and every order will be more perfect in point of poverty, the more its poverty is proportioned to its end. For manifestly man needs greater store of exterior goods for the exterior and corporal works of the active life: whereas for contemplation few things are requisite. Hence the Philosopher says: "For actions, one needs many things; and the greater and nobler the actions, the more: but the contemplative has need of none of these things for his special activity: rather we may say they are in his way, for contemplation: but he will need such things to live as a human being."[1] Thus it appears that a religious order which is intended for the corporal actions of the active life, as for military service or the exercise of hospitality, would be imperfect if it did not possess wealth held in common stock; but those religious orders that aim at the contemplative life are so much the more perfect, the less solicitude of temporal things their poverty puts upon them.

[1] These are the exact words of Aristotle, *Ethics*, X. viii. nn. 5, 6. St. Thomas quotes from an imperfect Latin version. (Trl.)

ARTICLE VIII.—*Is a religious order living in community more perfect than an order of solitaries?*

R. Solitude, like poverty, is not the essence of perfection, but an instrument of perfection. But plainly solitude is an instrument apt, not for action but for contemplation, according to the text: "I will lead her into the wilderness and I will speak to her heart."[1] Hence it suits not those orders that are meant for the works of the active life, whether corporal or spiritual, except it be for a time, after the example of Christ, who "went out into a mountain to pray, and he passed the whole night in the prayer of God."[2] But it does suit those orders that are intended for contemplation. However we must observe that the solitary ought to be self-sufficient, wanting in nothing; which is the attribute of him who is perfect: therefore solitude is proper for the contemplative who has already arrived at perfection. Therefore community life is necessary for training in perfection, while solitude befits those that are already perfect.[3] As then being already perfect is of superior excellence to being in training for perfection, so the life of solitaries, if duly entered upon, excels and is superior to community life. But if such a life be entered upon without training, it is most dangerous, unless divine

---

[1] Osee ii. 14.   [2] St Luke vi. 12.
[3] See the account of St. Cuthbert's solitude at Farne, *Life* by Consitt, c. x. When he entered upon it, he had lived fifteen years in a monastic community; and he was taken from it to be made a bishop: a good illustration of St. Thomas's doctrine of the achieved perfection of anchorites and bishops. (Trl.)

grace supply what in others is acquired by training, as in the case of Saints Antony and Benedict.

§ 4. A man's being set up upon a candlestick,[1] is no business of his own to bring about, but is the affair of his superiors. "And unless the burden of office be laid upon us," as Augustine says, "we should spend our time in the contemplation of the truth,"—whereunto solitude is a great help. At the same time solitaries are very useful to mankind. Hence Augustine says: "They seem to some overmuch to have abandoned the things of men: their critics not understanding how much their mind aids us in prayers, and their life for an example, whose bodily features we are not permitted to behold."

§ 5. A man may live as a solitary in two ways: in one way because he cannot brook the company of men on account of the savagery of his disposition; and that is brutish: in another way because he clings with all his being to the things of God; and that is something superhuman. Hence the Philosopher says that "he who lives away from the society of others is either a brute or a god," that is, a divine man.

[1] St. Luke xi. 33.

QUESTION CLXXXIX.

OF THE ENTRY INTO RELIGION.

ARTICLE I.—*Ought they to enter religion, who have not been exercised in the observance of the commandments?*

R. A man's affections becoming attached to the things of earth not only form a hinderance to the perfection of charity, but sometimes even bring about the destruction of charity, when through inordinate turning to temporal goods a man is turned away from the imperishable good by mortal sin. Hence, as the observances of religious life take away the obstacles to perfect charity, so do they also take away the occasions of sin. Thus by fasting, watching, obedience and the like, a man is withdrawn from gluttony, luxury, and all manner of sins besides. And therefore the entry into religion is not only expedient for those who have been trained in the observance of the commandments, that they may arrive at greater perfection, but also for those who have not been so exercised, that they more easily avoid sins and attain perfection.

§ 3. Holy orders presuppose sanctity, but the state of religion is an exercise for obtaining sanctity.

Hence the weight of orders is to be laid on walls already dried by sanctity; but the weight of religion dries the walls, that is, men, of the humour of vices.

§ 5. It is not necessary that the commandments should first be observed without the counsels and afterwards with the counsels, as it is not necessary for one to be an ass before he is a man, or married before he is a virgin. And in like manner one need not keep the commandments in the world before passing into religion, especially since life in the world does not dispose men for the perfection of religious life, but rather hinders them from it.[1]

ARTICLE III.

§ 3. It may be reasonably said that by entry into religion one obtains the remission of all his sins. For if by some almsgiving one can at once satisfy for his sins,[2] according to the advice:

---

[1] We read of criminals of olden time retiring to do penance in a monastery, of converted highwaymen turning monks, and the like. The ancient austere and cloistered orders afforded better ground for such transformations than do the orders and congregations of modern times, which have more of common life, of external activity, and of relations, sometimes sufficiently trying and dangerous, with the world about them. The limbs of such a body should be, not merely set and bandaged, but sound and whole. All that St. Thomas means in this Article is that it is well to enter religion young and innocent, and even inexperienced : there is no need for the aspirant's virtue to have been previously tested by contact with the world and its wickedness. (Trl.)

[2] Satisfy, that is, for the temporal punishment due to sin, true repentance for the same being supposed. So the entry into religion by the first pronouncing of the vows is taken to be a perfect satisfaction for all temporal punishment due at the time. (Trl.)

"Redeem thou thy sins with alms,"[1] much more does it suffice to satisfy for all sins, for a man to bind himself entirely to the divine service by entering religion, as religious life takes precedence of all manner of satisfaction, even that of public penance, in the same way that a holocaust exceeds a sacrifice. Hence we read in the Lives of the Fathers, that persons entering religion gain the same grace as the recipients of baptism.

ARTICLE VII.

§ 2. To the objection that if all priests having cure of souls were to enter religion, the people would be left without pastors,—it is to be said, as Jerome says, that "virtue is rare, and not coveted by the majority." Clearly then this is a foolish fear, as if one were to be afraid to draw water, lest the river should run dry.[2]

ARTICLE VIII.—*Is it lawful to pass from one religious order to another?*

R. To pass from one religious order to another, without great utility or necessity, is not a commendable thing to do: both because they who are left are generally scandalized at it; and also because, other things being equal, one more easily makes progress in an order that he is accustomed to than in one to

---

[1] Daniel iv. 24.

[2] There were more temporal inducements to undertake the cure of souls when St. Thomas wrote than in our age of lost endowments. His remark applies even better to laymen, and the fears expressed for the continuance of the race. (Trl.)

which he is unaccustomed. Still there are three causes for which a religious may laudably pass from one order to another. The first is zeal and desire of a more perfect order: on which we must remember that the excellence of an order does not go merely by strictness, but chiefly by the end that the order has in view, and secondly by the discretion shown in observances, and their due proportion as means to the end. The second cause is the falling away of an order from its due perfection: thus if in a more strict order the religious begin to live remissly, one may laudably pass even to an order less strict, if the observance is better. The third cause is infirmity or weakness; whence it sometimes comes to pass that one cannot observe the enactments of an order of greater strictness, but could observe the enactments of one that was less severe. But there may be a difference noticed in these three cases. In the first case one ought to ask leave for humility's sake; but the leave ought not to be refused, provided it is certain that the other order is more strict. In like manner the superior's judgment is to be sought in the second case. In the third case, even a dispensation is necessary.

ARTICLE X.—*Is it a praiseworthy thing to enter religion without seeking the advice of many persons, and without long previous deliberation?*

R. Long deliberation and the advice of many persons are requisite in great doubt, the Philosopher says. But in things fixed and certain, advice is not required. Now about the entry into religion three things may be considered. The first is the entry into religion as it is in itself; and for that, it is certain that entering religion is the better good. Whoever doubts of that, derogates so far as in him lies from the authority of Christ, who has given this counsel. Hence Augustine says: "The Orient calls thee, that is, Christ, and thou lookest to the west, that is, to a mortal and fallible man." Again, the entry into religion may be considered in reference to the strength of him who is thinking of entering religion; and upon this ground once more there is no room for doubt about the entry into religion: because they who enter religion trust not to stand in their own strength, but in the aid of the power of God, according to the text: "They that hope in the Lord shall renew their strength: they shall take wings as eagles: they shall run and not be weary, they shall walk and not faint."[1] If however there be any special obstacle, as bodily infirmity, or burden of debt, and the like, here deliberation is required, and counsel with those who may be expected to help you, and not stand in your way. Hence it is said: "Treat with a man without religion concerning holiness, and with an unjust man concerning justice,"[2] as much as to say, "Do not so." Hence the text goes on: "Give no heed to these in any matter of counsel, but be thou continually with a holy man."[3] Hence Jerome says: "Hasten, I pray thee, and cut rather than loosen the rope of thy skiff fastened on the beach." The

[1] Isaias xl. 31. [2] Ecclus. xxxvii. 12.
[3] Ecclus. xxxvii. 14, 15.

third thing that may be considered is the manner of entering religion, and what order you should enter; and on such points counsel also may be taken with persons who are not the men to stand in the way.

§ 1. When it is said, "Try the spirits if they be of God,"[1] the saying is to be understood to have place of proposals that are really doubtful, whether they are of the Spirit of God. Thus it may be doubtful to those who are already in religion whether a candidate for religion is led by the Spirit of God or by some interested motive; and therefore they ought to try the candidate, to see whether he is moved by the Divine Spirit. But to the candidate himself there can be no doubt, whether the purpose of entering religion has arisen in his heart from the movement of the Spirit of God, whose office it is to lead man "into the right land."[2] Nor is it shown to be not of God, because some go back upon their purpose: for not everything that is of God is incorruptible; nor is it other than heretical to assert that none who have grace from God can lose it. And therefore the purpose of entering religion needs no trial whether it be of God.

§ 3. By the building of the tower[3] is signified the perfection of Christian life. The renunciation of the things that are one's own is the estimated cost of building the tower. Now no one doubts or deliberates whether he wills to have in hand the estimate, or whether he can build the tower if he has the estimate in hand: but this is what comes

[1] 1 St. John iv. 1. [2] Psalm cxlii. 10. [3] St. Luke xiv. 29.

under deliberation, whether one has the estimate in hand. In like manner it ought not to fall under deliberation whether you should renounce all that you possess, or whether by doing that you can arrive at perfection; but this is what falls under deliberation, whether what you are doing is the renunciation of all that you possess: because without this renunciation—which is having the estimate in hand—you cannot, as the text goes on, "be the disciple" of Christ, which is building the tower.

But as for the fear of those who tremble and doubt whether they can arrive at perfection by entering religion, the unreasonableness of such fear is argued by the example of many. Hence Augustine says: "There opened upon my view in the direction to which I had turned my face, and trembled at the thought of passing over there, the chaste dignity of Continence, modestly alluring me to come and hesitate not, and stretching out to receive and embrace me her loving hands, full of flocks of good examples. There are so many boys and girls, there a numerous youth, and every age, grave widows, and virgins stricken in years. And she laughed at me, a laugh of encouragement, as much as to say: 'Cannot you do what these young men and maidens have done? Or can these young men and maidens do it in their own strength, and not rather in the strength of the Lord their God? Why do you stand upon your own strength, and upon that fail to stand? Throw yourself upon Him: He will not draw back, to let you fall. Throw yourself without fear: He will receive you and save you.'"

Now as to the example alleged of David unable to walk in the armour of Saul,[1] it makes not to the purpose: because "the arms of Saul," as the gloss says, "are the rites of the Old Law, burdensome ordinances;" but religious life is the sweet yoke of Christ. For, as Gregory says: "What heavy burden does He lay on the neck of our spirit, who bids the avoidance of every desire that could trouble us, and recommends the turning of our steps out of the toilsome ways of this world." And to those who take upon them this sweet yoke, He promises in recompense the refreshment of the fruition of God, and everlasting rest for their souls: to which may He bring us who has promised it, Jesus Christ our Lord, who is above all God blessed for ever. Amen.

[1] 1 Kings xvii. 39.

THE END.

INDEX.

I-II. First Division of the Second Part (Prima Secundæ).
II-II. Second Division of the Second Part (Secunda Secundæ).

A.

ACCESSORY, ways of being accessory to another's sin, II-II. q. 62, art. 7.
ACT, elicited and commanded, I-II. q. 6, art. 4; *ib.* q. 71, art 6; II-II. q. 10, art. 2; *ib.* q. 26, art. 7; *ib.* q. 124, art. 2, § 2; exterior and interior act, their relation, I-II. q. 20, artt. 3, 4; immanent and transient acts, I-II. q. 3, art. 2, § 3; *ib.* q. 31, art. 5; *ib.* q. 57, art. 4; human act, I-II. q. 1, art. 1.
ACTIVITY, the essence of happiness, I-II. q. 3, art. 2; the cause of pleasure, I-II. q. 32, art. 1; perfected by pleasure, I-II. q. 33, art. 4.
ADULTERY, a double sin, II-II. q. 154, art. 8.
AFFABILITY, II-II. q. 114, art. 1.
AFFIRMATIVE and negative precepts, II-II. q. 33, art. 2.
ALMSGIVING, precept of, II-II. q. 32, artt. 5, 6; *ib.* q. 66, art. 7; *ib.* q. 71, art. 1; propriety of religious living on alms, II-II. q. 187, art. 4.
ALTRUISM, II-II. q. 26, art. 4, with note.

AMBITION, II-II. q. 131, art. 1.
ANÆSTHETICS, II-II. q. 150, art. 2, § 3, with note.
ANGER, no passion contrary to it, I-II. q. 23, art. 3; anger in drunkards, I-II. q. 46, art. 4, § 3; anger contrasted with hatred, I-II. q. 46, art. 6; anger of God, I-II. q. 47, art. 1, § 1; anger the instrument of fortitude, II-II. q. 123, art. 10, §§ 2, 3; lawfulness of the passion, II-II. q. 158, art. 1; grievousness of the sin, II-II. q. 158, art. 4.
APPEALS, II-II. q. 69, art. 3.
APPETITE, sensitive, I-II. q. 23, art. 1, note; rational or intellectual, otherwise called the will, I-II. q. 31, art. 4; *ib.* q. 59, art. 4; II-II. q. 58, art. 4.
ART, in what sense a virtue, I-II. q. 57. art. 3.
ASSAULT AND BATTERY, II-II. q. 41.
ATTENTION in prayer, II-II. q. 83, art. 13.
ATTRACTIONS, display of, in whom unlawful, II-II. q. 169, art. 2.
AUSTERITIES, II-II. q. 88, art. 2, § 3; *ib.* q. 147.

B.

BEAUTY, I-II. q. 27, art. 1, § 3; II-II. q. 141, art. 2, § 3; *ib.* q. 145, art. 3.
BEGGING, II-II. q. 187, art. 5.
BELIEF AND KNOWLEDGE, II-II. q. 2, art. 1; *ib.* q 2, art. 9, § 3.
BENEDICT, St. his twelve degrees of humility, II-II. q. 161, art. 6.
BENEFICENCE, pleasure of, I-II. q. 32, art. 6.
BISHOPS, their state a state of perfection, II-II. q. 184, art 5; differing from the religious state, *ib.* q. 186, art. 3, § 5; bishops superiors of religious, *ib.* q. 186, art. 5, § 3.
BLASPHEMY, II II. q. 13; *ib.* q. 72, art. 2.
BLISS IN TEARS, I-II. q. 38, art. 2.
BOASTING, two sorts of, II-II. q. 112, art. 1.
BODY, its part in happiness, I-II. q. 4, art 6.
BRUTALITY, II-II. q. 159, art. 2.
BUYING AND SELLING, II-II. q. 77.

C.

CAPITAL VICES, I-II. q. 84, art. 4; II-II. q. 118, art. 7; *ib.* q. 132, art. 4; *ib.* q. 162, art. 8.
CARDINAL VIRTUES, I-II. q. 61.
CASE-LAW, I-II. q. 95, art. 1, § 2.
CHANGE, why pleasurable, I-II. q. 32, art. 2; change of laws, I-II. q. 97, artt. 1, 2.
CHARACTER, taking away of another's, II-II. q. 62, art. 2, § 2; *ib.* q. 73.
CHARITY, a friendship with God, II-II. q. 23, art. 1; charity to enemies, II-II. q. 25, artt. 8, 9; range and order of charity, II-II. q. 26, art 4; charity not the same for all objects, II-II. q. 26, art. 6; *ib.* q. 31, art. 3; never wholly self-regardless,

II-II. q. 26, art. 13, § 3; love of one's neighbour better in a certain sense than love of God, II-II. q. 27, art. 8; charity as meaning relief of the destitute, II-II. q. 71, art. 1; love of God the end to which all other virtue is the means, II-II. q. 44, art. 1.
CHASTITY, a special and a general virtue, II-II. q. 151, art. 2; modesty the expression of chastity, II-II. q. 151, art. 4; chastity of religious state, II-II. q. 186, artt. 4, 6.
CHEEK TO THE SMITER, II-II. q. 72, art. 3.
CHILDREN, religion of those of tender age, II-II. q. 10, art. 12; discipline of children, II-II. q. 142, art. 2.
CIRCUMSTANCES OF AN ACTION, I-II. q. 7; *ib.* q. 18, art. 3; aggravating and specific, I-II. q. 18, art. 11; *ib.* q. 73, art. 7.
CIVIL OBEDIENCE, duty of, I-II. q. 96, art. 4; II-II. q. 42, art. 2; *ib.* q. 104, art. 6.
COERCION, legal, I-II. q. 96, art. 5.
COMMERCE, II-II. q. 77, art. 4.
COMPULSION in the matter of religious belief, II-II. q. 10, art. 8; *ib.* q. 11, art. 3, with note.
CONCUPISCENCES, the three, I-II. q. 77, art. 5.
CONCUPISCIBLE AND IRASCIBLE faculties, I-II. q. 23, art. 1, with note.
CONFESSION, secret of, II-II. q. 70, art. 1, § 2.
CONSCIENCE, erroneous, how far a rule of action, I-II. q. 19, artt. 5, 6.
CONTEMPLATION, better than action, II-II. q. 182, artt. 1, 2; not all men fit for a contemplative life, II-II. q. 182, art. 4, § 3.
CONTINENCE, something short of a virtue, I-II. q. 58, art. 3, § 2;

INDEX.

II-II. q. 155, art. 1; continence in the will, temperance in the sensitive appetite, II-II. q. 155, artt. 3, 4.
CORPORATE PROPERTY of religious bodies, II-II. q. 188, art. 7.
CORRECTION, when an act of charity, when of justice, II-II. q. 33, artt. 1, 3.
COVETOUSNESS, II-II. q. 118; in what sense "the root of all evil," II-II. q. 119, art. 2, § 1.
CRUELTY, II-II. q. 159, art. 1.
CURIOSITY, II-II. q. 167, art. 2.
CURSING, II-II. q. 76.
CUSTOM, having the force of law, I-II. q. 97, art. 3.

D.

DANGERS, prudent and imprudent to encounter, II-II. q. 88, art. 4, § 2, with note.
DEBT, or DUE, two sorts of, II-II. q. 31, art. 3, § 3.
DECALOGUE, I-II. q. 100, art. 5.
DECEPTION, lawful and unlawful, II-II. q. 40, art. 3.
DENUNCIATION, II-II. q. 67, art. 3, § 2; how differing from accusation, II-II. q. 68, art. 1; ib. q. 68, art. 2, § 3.
DESIRE, what, I-II. q. 30, artt. 1, 2; physical and psychical desires, I-II. q. 30, art. 3; ib. q. 77, art. 5; II-II. q. 142, art. 2, § 2.
DESPAIR, sin of, II-II. q. 20.
DETACHMENT, II-II. q. 184, art. 2, note.
DETRACTION, II-II, qq. 73, 74.
DEVOTION, definition of, II-II. q. 82, art. 1; not necessarily diminished by high endowments, II-II. q. 82, art. 3, § 3; caused by meditation, II-II. q. 82, art. 3; causes both joy and sorrow, II-II. q. 82, art. 4.
DIFFICULTY of a work, not an absolute measure of its merit, II-II. q. 27, art. 8, § 3.

DD

DIRECTLY AND INDIRECTLY VOLUNTARY, I-II. q. 6, art. 3; ib. q. 73, art. 8; II-II. q. 62, art. 7; ib. q. 64, art. 8.
DISCORD, ordinary and incidental, II-II. q. 37, art. 1; discord the daughter of vainglory, II-II. q. 37, art. 2.
DISPENSATIONS, from laws, I-II. q. 97, art 4; ib. q. 100, art. 8; II-II. q. 147, art. 4; from vows; II-II. q. 88, artt. 10, 12; from oaths, II-II. q. 89, art. 7, § 3; ib. q. 89, art. 9.
DISSEMBLING, without lying, II-II. q. 40, art. 3; ib. q. 110, art. 3, § 4; ib. q. 111, art. 1, § 4; ib. q. 113, art. 1; ib. q. 169, art. 2, § 2.
DISTRACTIONS in prayer, II-II. q. 83, art. 13, § 3.
DIVINATION, II-II. q. 95, art. 1.
DIVINE ASSISTANCE, II-II. q. 17, art. 5, § 2.
DOWER, for entrance into religion, II-II. q. 100, art. 3, § 4.
DRESS, offences in, II-II. q. 169, art. 1; female dress, II-II. q. 169, art. 2.
DRUNKENNESS, as an excuse, I-II. q. 76, art. 4, §§ 2, 4; II-II. q. 150, art. 4; as a sin, II-II. q. 150, artt. 1, 2.
DULIA, II-II. q. 84, art. 1, § 1.
DUMB ANIMALS, not objects of charity, II-II. q. 25, art. 3; killed for human food, ib. q. 64, art. 1.

E.

EDUCATIONAL orders of religious, II-II. q. 188, art. 5, with note.
ELECTION, or choice, as distinguished from intention, I-II. q. 20, art. 2.
ELECTION TO DIGNITIES, obligation of choosing the most worthy, II-II. q. 63, art. 2, § 3.
END, does not justify the means, I-II. q. 20, art. 2.

VOL. II.

ENEMIES, love of, II-II. q. 25, artt. 8, 9; prayer for, II-II. q. 83, art. 8.
ENVY, II-II. q. 36, art. 2.
EQUITY, I-II. q. 96, art. 6; II-II. q. 120.
ETERNITY OF PUNISHMENT, I-II. q. 87, artt. 3, 4.
EXCHANGES, voluntary and involuntary, II-II. q. 61, art. 3.
EXECUTIONER of an innocent man, II-II. q. 64, art. 6, § 3.
EXTERIOR GOODS, useful to virtue, II-II. q. 129, art. 8.
EXTERNALS OF WORSHIP, II-II. q. 81, art. 7; *ib.* q. 83, art. 12; *ib.* q. 84, art. 2; *ib.* q. 91.
EXTERNAL COMPLIANCE with false religion, sinful, II-II. q. 94, art. 2.

F.

FAITH, formal motive of, II-II. q. 1, art. 1; faith and opinion, II-II. q. 1, art. 2; *ib.* q. 2, art. 1; faith the mental attitude of a scholar of God, II-II. q. 2, art. 3; faith voluntary and meritorious, II-II. q. 2, art. 9; more meritorious in intellectual men, as in martyrs, II-II. q. 2, art. 10, § 3; confession of faith, II-II. q. 3, art. 2; faith opposed to the eclecticism of private judgment, II-II. q. 5, art. 3; faith supernatural, II-II. q. 6, art. 1; when matter of compulsion, II-II. q. 10, art. 8.
FAME, not happiness, I-II, q. 2, art. 3.
FATHER AND SON, imperfect justice between, II-II. q. 57, art. 4.
FASTING, justification of, II-II. q. 147, art. 1; precept of, II-II. q. 147, artt. 3, 4.
FAVOURITISM, II-II. q. 63.
FEAR, as a stimulus, I-II, q. 44, art. 4; fear of God, II-II. q. 19; servile and filial, limits to the former, II-II. q. 19, artt. 6, 10; fear, when sinful, II-II. q. 125, art. 1; fear as an excuse, II-II. q. 125, art. 2; insensibility to fear, no virtue, II-II. q. 126.
FEES, professional, II-II. q. 71, art. 4; clerical, II-II. q. 100, art. 2; *ib.* q. 100, art. 3, § 2.
FIERY DARING, I-II. q. 45; II-II. q. 127.
FILTHY LUCRE, II-II. q. 32, art. 7; *ib.* q. 62, art. 5, § 2.
FLATTERY, II-II. q. 115.
FLOGGING, II-II. q. 65, art. 2.
FORTITUDE, how related to temperance, II-II. q. 123, art. 1; *ib.* q. 146, art. 1, § 3; spurious imitations of, II-II. q. 123, art. 1, § 2; fortitude properly appears in danger of a soldier's death, II-II. q. 123, artt. 4, 5; more in defence than in attack, II-II. q. 123, art. 6; not a pleasant virtue to exercise, II-II. q. 123, art. 8; parts of fortitude, II-II. q. 128.
FRATERNAL CORRECTION, II-II. q. 33.
FREEDOM AND BONDAGE in regard of justice and sin respectively (Cf. Rom. vi. 20), II-II. q. 183, art. 4.

G.

GAMBLING, II-II. q. 32, art. 7, § 2.
GIFTED MEN, their social function, II-II. q. 131, art. 1.
GLUTTONY, II-II. q. 148.
GOOD WORKS, necessary to salvation, I-II. q. 4, art. 7.
GRATITUDE, II-II. q. 106, artt. 4, 6; involves an interminable reciprocity, II-II. q. 106, art. 6, § 2.

H.

HABITS, in the sensitive appetite, I-II. q. 50, art. 3; in the will, I-II. q. 50, art. 5; the outcome

of acts, I-II. q. 51, art. 2; *ib.* q. 52, art. 3.
HABIT, clerical or religious, no hypocrisy, II-II. q. 111, art. 2, § 2.
HAPPINESS, object of, I-II. q. 2; happiness how related to pleasure, I-II. q. 2, art. 6; *ib.* q. 4, art. 1; what is happiness, I-II. q. 3; of the understanding or of the will, I-II. q. 3, art. 4; happiness open to man, I-II. q. 5, art. 1; natural and supernatural happiness, I-II. q. 5, art 5; *ib.* q. 62, art. 1; in contemplation rather than in action, II-II. q. 182, art. 1.
HARM DONE, not the sole measure of sin, I-II. p. 73, art. 8, § 2.
HATRED, as a passion, I-II. q. 29; as a vice, II-II. q. 34, art. 3; hatred of God, II-II. q. 34, artt. 1, 2.
HEAVEN, II-II. q. 28, art. 3.
HERESY, II-II. q. 11, art. 1; he is no heretic, who is not pertinacious, II-II. q. 5, art. 3; *ib.* q. 10, art 1.
HERMITS, II-II. q. 188, art. 8.
HEROISM, sometimes necessary to salvation, II-II, q. 124, art. 3, § 1.
HIDDEN SINS, not within the province of human control, II-II. q. 25, art. 8, § 3.
HOLINESS, II-II. q. 81, art. 8.
HONOUR, not happiness, I-II. q. 2, art. 2; how differing from fame and glory, II-II. q. 73, art. 1; *ib.* q. 132, art. 2, note; three modes of undue seeking of honour, II-II. q. 131, art. 1; renunciation of honour by religious, II-II. q. 186, art. 7, § 4.
HOPE, as a passion, I-II. q. 40; as a virtue, II-II. q. 17; its relation to love, I-II. q. 40, art. 7.
HUMAN BODY, love of, II-II. q. 25, art. 5; *ib.* q. 26, art. 5.

HUMILITY, idea of the virtue, II-II. q. 161, art. 1, § 2; not in Aristotle, II-II. q. 161, art. 1, § 5; comparisons drawn in humility, II-II. q. 161, art. 1, § 3; why humility is specially commended to Christians, II-II. q. 161, art. 5, § 4; degrees of humility, II-II. q. 161, art. 6.
HYPOCRISY, II-II. q. 111, artt. 2, 4.

I.

IDOLATRY, II-II. q. 94.
IGNORANCE, antecedent, consequent, concomitant, I-II. q. 6, art. 8; when ignorance is sinful, I-II. q. 76, art. 2; II-II. q. 156, art. 3, § 1; when an excuse, I-II. q. 76, art. 4.
ILL-GOTTEN GOODS, II-II. q. 32, art. 7.
IMAGES, worship of II-II, q. 81, art. 3, § 3; *ib.* q. 94, art. 2, § 1, with the subsequent Article.
IMMORAL CONTRACT, II-II. q. 32, art. 7; *ib.* q. 62, art. 5, § 2.
IMMUTABILITY of natural law, I-II. q. 94, art. 5; *ib.* q. 100, art. 8.
IMPERIUM IN IMPERIO, II-II. q. 60, art. 6.
IMPURITY, its effects on character, II-II. q. 153, art. 5.
IMPRECATIONS, in Scripture, II-II. q. 76, art. 1; *ib.* q. 83, art. 8, § 1.
IMPRISONMENT, II-II. q. 65, art. 3.
INACTION, how voluntary, I-II. q. 6, art. 13; *ib.* q. 71, art. 5.
INCIDENTAL and ORDINARY, distinction of, II-II. q. 37, art. 1.
INCRIMINATION, of oneself, II-II. q. 69, artt. 1, 2.
INDIFFERENCE, of acts, I-II. q. 18, artt. 8, 9.
INFUSED VIRTUES, I-II. q. 65, art. 2; *ib.* q. 92, art. 1, § 1; II-II. q. 47, art. 14, § 3.

INGRATITUDE, three degrees of, II-II. q. 107, art. 2.
INNOCENCE, thankfulness for, II-II. q. 106, art. 2.
INSULTS, patience under, II-II. q. 72, art. 3; ib. q. 108, art. 1.
INTEGRAL PARTS of a virtue, II-II. q. 48, art. 1.
INTEMPERATE man compared with the incontinent, I-II. q. 58, art. 3, § 2; II-II. q. 156, art. 3; intemperance more sinful than cowardice, II-II. q. 142, art. 3.
INTENTION, I-II. q. 12.
INTEREST, on capital, justification of, II-II. q. 62, art. 4, note; ib. q. 78, art. 2, § 2, with note; ib. q. 78, art. 2, § 5, with note.
INTOXICATING LIQUORS, II-II. q. 149.
INTUITION, or INSIGHT, I-II. q. 57, art. 2.

J.

JEWISH CHILDREN, baptism of, II-II. q. 10, art. 2.
JOBBERY, II-II. q. 63.
JOY, as distinguished from pleasure, I-II. q. 31, artt. 3, 4; spiritual joy, II-II. q. 28.
JUDGE, must give sentence according to the evidence, II-II. q. 64, art. 6, § 3; ib. q. 67, art. 2.
JURIDICAL INTERROGATORIES, II-II. q. 69, art. 1.
JUSTICE, definition of, II-II. q. 58, art. 1; justice always to another, II-II. q. 57, art. 1; ib. q. 58, art. 2; a habit in the will, II-II. q. 58, art. 4; legal, or general, justice, II-II. q. 58, artt. 5, 6; commutative and distributive justice, II-II. q. 61; virtues annexed to justice, II-II. q. 80, art. 1; justice of man towards God, II-II. q. 57, art. 1, § 3; golden mean of justice, I-II. q. 64, art. 2, with note.

K.

KINDRED, affection for, II-II. q. 26, artt. 7, 8; ib. q. 32. art. 9; ib. q. 101.

L.

LABOUR, manual, duty of, II-II. q. 117, art. 3.
LAST END, I-II. q. 1.
LATRIA, II-II. q. 84, art. 1, § 1; ib. q. 94, art. 2.
LAW, definition of, I-II. q. 90, art. 4; the Eternal Law, I-II, q. 91, art. 1; ib. q. 93; the natural law, I-II. q. 91. art. 2; ib. q. 94; immutability of the natural law, I-II. q. 94, art. 5; ib. q. 100, art. 8; positive law, need of, I-II. q. 94, art. 3. with note: ib. q. 95, artt. 1, 2; II-II. q. 57, art. 2, § 2; the divine law, I-II. q. 91, art. 4; ib. q. 100, art. 2; law how binding on the Sovereign, I-II. q. 96, art. 5.
LAWYERS, duties of, II-II. q. 71, artt. 1, 3.
LIBERALITY, conversant with gifts and expenses, II-II. q. 117, art. 3, § 3.
LIFE, contemplative and active, I-II. q. 3, art. 2, § 4; ib. q. 3, art. 5; II-II. q. 182.
LIKENESS, a cause of love, I-II. q. 27, art. 3.
LINGERING DELECTATION, I-II. q. 74, art. 6; how a mortal sin, I-II. q. 74, art. 8.
LOTS, drawing of, II-II. q. 95, art. 8.
LOVE, of friendship and of desire, I-II. q. 26, art. 4; love of God above all things, II-II. q. 44, art. 4, § 2; ib. q. 44, art. 6; love of neighbour as self, II-II. q. 44. art. 4, § 7.
LUSTFUL CARESSES, mortal sins, II-II. q. 154, art. 4.

LYING, II-II. q. 69, art. 1; *ib.* q. 70, art. 4; *ib.* q. 100; material and formal lies, II-II. q. 110, art. 1; essence of a lie, not the deceiving of one's neighbour, II-II. q. 110, art. 1; sinfulness of lying, II-II. q. 110, art. 3; lies in jest, II-II. q. 110, art. 3, § 6; a lie not a mortal sin except under special circumstances, II-II. q. 110, art. 4; lying by other signs than by words, II-II. q. 111, art. 1.

M.

MAGNANIMITY, in bearing honours, II-II. q. 129, art. 1; and those, great honours, II-II. q. 129, art. 2, § 3; *ib.* q. 129, art. 4, § 1; consistent with humility, II-II. q. 129, art. 3, § 4; *ib.* q. 161, art. 1; external mien of the magnanimous man, II-II. q. 129, art. 3, §§ 3, 5.

MAGNIFICENCE, or MUNIFICENCE, in the matter of great expenses, II-II. q. 134, art. 3; especially for the honour of God, II-II. q. 134, art. 2, § 3; differs from liberality, II-II. q. 134, art. 3, § 2.

MALEVOLENCE, pleasure of, I-II. q. 32, art. 6, § 3.

MALICE, I-II. q.78.

MARTYRDOM, II-II. q. 123, art. 5, § 1; *ib.* q. 124.

MATRIMONY, an institution of natural law, II-II. q. 154, art. 2.

MEAN, the golden, theory of, I-II. q. 64, art. 1; II-II. q. 92, art. 1; not made for theological virtues, I-II. q. 64, art. 4; II-II. q. 27, art. 6.

MEDITATION, causes devotion, II-II. q. 82, art. 3.

MEEKNESS AND CLEMENCY, II-II. q. 157.

MERCY, works of, when obligatory, II-II. q. 71, art. 1.

MERIT, I-II. q. 21, artt. 3, 4.

MILITARY ORDERS, II-II. q. 188, art. 3.

MINORS, vows of, II-II. q. 88, art. 8.

MISCHIEF-MAKING, between friends, worse than detraction, II-II. q. 74, art. 2.

MODESTY, the outward mien of chastity, II-II. q. 151, art. 4; *ib.* q. 168, art. 1; modesty in dress, II-II. q. 169.

MORTAL SIN, what, I-II. q. 72, art. 5; *ib.* q. 88, art. 1; destructive of supernatural virtue, I-II. q. 71, art. 4; II-II. q. 24, art. 12; sin *mortal of its kind*, I-II. q. 88, art. 2; II-II. q. 35, art. 3.

MURDER, II-II. q. 64, art. 6.

MUSIC, in churches, II-II. q. 91, art. 2.

MUTILATION, II-II. q. 65, art. 1.

N.

NATURAL, two meanings of the word, I-II. q. 31, art. 7; two other meanings, I-II. q. 63, art. 1; natural as opposed to supernatural, I-II. q. 62, art. 1; natural inclinations, II-II. q. 69, art. 4, § 1; *ib.* q. 108, art. 2; *ib.* q. 126, art. 1; *ib.* q. 133, art. 1; *ib.* q. 141, art. 1, § 1; *ib.* q. 142, art. 1; natural order the moral order, II-II. q. 130, art. 1; *ib.* q. 154, art. 12.

NECESSARIES OF LIFE, II-II. q. 32, art. 6; *ib.* q. 141, art. 6, § 2; *ib.* q. 169, art. 1.

NEEDY, relief of, II-II. q. 71, art. 1.

NEPOTISM, II-II. q. 63, art. 2, § 1.

O.

OATH, why required, II-II. q. 70, art. 4, § 3; *ib.* q. 89, art. 1;

conditions of lawfulness, II-II. q. 89, art. 3; not a thing desirable in itself, II-II. q. 89, art. 5; oath and affirmation, how different, II-II. q. 89, art. 7, § 1; unlawful oaths, keeping of, II-II. q. 89, art. 7, § 2; oath less binding than vow, II-II. q. 89, art. 8; dispensation from oath, II-II. q. 89, art. 7, § 3; *ib.* q. 89, art. 9; oath to observe college statutes, II-II. q. 98, art. 2, § 4; compulsory oaths, II-II. q. 98, art. 3, § 1.

OBEDIENCE, true idea of, II-II. q. 104, art. 2, § 3; obedience of religious state, II-II. q. 186, artt. 5, 6; merit of such obedience, II-II. q. 186, art. 5, § 5; limits to obedience, II-II. q. 104, art. 5; even in religious, II-II. q. 104, art. 5, § 3; *ib.* q. 186, art. 5, § 4, with note: obedience chief vow of religion, II-II. q. 186, art. 8.

OFFERINGS, to the clergy, threefold purpose of, II-II. q. 86, art. 2.

OMENS, II-II. q. 96, art. 3.

OMISSIONS, possibility of a sin of pure omission, I-II. q. 6, art. 3; *ib.* q. 71, art. 5; II-II. q. 79, art. 3, § 4; moment when the omission becomes sinful, II-II. q. 79, art. 3, § 3.

OPINION, differences of, not dissensions, II-II. q. 29, art. 3, § 2.

ORDEAL, II-II. q. 95, art. 8, § 3.

ORDINARY and INCIDENTAL, distinction of, II-II. q. 37, art. 1.

P.

PAIN, how different from sorrow, I-II. q. 35, art. 2; pain of body and mind compared, I-II. q. 35, art. 7; bodily pain not the worst of evils, I-II. q. 39, art. 4; pain of loss and pain of sense, I-II. q. 87, art. 4.

PAINTING, in the toilet, II-II. q. 169, art. 2, § 2.

PARENTS, duties to, II-II. q. 101, artt. 1, 2; their claims on children already in religion, or called thereto, II-II. q. 101, art. 4.

PARTIALITY, II-II. q. 63.

PASSION, what, I-II. q. 22, art. 3; mutual contrariety of passions, I-II. q. 23, art. 2; voluntary element in, I-II. q. 24, art. 1; passion antecedent and consequent, I-II. q. 24, art. 3, § 1; *ib.* q. 77, art. 6; morality of acts done under passion, I-II. q. 24, art. 3; enumeration of passions in the concupiscible faculty, I-II. q. 30, art. 2; in the irascible faculty, I-II. q. 45, art. 2; passions not to be entirely suppressed, I-II. q. 24, art. 2; II-II. q. 158, artt. 1, 8; how passions come to be at times synonymous with sins, II-II. q. 127, art. 1.

PATIENCE, II-II. q. 136.

PATRIOTISM, II-II. q. 101, art. 1.

PEACE, effect of charity, II-II. q. 29, art. 3.

PERFECTION, how far possible in this life, II-II. q. 184, art. 2; consists essentially in the precepts of charity, instrumentally in the counsels, II-II. q. 184, art. 3; *ib.* q. 186, art. 7; state of perfection, not the perfection of the individual, II-II. q. 184, art. 4; degrees of perfection, II-II. q. 186, art. 2; contempt of perfection, II-II. q. 186, art. 2, § 2; *ib.* q. 186, art. 9, § 3; *ib.* q. 186, art. 10, § 3.

PERJURY, II-II. q. 98.

PERSEVERANCE, II-II. q. 137.

PETTY ECONOMY, a vice, II-II. q. 135, art. 1.

PHILOSOPHICAL SIN, I-II. q. 71, art. 6, § 5; *ib.* q. 74, art. 7, § 2; II-II. q. 20, art. 3.

PLACE OF WORSHIP, II-II. q. 84, art. 3, § 2.

PLATO, his notion of the pre-existence of knowledge and virtue in the soul, I-II. q. 63, art. 1 : Platonic theology, II-II. q. 94, art. 1.
PLEASURE, not happiness, I-II. q. 2, art. 6; nor always joy, I-II. q. 31, art. 3; pleasures of mind and body compared, I-II. q. 31, art. 5; pleasure medicinal, I-II. q. 31, art. 5, § 1; *ib.* q. 35, art. 5; a need of man, I-II. q. 34, art. 1; II-II. q. 168, art. 2; pleasure perfects activity, I-II. q. 33, art. 4; good and evil pleasures, I-II. q. 34, art. 1; temperate use of pleasures, II-II. q. 141, art. 6, § 2; abstinence from pleasure, II-II. q. 142, art. 1; *ib.* q. 149, art. 3, § 1; *ib.* q. 152, art. 2; no mere intensity of pleasure ever of itself a sin, II-II. q. 153, art. 2, § 2.
POISONS, sale of, II-II. q. 169, art. 2, § 4, with note.
POOR, gratuitous professional aid of, II-II. q. 71, art. 1.
POSITIVE LAW, as a further determination of the law of nature, I-II. q. 94, art. 3; *ib.* q. 95, art. 2; II-II. q. 81, art. 2, § 3; *ib.* q. 85, art. 1, § 1; *ib.* q. 147, art. 3.
POTENTIAL PARTS of a virtue, II-II. q. 48, art. 1.
POVERTY, religious, II-II. q. 186, artt. 3, 6; *ib.* q. 188, art. 7.
POWER, not happiness, I-II. q. 2, art. 4.
PRAYER, theory of, II-II. q. 83, art. 2; what to pray for, II-II. q. 83, art. 5; prayer for temporals, II-II. q. 83, art. 6; for enemies, II-II. q. 83, art. 8; vocal prayer, II-II. q. 83, art. 12; attention in prayer, II-II. q. 83, art. 13; long prayers, II-II. q. 83, art. 14; conditions under which prayer is heard, II-II. q. 83, art. 15, § 2; sinners' prayers, II-II. q. 83, art. 16.

PRESUMPTION, on God's mercy, II-II. q. 21; on one's own strength, II-II. q. 130.
PRIDE, essential idea of, insubordination to God, II-II. q. 162, art. 5; the most grievous of sins, II-II. q. 162, art. 6; capable of causing all sin, though not the actual cause of all, II-II. q. 162, art. 2; pride and unbelief, II-II. q. 162, art. 6, § 2; pride and impurity, II-II. q. 162, art. 6, § 3; pride and vainglory, II-II. q. 162. art. 8, § 2.
PRIESTHOOD, II-II. q. 86, art. 2; compared with religious state, II-II. q. 184, art. 8.
PRIVATE INDIVIDUAL, not to usurp functions of authority, I-II. q. 90, art. 3, § 2.
PRIVATE WAR, II-II. q. 40, art. 1, note.
PRODIGALITY, II-II. q. 119.
PROMISES, II-II. q. 110, art. 3, § 5.
PROPERTY, private, I-II. q. 94, art. 5, § 3; II-II. q. 66, art. 2; avaricious greed of, II-II. q. 118, art. 1.
PRUDENCE, what, II-II. q. 47, artt. 12, 13; *ib.* q. 119, art. 3, § 3; differs from art, I-II. q. 57, art. 4; prudence of the flesh, II-II. q. 55, art. 1.
PUNISHMENT, three sources of, I-II. q. 87, art. 1; retributive and preventive, II-II. q. 108, art. 4; when preventive punishment should be withheld, II-II. q. 43, art. 7, § 1; punishment of the community for the individual, II-II. q. 108, art. 1, § 5; *ib.* q. 108, art. 4, §§ 1, 2; punishment as making satisfaction, I-II. q. 87, art. 6; capital punishment, II-II. q. 25, art. 6, § 2; *ib.* q. 64, art. 2, 3; *ib.* q. 108, art. 3; for what crimes, II-II. q. 66, art. 6, § 2; eternal punishment, II-II. q. 87, artt. 3, 4.

PURGATORY, philosophy of, I-II. q. 87, art. 6.
PUSILLANIMITY, a sin, II-II. q. 133, art. 1.

R.

RASH JUDGMENT, II-II. q. 60, artt. 3, 4.
READINESS OF HEART, sometimes a sufficient observance of the precept, II-II. q. 25, artt. 8, 9; *ib.* q. 40, art. 1, § 2; *ib.* q. 72, art. 3; *ib.* q. 83, art. 8; *ib.* q. 108, art. 1, § 4.
REASON, sin in, I-II. q. 74, art. 5; upper and lower, I-II. q. 74, art. 7.
RECREATION, II-II. q. 168, artt. 2, 3, 4.
RELAPSING PENITENTS, II-II. q. 156, art. 3.
RELICS, wearing of, II-II. q. 96, art. 4, § 3.
RELIGION, virtue of, II-II. q. 81, artt. 3, 4, 5; externals of, II-II. q. 81, art. 7; *ib.* q. 83, art. 12; *ib.* q. 84, art. 2; *ib.* q. 85, art. 1; *ib.* q. 91.
RELIGIOUS DISCUSSION, II-II. q. 10, art. 7.
RELIGIOUS STATE, why so called, II-II. q. 81, art. 1, § 5; *ib.* q. 186, art 1; a state of perfection, II-II. q. 184, art. 5; how compared with the order and office of parish-priests, II-II. q. 184, art. 8; religious poverty, II-II. q. 186, art. 3; religious chastity, II-II. q. 186, art. 4; religious obedience, II-II. q. 186, art. 5; why vows in religion, II-II. q. 186, art. 6; subjection of religious to bishops, II-II. q. 186, art. 5, § 3; renunciation of honour by religious, II-II. q. 186, art. 7, § 4; the sacred ministry a proper function for religious, II-II. q. 187, art. 1; *ib.* q. 188, art. 4; also study, II-II. q. 188, art. 5; variety of religious orders, II-II. q. 188, art. 1; not all religious are monks, II-II. q. 188, art. 2, § 2; observance better than strictness of rule, II-II. q. 189, art. 8; corporate property of religious, II-II. q. 188, art. 7; entry into religion, like a second baptism, II-II. q. 189, art. 3, § 3; this entry well made young, II-II. q. 189, art. 1; and without long previous deliberation, II-II. q. 189, art. 10.
RENUNCIATION, universal, obligatory on all Christians, II-II. q. 189, art. 10, § 3.
REST, pleasure of, I-II. q. 32, art. 1, § 3.
RESTITUTION, II-II. q. 62.
REVELATION, *a priori* reasons for, II-II. q. 2, art. 4.
RICHES, not happiness, I-II. q. 2, art. 1.
RIGHTS, natural and positive, II-II. q. 57, art. 2.
ROBBERY, II-II. q. 66, art. 8; more grievous than theft, II-II. q. 66, art. 9.
ROBES OF OFFICE, II-II. q. 169, art. 1, § 2.

S.

SABBATARIANISM, II-II. q. 40, art. 4.
SACRED persons, places, and things, II-II. q. 99, art. 3.
SACRIFICE, to God alone, II-II. q. 84, art. 1, § 1; *ib.* q. 85, art. 2; a duty of the law of nature, II-II. q. 85, art. 1; sacrifice different from simple offering, II-II. q. 85, art. 3, § 3; *ib.* q. 86, art. 1; three sorts of sacrifices, by whom severally offered, II-II. q. 85, art. 4.
SACRILEGE, II-II. q. 99.
SALES, fraudulent, II-II. q. 77, artt. 2, 3.

INDEX.

SATISFACTION, to God for sin, I-II. q. 87, art. 6.
SCANDAL, active and passive, II-II. q. 43, art. 1; not easily taken by good men, II-II. q. 43, art. 5; scandal of Pharisees and of little ones, II-II. q. 43, art. 7.
SCIENCE, what, I-II. q. 57, art. 2; pursuit of science, when inordinate, II-II. q. 167, art. 1.
SECRETS, II-II. q. 68, art. 1, § 3; ib. q. 70, art. 1, § 2.
SELF, well-ordered love of, II-II. q. 25, artt. 4, 7; ib. q. 26, artt. 3, 4.
SELF-LOVE, source of all sin, I-II. q. 77, art. 4; in what sense consonant with charity, II-II. q. 19, art. 6; ib. q. 25, art. 7.
SELF-APPRECIATION, II-II. q. 35, art. 1, § 3; ib. q. 161, art. 3.
SELF-DEPRECIATION, when sinful, II-II. q. 113, art. 1; ib. q. 161, art. 3.
SELF-DEFENCE and killing, II-II. q. 64, art. 7; self-defence in a condemned felon, II-II. q. 69, art. 4.
SENECA, on anger, no reliable authority, II-II. q. 123, art. 10, § 2.
SERVILE FEAR, use of, I-II. q. 92, art. 2, § 4; II-II. q. 19, art. 4, § 1; ib. q. 19, art. 6.
SEXUAL ACT, not of itself sinful, II-II. q. 153, art. 2.
SIMONY, II-II. q. 100.
SIMULATION, always sinful, II-II. q. 111, art. 1; ib. q. 169, art. 2, § 2.
SIN, definition of, I-II. q. 71, art. 6; sin as *turning away* and *turning to*, I-II. q. 72, art. 5, § 1; ib. q. 73, art. 5; ib. q. 87, art. 4; II-II. q. 20, art. 1, § 1; ib. q. 20, art. 3; ib. q. 162, art. 6; sin not a pure privation, I-II. q. 72, art. 1, § 2; ib. q. 73, art. 2; ib. q. 75, art. 1, § 1; sin viewed differently by the philosopher and by the theologian, I-II. q. 71, art. 6, § 5; sin worse than vice, I-II. q. 71, art. 3; sins of omission, I-II. q. 71, art. 5; II-II. q. 79, art. 3; spiritual and carnal sins, I-II. q. 72, art. 2; the former the more culpable, I-II. q. 73, art. 5; the more shameful not always the more grievous sin, II-II. q. 116, art. 2, §§ 2, 3, comparative gravity of sins, II-II. q. 20, art. 3; ib. q. 118, art. 5; ib. q. 162, art. 6; sin in the privileged classes, I-II. q. 73, art. 10; sin in a religious, II-II. q. 186, art. 10; sins against God, self, and neighbour, I-II. q. 72, art. 4; mortal and venial sin, I-II. q. 72, art. 5; ib. q. 88, art. 1; sins mortal and venial *of their kind*, I-II. q. 88, art. 2; sin always in the will, yet not always in the will only, I-II. q. 74, art. 2; II-II. q. 10, art. 2; sin in the reason, I-II. q. 74, artt. 5, 6; no sin that is not in some measure voluntary, I-II. q. 74, art. 10, note; II-II. q. 162, art. 5, note; causes of sin, I-II. qq. 75, 76; stain of sin, I-II. q. 86; sin how an object of the will, II-II. q. 46, art. 2, § 2.
SINGULARITY, II-II. q. 187, art. 6, § 3.
SINNERS, charity to, II-II. q. 25, art. 6; value of their prayers, II-II. q. 83, art. 16.
SLAVERY, II-II. q. 104, art. 5; ib. q. 104, art. 6, § 1.
SLEEP, what happens in, never a sin, but sometimes the consequence of a sin preceding, II-II. q. 154, art. 5; sleep and baths, a cure for sorrow, I-II. q. 38, art. 5.
SLOTH, II-II. q. 35.
SOCIETY, as an element of happiness, I-II. q. 4, art. 8, with note.
SOCRATES, his doctrine that virtue is knowledge, I-II. q. 58, art. 2;

ib. q. 77, art. 2; Socrates on prayer, II-II. q. 83, art. 5.
SOLICITUDE, II-II. q. 55, artt. 6, 7.
SOVEREIGN, how far bound by law, I-II. q. 96, art. 5.
SOVEREIGNTY OF THE PEOPLE, I-II. q. 97, art. 3, § 3, with note.
SPIRITUALISM, principles by which to judge of, II-II. q. 95, art. 4; *ib.* q. 96, art. 2; *ib.* q. 96, art. 3, § 2.
SPORTIVENESS (*eutrapelia*), II-II. q. 168, art. 2.
STAGE-PLAYERS, moral position of, II-II. q. 168, art. 3, § 3.
STATE, or STATUS, legal meaning of, II-II. q. 183, art. 1; variety of states, the beauty of God's house, II-II. q. 183, art. 2; state of perfection, II-II. q. 183, art. 4; *ib.* q. 184, artt. 4, 5.
STOICS, their condemnation of all passions, I-II. q. 24, art. 2; *ib.* q. 59, artt. 3, 5; their assertion of the equality of all sins, I-II. q. 73, art. 2.
STUDY, application to, II-II. q. 166; *ib.* q. 188, art. 5.
STUPIDITY, how sinful, II-II. q. 46, art. 2.
SUBJECTIVE PARTS, of a virtue, II-II. q. 48, art. 1.
SUICIDE, II-II. q. 64, art. 5.
SUPERFLUITIES, what, II-II. q. 32, art. 5.
SUPERHUMAN POWER, universal recognition of some, II-II. q. 85, art. 1.
SUPERIORS, why honoured, II-II. q. 63, art. 3.
SUPERNATURAL, what, I-II. q. 5, art. 5; *ib.* q. 62, art. 1; *ib.* q. 91, art. 4; supernatural virtue, I-II. q. 65, art. 2; destroyed by one mortal sin, I-II. q. 71, art. 4.
SUPERSTITION, II-II. qq. 92, 93.
SYMPATHY, short of charity, II-II. q. 27, art. 2.

T.

TEMPERANCE, proper matter of, II-II. q. 141, art. 4, with note; parts of, II-II. q. 143.
TEMPORAL BLESSINGS, prayer for, II-II. q. 83, art. 6.
TEMPTATIONS, some to be fled from, others to be thought out, II-II. q. 35, art. 1, § 4.
TEMPTING GOD, II-II. q. 97, art. 1.
TESTIMONY, conflicting, II-II. q. 70, art. 2, § 2.
THEFT, II-II. q. 66, artt. 3, 6, 7.
THEISM, perfective of humanity, II-II. q. 81, art. 7.
THEOLOGICAL VIRTUES, I-II. q. 62.
TIME, its effect on anger and on love, I-II. q. 48, art. 2, § 2.
TOLERATION, II-II. q. 10, art. 11; *ib.* q. 11, art. 3.
TRANSGRESSION, as opposed to omission, II-II. q. 79, art. 2; usually a worse sin than omission, II-II. q. 79, art. 4.
TREATIES, observance of, II-II. q. 89, art. 7, § 3, note.
TRUTHFULNESS, II-II. q. 109.

U.

UNION OF LOVE, I-II. q. 28, art. 1, § 2.
UNITY, yearning after, I-II. q. 36, art. 3.
UNBELIEF, temptation to, I-II. q. 74, art. 10; sin of, II-II. q. 10; *ib.* q. 162, art. 7, § 3.
USURY, what, and why sinful, II-II. q. 78, art. 1.
UTILITARIANISM, II-II. q. 145, art. 3, with note.

V.

VAINGLORY, why so called, II-II. q. 132, art. 1; opposed to mag-

nanimity, II-II. q. 132, art. 2; vainglory and pride, II-II. q. 162, art. 8, § 2; how far lawful to seek for glory, II-II. q. 132, art. 1.
VALUE, II-II. q. 77, art. 1.
VENGEANCE, when lawful, II-II. q. 108, art. 1; ib. q. 158, art. 1, § 3; how virtuous, II-II. q. 108, art. 2.
VENIAL SIN, I-II. q. 72. art. 5.
VICARIOUS PUNISHMENT, I-II. q. 87, artt. 7, 8; II-II. q. 108, art. 4, § 1.
VICE, I-II. q. 71.
VIRGINITY, praiseworthy, II-II. q. 152, art. 2; better than marriage, state for state, not individual for individual, II-II. q. 152, art. 4; inferior to the theological virtues, to religion, and to martyrdom, II-II. q. 152, art. 5; loss of virginity, how far reparable, II-II. q. 152, art. 3, § 3.
VIRTUE, a habit, I-II. q. 55, art. 1; how natural, how acquired, I-II. q. 63, art. 1; how compatible with a sinful act, I-II. q. 63, art. 2, § 2; ib. q. 71, art. 4; virtue lies in the mean, I-II. q. 64; natural and supernatural virtues, I-II. q. 65, art. 2; ib. q. 92, art. 1, § 1; division of natural virtues, II-II. q. 123, art. 1; intellectual virtues, I-II. q. 56, art. 3; virtues in the sensitive appetite, I-II. q. 56, art. 4; virtues in the will, I-II. q. 56, art. 5; difference of moral from intellectual virtues, I-II. q. 58, artt. 1, 2; inseparability of the virtues, I-II. q. 58, artt. 4, 5; ib. q. 65; cardinal virtues, I-II. q. 61; theological virtues, I-II. q. 62; II-II. q. 17, art. 6; order of precedence among virtues, II-II. q. 104, art. 3; ib. q. 136, art. 2; ib. q. 161, art. 5; mode of virtue, I-II. q. 100, art. 9; virtue without charity, what, I-II q. 65, art. 2; II-II. q. 23, art. 7; ib. q. 32, art. 1, § 1; parts of virtue, integral, subjective, potential, II-II. q. 48; ib. q. 128; ib. q. 143; outward act of virtue sometimes not of the virtue, II-II. q. 123, art. 1, § 2; virtue at times unpleasant to exercise, II-II. q. 123, art. 8.
VOCAL PRAYER, II-II. q. 83, art. 12.
VOCATION, to religious life, II-II. q. 189, art. 10.
VOLUNTARY, directly and indirectly, I-II. q. 6, art. 3; ib. q. 73, art. 8; ib. q. 77, art. 7; voluntariness diminished by ignorance, I-II. q. 6, art. 8; ib. q. 76, art. 4; by fear, I-II. q. 6, art. 6; by passion, I-II. q. 77, artt. 6, 7.
VOW, three essentials of II-II. q. 88, art. 1; of the better good, II-II. q. 88, art. 2; wisdom and merit of vows, II-II. q. 88. artt. 4, 6; vows of religion, II-II. q. 186, art. 6; dispensation from vows, II-II. q. 88, art. 10; limits of the dispensing power, II-II. q. 88, art. 12, § 2.

W.

WAR, II-II. q. 40; ib. q. 188, art. 3.
WILL, sin not confined to the will, I-II. q. 74, art. 2; will regulated by the will of God, a rule for other wills, II-II. q. 37, art. 1, § 1.
WISDOM, distinct from science, I-II. q. 57, art. 2.
WIT at another's expense, II-II. q. 72, art. 2, § 1.
WITNESSES, reconciliation of, II-II. q. 70, art. 2, § 2.
WORSHIP, II-II. qq. 81, 84, 85, 91.

Y.

YOUTH, hopeful, I-II. q. 40, art. 6.

Z.

ZEAL., I-II. q. 28, art. 4.

Made in the USA
Columbia, SC
17 February 2023